The Cruiser's Compendium

The Cruiser's Compendium

a complete guide
to coastal, inland, and
gunkhole cruising

RICHARD HENDERSON

HENRY REGNERY COMPANY·CHICAGO

Library of Congress Cataloging in Publication Data

Henderson, Richard, 1924-
  The cruiser's compendium.

  Bibliography: p.
  1. Sailing. 2. Sailboats. I. Title.
GV811.H3598   797.1'24   73-6473

Published by Henry Regnery Company
180 North Michigan Avenue, Chicago, Illinois 60601
Manufactured in the United States of America
Library of Congress Catalog Card Number: 73-6473
International Standard Book Number: 0-8092-8923-7

In memory of
Thomas R. Symington

Acknowledgments

The author is very grateful for valuable advice, suggestions, and wrinkles from many boating and cruising friends. Particular thanks are due to Harold R. ("Buzz") White, yacht yard manager par excellence. Buzz never is too busy to answer a question or to investigate a boat problem, and he carefully checked the accuracy of Chapter 5, "Mechanical Matters and Basic Instruments." Also, I am grateful to Captain George E. White, former merchant ship's captain and navigation instructor, for reading and checking Chapter 8, "Thoughts on Small Boat Navigation." My old friend Arthur W. Sherwood, director of the Chesapeake Bay Foundation, was most generous in allowing me to use the Ecology Cruise Guide, which is reproduced in Appendix B. As usual, Dr. Roger P. Batchelor has been very helpful in supplying me with many old books and articles. I am very much obliged to David Q. Scott, executive director of the U.S. Naval Institute, for his fine photographs and caption suggestions, and, in addition, I appreciate permission to use two diagrams from the book *Sail and Power*, published by the Naval Institute Press. My English friend, John Rock, contributed a great deal of his time to photographic work and to broadening my knowledge of self-steering gears. Thanks are due to Roger C. Taylor, president of International Marine Publishing Company, for certain suggestions and for firsthand instruction in fog piloting. Once again, I want to thank Patty M. Maddocks of the U.S. Naval Institute for a splendid job of typing the manuscript. Others who have been helpful in one way or another are Nancy and Harry C. Primrose, Edmund H. Henderson, Richard F. Jablin, Paul Hagan, Edward Karkow, Commander Richard Brooks, Donald J. Kerlin, John F. Quinn, Robert S. Cockran, Henry C. Strong, Louise Gerretson, Victor Jorgensen, and Wright Britton. I apologize for any others I may have overlooked.

Photograph Credits

Page 1: Fred Thomas
Page 8: Courtesy of Morgan Yacht Corporation
Page 10: Courtesy of Irwin Yacht and Marine Corporation
Page 13: *Motor Boating & Sailing* photo by Tony Gibbs; courtesy of Symons-Sailing, Inc.
Page 14: *Motor Boating & Sailing* photo by Tony Gibbs; courtesy of Symons-Sailing, Inc.
Page 15: Courtesy of Cross Trimarans
Page 17: Courtesy of Islander Yachts
Page 22: *National Fisherman*
Page 30: Courtesy of O'Day Yachts
Page 32: Fred Thomas
Page 34: Courtesy of Allied Boat Company, Inc.
Page 38, left: Courtesy of Coastal Recreation, Inc.
Page 38, right: Courtesy of Robert G. Henry
Page 42: David Q. Scott
Page 62: Courtesy of Robert G. Henry
Page 75: David Q. Scott
Page 79: Courtesy of Irwin Yacht and Marine Corporation
Page 80: David Q. Scott
Page 82: David Q. Scott
Page 95: David Q. Scott
Page 96: Courtesy of Jensen Marine Corporation
Page 99, top: Mystic Seaport photograph by Sandra DeVeau
Page 99, bottom: David Q. Scott
Page 100: Fred Thomas
Page 103: Courtesy of *National Fisherman* and Pratt's Photo Service
Page 110: Courtesy of Islander Yachts
Page 126: David Q. Scott
Page 129: Fred Thomas
Page 134: Courtesy of Wright Britton
Page 136: Courtesy of Pete Smythe, *Motor Boating & Sailing*
Page 139: John Rock
Page 143: David Q. Scott
Page 149: David Q. Scott
Page 150: David Q. Scott
Page 152: David Q. Scott

Contents

Author's Introduction   *xiii*

1. Cruising Sailboat Types and Design Considerations   1
   Deep-Keel Boats
   Variable Draft
   Twin-Keelers
   Multihulls
   Motor Sailers

2. Construction and Safety Features   18
   Construction Features
   Safety Features

3. Accommodation, Galley, and Comfort Features   28
   Small Cruisers
   Medium-Sized Cruisers
   Large Cruisers
   Berths and Seats
   Heads
   Stowage and Tanks
   Cockpit Comfort
   The Galley

4. Inspecting and Testing a New Boat   48
   Inspection
   A Trial Sail
   Summary Inspection List
   Trial Sail Checklist

5. Mechanical Matters and Basic Instruments   60
   Batteries
   Engines
   Tanks and Piping
   Radiotelephones
   Depth Sounders
   Speedometers and Logs
   Refrigeration

6. Fitting Out for Cruising   72
   Safety Equipment
   Deck Gear
   Comfort Equipment
   The Dinghy
   Stowing the Gear

7. Cruise Planning and Activities   86
    Preliminary Knowledge of the Cruising Area
    Tide and Current
    Regional Weather
    Fog
    Distant Cruising Areas
    Miscellaneous Activities on a Cruise
    Stocking Up

8. Thoughts on Small Boat Navigation   109
    Basic Tools
    Charts
    The Compass
    Taking Bearings
    Lines of Position and Fixes
    Dead Reckoning
    Fog Piloting
    Eyeball Navigation
    U.S. Buoyage Systems
    Grounding

9. Cruising Rigs and Sailing Short-Handed   127
    Popular Cruising Rigs
    Sail Selection
    Trouble-Free Rigging
    Labor-Saving Gear and Sail Reduction
    Sailing in Comfort
    Sailing Short-Handed and Simple Self-Steering

10. Marinas, Yacht Clubs, and Anchorages   143
    Marinas
    Yacht Clubs
    Anchorages

    Appendix A: Federal Equipment Requirements   *157*

    Appendix B: Chesapeake Bay Foundation Ecology
       Cruise Guide   *165*

    Index   *179*

Author's Introduction

It has often been said that cruising is not merely a sport but a way of life. This is very true, and yet there are wide variations in the basic concept of the cruising way of life. To some boatmen, powering in the quickest time from one crowded marina to another is the ultimate in cruising, but to others, cruising involves poking into quiet, relatively secluded creeks or making longish but leisurely runs under sail between snug, attractive anchorages. The latter notion coincides with my own of what real cruising should be.

Pace is an important element, I think. There should be no great rush to get where you're going, except for the sake of deriving maximum pleasure from sailing efficiently, for there should be as much enjoyment from a fair weather passage as from a stay in port. Also, cruising should allow one to relax and escape the rush and worries of the normal life ashore. Even ports of call, it seems to me, should afford ample opportunity to "get away from it all." Sailors who spend most of their time tied up in a crowded marina may enjoy television and other modern conveniences, but if this is the goal of cruising, it hardly seems worthwhile leaving home. In contrast, a snug anchorage in an unspoiled cove, as far as possible from the beaten track, can offer peaceful contentment and the rare opportunity for quiet reflection. In such a place, furthermore, one has a chance to enjoy nature, have undisturbed conversations with family or friends, and escape, at least momentarily, from the cares of civilization.

The Cruiser's Compendium deals with cruising on soundings — that is, wherever the normal lead line can strike bottom. Obviously, this does not include the sea far offshore, but it does include, as the book's subtitle states, inland and coastal waters and those very protected waters commonly known as gunkholes.

Although the word *gunkhole* may sound peculiar to the uninitiated, it evokes delightful images to most veteran cruising sailors. My own image would include a languid creek with a background of rolling fields, a fringe of woods along the shore with at least one dead tree bleached white and crowned with an osprey's nest, a heron stalking its dinner in the reeds, and the reflections of foliage shimmering at the water's edge. There would be the scent of honeysuckle mixed with the slightly musky smell of low tide and the sounds of fish crow calls, the buzz of cicadas, the lap of ripples against the topsides, and the occasional plop of a jumping fish.

Other sailors might envision northern coves bound by spruce-covered rocky shores, or perhaps landlocked southern bays ringed by white sand beaches with overhanging palms. But no matter what the particular image, all gunkholes are alike in being idyllic harbors.

Of course, secret anchorages are almost nonexistent now; they must be shared with others. Still, reasonably uncrowded harbors can be found away from cities, especially by those who can cruise off-season or during the middle of the week rather than during midsummer weekends or holidays. Many delightful anchorages are available to U.S. yachtsmen in such areas as New England (especially along the coast of Maine), the Chesapeake Bay, the Florida Keys, the Bahamas, the Virgin Islands, the bayous of the southern United States, the Gulf of California, Puget Sound and points north, and on numerous midwestern lakes, including, of course, the Great Lakes. If the prospective cruising sailor is not close to suitable cruising grounds, he can either charter a boat there, take his own boat through an inland waterway or along a coast in fair weather when there are accessible inlets, or, if the boat is small, he can tow her to the cruising area on a trailer behind his automobile. In addition, there are yacht delivery services, and there is at least one organization that arranges boat swaps, whereby boat owners in different parts of the country exchange yachts for a time.

The purpose of this book is to help the prospective cruising sailor in selecting a suitable boat, suggest important requirements and interesting activities, and present the knowledge needed to begin cruising. This book does not cover the elementary principles and terminology of sailing, for these have been covered in the author's earlier book *Hand, Reef and Steer*, published by the Reilly & Lee division of Henry Regnery Company. The system used for defining or explaining nautical terms and nomenclature is the same in both books. All new terms (those not defined in *Hand, Reef and Steer*) are italicized and explained in the text when first used. In addition, there is an index of the terms at the back of the book. *The Cruiser's Compendium* might be considered a companion to *The Racing-Cruiser,* another book by the author published by Reilly & Lee. The latter book concentrates on racing, while this present one specializes in sailboat cruising and related subjects.

The Cruiser's Compendium

1

Cruising Sailboat Types and Design Considerations

Many prominent sailors say the best kind of cruising sailboat is one that is competitive on the race course, while others believe some features that are desirable for racing are detrimental to cruising. There is truth in both points of view. Some very fast boats are good cruisers, and smart sailing ability, good maneuverability, and close-windedness are valuable assets for a cruiser. It is desirable that each kind of boat have reasonably low *wetted surface* (the immersed surface area of the hull producing skin friction) and reasonably light *displacement* (weight), because these characteristics enable the boat to carry a small, easy-to-handle rig without undue sacrifice of performance.

On the other hand, some highly competitive boats have extremely short keels that may cause *directional instability* (an inability of the boat to hold a steady course) and an excessively quick helm for cruising. Then, too, many hot racers are very light and beamy and have *hard* (fairly flat) bilges for speed downwind in a blow and for high initial stability so that they can stand up to a lot of sail. This feature, however, often produces a quick rolling motion in beam seas, especially when at anchor or under power with the sails lowered, and a light boat with hard bilges will very often pound when she is driven into choppy head seas. Rounded or *slack bilges* (those having a gradual turn and considerable deadrise) will not afford high initial stability, but they usually produce an easier motion. Bilges should not be so slack or narrow, however, that they encourage excessive *accumulative rolling*, an increasing motion due to the coincidence of the boat's period of roll with commonly encountered wave periods. Extremely slack bilges also may cause excessive tenderness. Some of these points are illustrated in Figures 1-1, 1-2, and 1-3.

Size and special features needed for personal requirements will have an important influence on hull design. For instance, many very small cruisers have fairly flat bilges and retractable keels so that they can be launched with ease from ramps or trailers, and some boats have twin keels (see Figure 1-10) so that they can sit upright for easy trailering or for use in areas of extreme tide where they must sit on the ground. Then, too, small boats have different proportions from large boats. Generally speaking, a small conventional sailing cruiser will have greater relative beam and freeboard but lesser overhangs than her larger sister. Disregarding for the moment special-purpose craft and considering sizes larger than boats intended for trailering, however, I would recommend a normal cruiser of moderate design, one that is not extreme in form or dimension. In other words, the hull's draft, beam, deadrise, overhangs, freeboard, displacement, and keel size should not be extremely large or extremely small. This concept of moderation will be expanded later.

Deep-Keel Boats

Extreme and moderate lateral planes for deep single-keel boats are shown in Figure 1-4. My choice for a good combination of easy handling, smart sailing ability, and sea-kindliness are the moderate hulls A and B. Both of these types should

The "Seawind" ketch, a sea-kindly, 30-foot deep-keel cruiser designed by Thomas Gilmer.

1

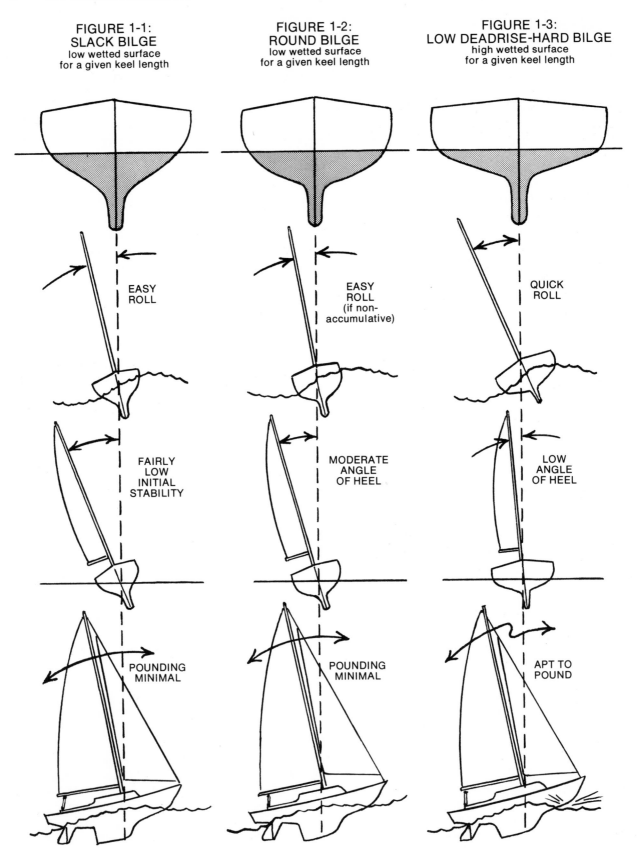

FIGURE 1-1:
SLACK BILGE
low wetted surface
for a given keel length

FIGURE 1-2:
ROUND BILGE
low wetted surface
for a given keel length

FIGURE 1-3:
LOW DEADRISE-HARD BILGE
high wetted surface
for a given keel length

EASY
ROLL

EASY
ROLL
(if non-
accumulative)

QUICK
ROLL

FAIRLY
LOW
INITIAL
STABILITY

MODERATE
ANGLE
OF HEEL

LOW
ANGLE
OF HEEL

POUNDING
MINIMAL

POUNDING
MINIMAL

APT TO
POUND

be quite fast and responsive as compared with type C, the traditional heavy-displacement, long-keel cruiser. Type C represents one extreme in the spectrum of cruiser designs, the sea-kindly, directionally stable hull that is usually sluggish in light winds and a mediocre performer to windward. Types D and E represent the opposite extreme. They are designed for speed over the race course, yet in my opinion they have certain drawbacks for cruising.

Both D and E have very short keels for minimal wetted surface, but they might be excessively quick on the helm for cruising and require that the helmsman give his undivided attention to steering. Furthermore, these particular boats have *balanced rudders,* meaning that part of the rudder is forward of the rudder post or steering axis (see Figure 1-4) in order that water force can assist in turning the rudder. This means that if the helmsman leaves his post even momentarily, the boat might make a sudden, sharp turn. Of the two types D and E, the latter will probably have more directional stability, because she has a small skeg and only the bottom half of her rudder is balanced. One practical drawback of type E, however, is her sharp, scimitar-shaped keel. This kind of keel minimizes forward resistance, but it makes *hauling* (or *slipping* as the British say) on a marine railway quite difficult, and it may necessitate using a boat yard that is equipped with a *travel lift* (a lifting device on wheels that pulls a boat out of the water vertically with slings). Furthermore, in areas of extreme tide the keel shape might prevent intentional grounding while tied to a pier for bottom cleaning or another purpose. The keel on boat D has a fairly flat bottom, which facilitates intentional grounding or hauling on a railway (although her bow and stern would have to be carefully supported), and its shape allows constant *camber* (a curved surface similar to that on the top of an airplane's wing) for hydrodynamic efficiency when beating to windward. Directional stability is sacrificed, however, and the leading edge of the keel is so vertical that it might tend to catch seaweed or lobster pot anchor lines in many cruising areas.

Profiles A and B fulfill the practical considerations of easy hauling and nonfouling at the keel's leading edge, and they should produce good directional stability. Although these lateral planes are greater in area than those of D and E, wetted surface areas of A and B should not be high when the bilges are either rounded or are fairly slack. A round bilge (see Figure 1-2) gives a low wetted surface, because

a sphere has the least area for a given volume; while a slack bilge with ample deadrise (see Figure 1-1) minimizes wetted surface, because it shortens the girth distance from the waterline to the bottom of the keel. In addition, both the round and slack bilges minimize pounding in a seaway.

Of the two profiles A and B, the latter has the shortest keel, and for a given *midship section* form (the shape of the hull's cross section at the middle of the load waterline, as shown in Figures 1-1, 1-2, and 1-3), B has less wetted surface area. Her rudder has been detached from the keel and moved aft, a long distance from the boat's vertical turning axis, so that a long lever arm is produced for easy steering (see Figure 1-4). Separated rudders of the *balanced spade* type (illustrated in Figure 1-4, D), having no skeg ahead of them, are subject to early *stalling* (great turbulence on one side and a sudden loss of lateral force) when the rudder is turned sharply, especially when the boat is heeled. When a keel-separated rudder is attached to a deep skeg as exemplified by B in Figure 1-4, however, there is less chance of the rudder stalling, and the rudder is better supported and protected from grounding, striking a drifting object, or running over a fish net cable. If one wants to race his cruiser occasionally, types A and B may not be the most competitive, but they are wholesome designs that should rate well under a stable, time-tested handicap rule that has no glaring loopholes. Boats designed to exploit loopholes in handicap rating rules will enjoy only temporary success before the rules are changed to plug the loopholes. Boats of the B type profile are still enjoying fairly consistent success over closed racecourses. One example of such a boat is the "Ohlson 38."

Although type A may not be the most competitive kind of boat for today's racing, she need not be slow. Indeed, the "Luders 33," having this kind of profile, has been fairly competitive in recent years. Furthermore, the type has many advantages for cruising, including the ability to hold a steady course, ease of maintaining good balance over a wide range of conditions, a well-protected rudder that will enhance keel lift when the boat carries a slight weather helm, a profile that permits an after-raking rudder axis for maximum steering effectiveness when the boat is heeled, ample lateral plane area without the need for resorting to deep draft, and a keel form that will allow easy hauling and a level attitude when grounded or cradled. Type A also offers some advantages in propeller installation.

FIGURE 1-4: DEEP-KEEL BOATS

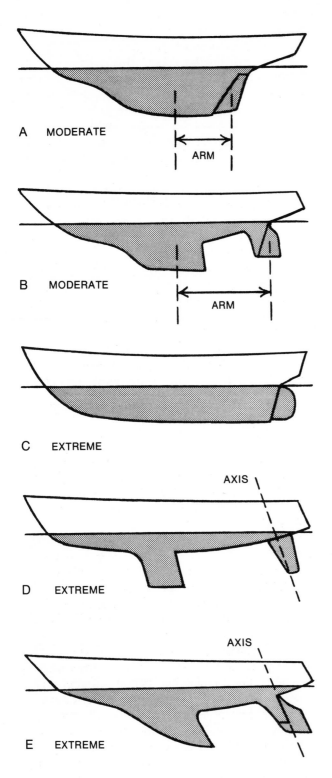

A   MODERATE

ARM

B   MODERATE

ARM

C   EXTREME

AXIS

D   EXTREME

AXIS

E   EXTREME

Figure 1-5 illustrates how the keel-attached rudder with a raked axis can enhance the keel's lift (that is, reduce leeway) and how the rudder's side force acts in a more or less horizontal direction when the boat is heeled. Notice that when the rudder is turned very slightly to correct for the moderate weather helm normally induced by heeling, side force is about parallel to the water's surface, and the water flow on the windward side of the keel speeds up, thereby lowering the pressure on that side, all of which tends to discourage leeway and increase the keel's and rudder's effectiveness when beating or reaching. Of course, the keel on this type of boat should be sufficiently long that the rudder is well aft for ample arm length between the hull's turning axis and the rudder's center of pressure. On the other hand, the keel should not be so long that the boat has a sluggish helm and excessive wetted surface, as exemplified by boat C in Figure 1-4.

Other moderate parameters for small- to medium-sized deep-keel boats are suggested in Figure 1-6. The proportions illustrated are by no means hard and fast design dictums, but they are intended to represent average, wholesome dimensions for a modern, normal boat of the kind being discussed.

Moderate overhangs are not only helpful to a boat's appearance, but they afford reserve buoyancy when she is pitching in a seaway. A boat with a sharp, plumb bow is subject to plowing into rather than lifting to a head sea. Overhang aft also damps pitching, especially when the sections are somewhat U-shaped, as illustrated in Figure 1-6. Sections forward should be more flaring and V-shaped in order that the boat can knife through head seas, but the bow and stern sections should not be extremely dissimilar, or else the boat may develop a bad weather helm when heeled. Then, too, extremely flat sections aft should be avoided because they may pound in following seas or when the boat is pitching. Overhangs forward are often greater than those aft, but the difference should not be so great that the boat appears aesthetically unbalanced. Long overhangs will pound in a seaway and add unnecessary weight to the ends, which may adversely affect pitching or cause *hobbyhorsing* (extreme pitching up and down, violently turning around her transverse axis). A good rule of thumb is that, for a small- to medium-sized cruiser, the forward plus after overhangs should not be over a third of the load waterline (LWL) length. Small, light boats generally have lesser overhangs than smart sailers that are large and heavy.

FIGURE 1-5: RUDDER FORCES

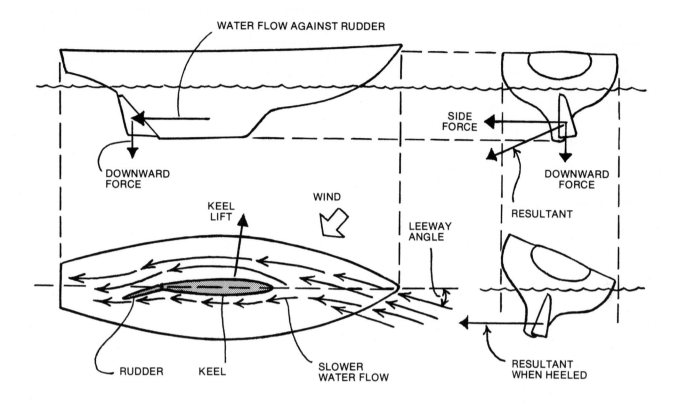

FIGURE 1-6: MODERATE PROPORTIONS (FOR A DEEP-KEEL BOAT
OF MEDIUM SIZE)

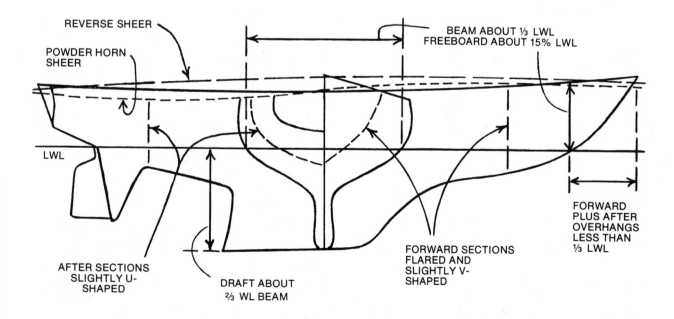

Beam is obviously dependent on length, but there is also a close relationship between beam and draft (when the keel is ballasted), since both of these dimensions have an important effect on stability. More will be said about this later, but as a general rule the less draft a boat has, the greater her beam should be. This is why centerboard boats usually have greater beam than those with deep keels. Beam for normal cruisers may vary between 25 percent of the LWL for large keel boats to 40 percent of the LWL for small centerboarders, but for an average, smart-sailing, deep-keel cruiser similar to the type illustrated in Figure 1-6, the waterline beam will be in the neighborhood of one-third of her LWL. Large boats are naturally *stiffer* (more stable) than small ones; thus the latter generally require greater proportional beam. Very generally speaking, draft for deep-keel cruisers will be in the vicinity of two-thirds waterline beam. Small boats will have slightly less draft in proportion to their beam, while large boats will have slightly greater proportional draft.

Another important parameter is freeboard, because this has an effect on safety, comfort, performance, and appearance. On modern cruisers, freeboards seem to be growing higher and higher. Reasonably high freeboard provides room, especially headroom, below decks; it helps keep spray and solid water off the decks; and it adds to the boat's reserve stability at moderate heel before her rail is submerged. Excessively high freeboard, however, can be ugly; it can cause harmful windage that will be detrimental to windward performance; and it may lessen initial stability because a heavy deck is carried high above the waterline. Perhaps the most important point for freeboard measurement is at the forward end of the LWL, as this is in the region of the bow wave. For a small- to medium-sized cruiser, I would suggest as a rough guide that the freeboard at this point be somewhere around 15 percent of the LWL. For the type of boat under discussion, I don't think freeboard should be below 12 percent, nor should it be a great deal higher than 15 percent. One should remember, however, that small cruisers generally have greater proportional freeboard than large boats.

Once the freeboard is established at the forward end of the LWL, freeboard dimensions will vary at other points along the LWL in accordance with the boat's sheer line. The boat illustrated in Figure 1-6 has a conventional sheer, but the dashed line shows a reverse sheer, and the dotted line shows a *powder horn sheer* (reversed forward and conventional aft).

The latter has the advantage of having its highest point at the forward end of the LWL, but the deck line is usually not very pleasing aesthetically. Reverse sheer may give more room below decks, and it helps keep the lee rail above water when heeling; but the windward rail appears extremely humped when heeling, and the stern will be quite low and possibly subject to being *pooped* (overrun by following seas) in heavy weather. Conventional sheer is usually the most desirable, because the bow and stern are elevated to help prevent head seas or following seas from coming aboard, the deck line is generally considered most aesthetically pleasing, and the windward rail is kept low and thus causes little windage when heeled. For appearance and prevention of early immersion of the lee rail, however, conventional sheer should be very moderate. I prefer a slight conventional sheer with the bow a bit higher than the stern.

Variable Draft

A handy boat for shallow water cruising is the keel-centerboarder, the boat with a shoal-draft, ballasted keel into which a centerboard retracts (see Figure 1-7, A). Many of the best gunkholes are quite shallow, so obviously shoal draft is highly advantageous. I would not recommend a centerboard cruiser with no ballasted keel because of the possibility of capsizing in heavy weather, but a keel-centerboarder similar to type A has reasonably shallow draft and yet provides assurance against capsizing except, perhaps, in the very worst weather at sea.

Of course, since boat designing nearly always involves compromises, there are some drawbacks in the keel-centerboard concept. Boats of this type must have ample beam for stability, and unless the rudder is retractable, it must be shallow in order that it won't be damaged by running aground. A very beamy boat will tend to *roll out* or slightly rise up in the water when she heels, and very often the helmsman loses steering control, especially when the rudder is shallow. An exaggerated example of roll out is illustrated in Figure 1-8. Notice that when the boat heels without lifting up, the additional immersed area is greater than the area on the opposite side of the hull that rises out of the water. The additional immersed and emersed areas, which are shown as "in" and "out" wedges in the sectional view of the hull, cannot be unequal so long as the boat's displacement remains constant; so in actuality, the hull must roll out to equalize the wedges.

FIGURE 1-7: VARIABLE DRAFT

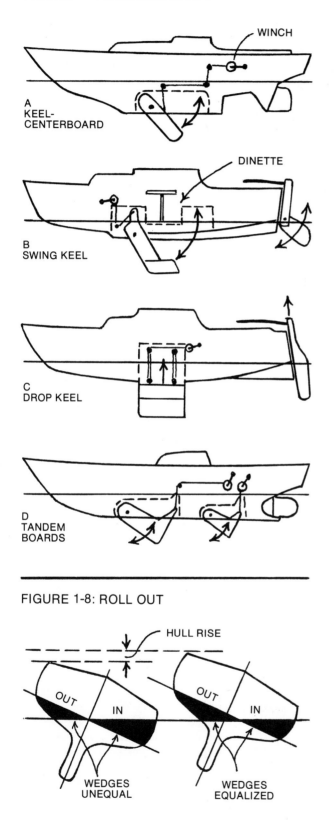

A
KEEL-
CENTERBOARD

B
SWING KEEL

C
DROP KEEL

D
TANDEM
BOARDS

FIGURE 1-8: ROLL OUT

HULL RISE

OUT   IN   OUT   IN

WEDGES   WEDGES
UNEQUAL   EQUALIZED

In addition to the possible problem with excessive roll out on the very beamy keel-centerboarder, there may be certain maintenance problems for some centerboards—wearing or erosion of the pin on which the board pivots and jamming or wearing of the wire pendant by which the board is lifted. Furthermore, there might be some difficulties in servicing, cleaning, and painting centerboards when the boat must be hauled on a marine railway. For a boat that will be cruised offshore in exposed waters, many experienced sailors prefer a fairly deep-draft, heavily ballasted keel because of the reserve stability it affords. A very shoal-draft keel-centerboarder could capsize if she took an extreme knockdown in heavy weather offshore in high seas.

For those sailors who want the advantages of controllable draft in a keel-centerboarder, I would suggest that the ballasted keel be sufficiently deep for reasonable reserve stability, for ample depth of a nonretractable rudder (which needs to be protected by the keel), and for a lateral plane sufficiently deep that the boat can be sailed to windward with the board fully housed (in case the board should happen to drop out or jam in the up position). A good rule of thumb is that the draft should be at least one-seventh of the load waterline length for a small- to medium-sized boat.

Many small trailerable boats, up to about twenty-six feet in overall length, are equipped with retractable ballasted keels. Normally, such a keel swings on a pivot pin as shown in Figure 1-7, B, and a winch is provided for lifting purposes. In some cases the retracted keel is housed in a shallow well at or under the inboard edge of a *dinette* (a sitting area with a table and seats), where there is minimal interference with the accommodations. Most retractable swing keels on small boats can be locked in the fully down position, and for the sake of assuring reasonable reserve stability and self-righting ability, trailerable boats should never be cruised or raced without the keel being fully down and locked.

A few large sailing cruisers have fully retractable keels, and these are often vertical drop keels as illustrated by C in Figure 1-7. When racing, drop-keel boats alter their draft by beating with the keel down but sailing downwind with the keel up in order to keep wetted surface friction to an absolute minimum. This practice could be dangerous, however, in very heavy weather in exposed waters. Obviously, the boat's range of stability would be much less with the keel up than with it down. Some sailors argue that a large drop-keel boat is almost impossible

Ideal for gunkhole and inland cruising, the "Morgan 34" is a popular keel-centerboarder that has shallow draft when conditions require it.

to capsize even with the keel retracted, because, without a deep appendage to trip on, she will merely slide off to leeward instead of rolling over on her side. It is true that yacht designer Richard Carter could not knock down his famous retractable-keel forty-footer *Red Rooster* during sea trials, but he says the boat has a stability range of only slightly more than 90 degrees with the keel up. Of course, this is more than ample stability for normal sailing, but to allow for the possibility of being caught offshore in a gale with high seas that could roll the boat over, the stability range should be greater. In my opinion, every sailboat that will ever venture into exposed waters should have *positive stability* (the ability to self-right) to 110 degrees heel at the very minimum. As a very general rule of thumb, at least a third of a sailing cruiser's displacement should be consigned to keel ballast that will be carried outside the hull. A drop-keel boat may enter a protected gunkhole with her keel retracted, but if she ventures into exposed waters, especially in heavy weather, it would certainly be prudent to keep the keel fully down.

Another variable draft configuration occasionally seen is the tandem centerboard arrangement illustrated by D in Figure 1-7. Basically, D is a keel-centerboarder (similar to A in the same figure) but she has two centerboards, one ahead of the other, on the boat's centerline. The forward board is usually the larger, and its main function is to supply lateral resistance for the prevention of leeway. The after board is trimmed according to wind and sea conditions and the particular point of sailing for optimal steering control. Advantages are that the helm can be balanced easily under almost all sailing conditions, and the boat can be made to steer herself. Disadvantages are that tacking is more difficult, and some of the possible centerboard problems mentioned earlier—worn pins, broken pendants, bent boards, and servicing difficulties—may be doubled when there are two boards instead of one.

Twin-Keelers

Thus far, this chapter has concentrated on common types of *monohull* (single-hulled) cruising sailboats having their lateral resistance appendages, those needed to inhibit leeway, located on the boat's centerline. Other craft, less often seen on American waters but having some degree of popularity, are twin-keelers (mentioned earlier) and *multihulls* (craft having more than one hull—see Figure 1-9).

Although I personally prefer the monohull for ordinary use, there are admittedly some special advantages in the twin-keel and multihull concepts.

The usual twin-keeler has side-by-side identical fins widely separated from each other on either side of the boat's centerline as shown in Figure 1-10. Notice that the keels are angled away from a vertical to the load waterline in such a way that when the boat heels, her draft becomes deeper, and the leeward keel presents a more vertical surface to the water's side force, thereby discouraging water flow under the keel's bottom from the leeward to windward side, all of which is helpful in reducing leeway without resorting to deep draft. Also, it may be possible to gain efficiency to windward when heeled if the keels are slightly angled away from the boat's centerline so that the leeward keel can have an angle of leeway, necessary for hydrodynamic lift (the side force at right angles to the water flow, which prevents excessive leeway) without the need of dragging a bulky hull at a considerable angle of leeway (see Figure 1-10). The principal advantage of a twin-keeler, however, is that she will stand upright when high and dry in regions of extreme tide, and, of course, she draws less when floating upright than a normal single-keel boat. For these reasons, and the fact that many small twin-keelers are readily trailerable, boats of this configuration may gunkhole cruise in some areas that are not accessible to deep single-keel boats and even keel-centerboarders.

Despite these advantages, many of the stock twin-keelers being produced today have drawbacks. As compared with a boat with a single fin keel, the boat with twin keels will generally have more wetted surface, and this obviously will affect performance, especially in light airs. Then, too, despite some theoretical arguments for the superiority of a twin-keeler in windward performance, a boat with a single fin will nearly always reach the windward mark ahead of the twin-keeler during a race. The main reason for this, aside from the wetted surface consideration, is that the *aspect ratio* (the ratio of depth to fore-and-aft length) of the single fin is higher and therefore more effective in producing lift at a low cost in drag. Some sailors argue that windward ability is not important for a cruiser that will never be raced, but I strongly disagree. Not only will a weatherly boat be more fun to sail, but her ability to make progress to windward against head seas and a foul tide could be a great convenience and even a safety factor when it is necessary to make

Some boats, such as the "Irwin 32," can be ordered with either a deep, fairly long fin keel or with a shallow keel and centerboard.

port before dark or before a storm or to work away from a lee shore. Certainly twin-keelers are not all bad performers when beating, but in general they are not superior on this point of sailing.

In considering all the pros and cons of the twin-keel concept, I would question the advisability of selecting a twin-keeler for cruising except in regions of extreme tide when the boat must sit on the bottom. The other main plaudit for the design is shoal draft without excessive sacrifice to reserve stability. Figure 1-11 compares the general characteristics of stability curves for a typical single-keel boat, a keel-centerboarder, and a twin-keeler. Notice that the twin-keeler has slightly less initial stability but quite a bit more reserve stability than the keel-centerboarder. Thus in localities where long stretches of rough, exposed waters occur between very shallow gunkholes, the advantages of the twin-keel design might very well outweigh its disadvantages.

Multihulls

There are also good arguments for and against multihulls. These boats are usually extremely fast on runs and reaches but not very efficient when beating, and coming about can be somewhat difficult. Furthermore, multihull performance on any point of sailing will suffer from heavy loading of supplies or gear; thus, cruisers of this type will seldom have the speed of those intended for racing or day sailing.

Perhaps the most serious drawback of the multihull is the lack of ultimate stability. These craft depend on extreme beam—actually a wide spread of distance between hulls—rather than low placement of ballast for transverse stability, and this gives them tremendous resistance to initial heeling. After a moderate angle of heel, however, stability decreases rapidly. The general character of stability curves for a *catamaran* (a two-hulled boat) and a *trimaran* (a three-hulled boat) are shown in Figure 1-11. Resistance to heeling is indicated by the vertical height of the curves, which show the boats' *righting moments* at various angles of heel, from 0 to more than 130 degrees. A boat's righting moment is her displacement times her *righting arm* (the distance between the upward, buoyant force acting through the center of buoyancy of a heeled hull and the downward force, the boat's weight, acting through the center of gravity). Notice that the catamaran in Figure 1-11 has a tremendous righting moment at about 18 degrees of heel, and the trimaran has almost as much stability at about 38 degrees, but after further heeling the curves of both multihulls drop off quickly. Comparing the multihull curves with those of the monohulls, one can see that the former have far greater righting moments, but the latter have positive stability through much greater

FIGURE 1-9: MULTIHULLS

FIGURE 1-10: TWIN KEELERS

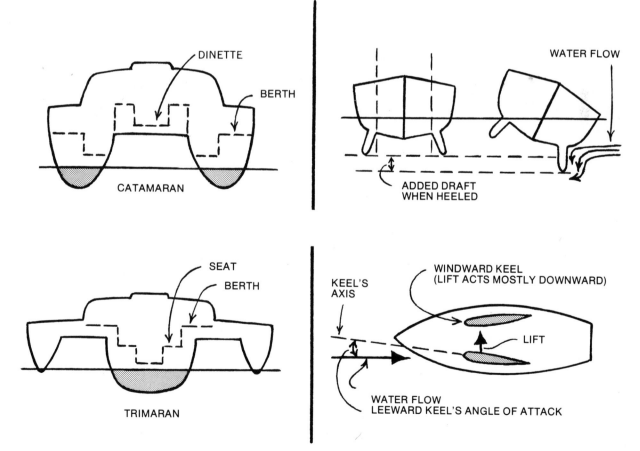

FIGURE 1-11: CHARACTER OF STABILITY CURVES

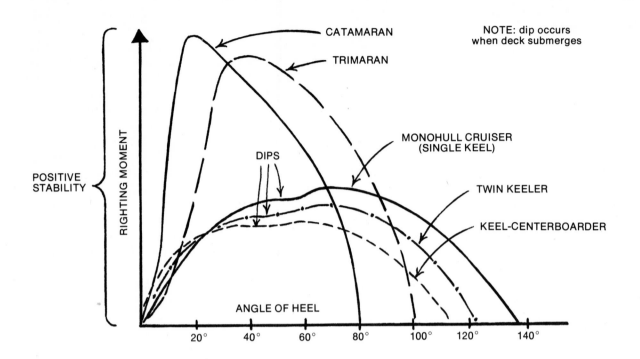

angles of heel. In other words, if a multihull is knocked down to the point where her mast touches or nearly touches the water, her stability will become negative, and she will capsize and most probably *turn turtle* (roll over until completely upside down). In this position she will be more stable than if she were right side up, and therefore extremely difficult to right. There is safety in the fact that the average multihull, being unballasted, will float and thus serve as a crude life raft when upside down, but the crew would be safer in a watertight boat with self-righting capabilities in weather sufficiently heavy to cause a severe knockdown. A properly ballasted monohull, though usually sinkable if she is allowed to fill with water, can turn nearly bottom side up before her stability becomes negative; and even if she should happen to turn turtle, she can be righted very easily. In fact, a wave washing against her keel could possibly exert sufficient force to right her. The foregoing is not to say that multihulls are dangerous, but in general they must be sailed with greater caution than monohulls.

Another, perhaps less serious, disadvantage of the multihull is that high initial stability imposes great strain on the rigging. When a strong gust of wind strikes a ballasted monohull, she will heel and spill the wind from her sails before the rigging is strained excessively, but a multihull may be so unyielding that her rig could be damaged in a sudden squall. The usual solution is to put far stronger rigging on a multihull than on a monohull of similar mast height and sail area and to have jam cleats that will automatically release the sheets in puffs strong enough to capsize the boat.

As mentioned earlier, high initial stability can cause an uncomfortably quick roll in beam seas. Multihulls are subject to this motion, but in many instances their extreme beam allows them to fit comfortably on top of or to straddle a wave that would roll a monohull considerably. Indeed, I have seen some harbors that were subject to *surge* (a term commonly given to swells entering an anchorage) in which single-hulled craft experienced a disagreeable roll while multihulls lay to their anchors placidly. In addition, multihulls do not suffer from the accumulative rolling that sometimes bothers narrow monohulls. To draw a very general conclusion on the matter of rolling, I prefer the motion of a mono-hull for most passages offshore, but for coastal or gunkhole cruising, the motion of the multihull might

One example of a cruising catamaran is the "Hirondelle 24," shown under sail. The twin companionways are perfectly safe on a multihull because of its low angle of heel.

be quite comfortable, perhaps more so than that of the average monohull in certain conditions.

The very high initial stability of a multihull also means that she will sail upright with very little heel. Whether or not this is an advantage is a matter of personal preference. Some people like level sailing so that articles will not slide off tables, shelves, or the galley stove; but many sailors prefer the feeling of natural responsiveness to the wind and the apparent speed to windward induced by heeling, even if this

Below, the "Hirondelle 24" has a dinette and galley amidships with sitting headroom; the hulls, which hold bunks, have full headroom.

means extra care in stowing loose articles, the installation of *fiddles* (rails) around tables and shelves, and the mounting of the galley stove on *gimbals* (swivels that allow an object to remain level). My own personal preference is for a boat that has a moderate heel, but I abhor excessive tenderness in any boat.

Compared with a monohull, a cruising multihull of the same length usually affords greater deck and accommodation space. In a fairly large catamaran, for instance, both hulls can be used for cabin space, though it might be very narrow, and on a trimaran, the space under a *wing deck* (the deck connecting the hulls) might be used for upper berths to allow a great deal of room in the central passageway. The trade-off for space above and below decks, however, is that a multihull's extreme beam can make hauling on a marine railway or mooring in a marina slip rather difficult.

For gunkhole cruising most multihulls have the advantage of very shallow draft. Indeed, many of these craft can be run up on the beach in protected areas with no surf. This beaching capability is also a safety factor if one gets caught on a lee shore in a blow and cannot work his boat off. On a rocky coast or any shore with even moderate surf, however, a beached boat is very apt to break up or at least sustain serious damage.

Very shoal-draft multihulls should usually be fitted with centerboards lest windward performance suffer. I have sailed a thirty-five-foot, V-bottom trimaran without a centerboard, and her windward performance was abominable. Since a cruising catamaran sails at a low angle of heel, and since she should never be allowed to lift either hull clear of the water because of the capsize risk, it is very probable that only one centerboard placed in one hull will be needed.

This small cruising trimaran, the "Cross 26," has safety nets forward to prevent crew members from falling between the hulls. Notice the ample space for quarters below.

Motor Sailers

The vast majority of modern cruising sailboats have some sort of auxiliary engine power. This may be in the form of outboard motors on small boats or inboard gasoline or diesel engines on large boats, but on the sailing cruisers previously discussed, sail is considered the prime motivating power, and the engine is merely a secondary means of propulsion used during calms or when maneuvering into a tight spot such as a marina slip. (Auxiliaries will be discussed in Chapter 5.)

When a sailboat is designed with emphasis on mechanical propulsion, she is usually termed a *motor sailer*. This type of cruiser is often classified according to the approximate percentage of sail power to mechanical power allocated to propulsion. For instance, a *thirty-seventy* might be considered a motorboat with sails, a *fifty-fifty* has almost equal emphasis on sail and engine power, and a *seventy-thirty* could be considered a heavily powered sailboat.

With the thirty-seventy type, sail adds little to propulsion, its principal function being to dampen rolling or to help hold the boat at a favorable attitude to the wind and seas in heavy weather. Even when there is little wind, a sizable sail sheeted flat can help alleviate the tiresome rolling sometimes experienced in beam seas during a long passage. Also, a sail far aft can be used to help hold the vessel's head into the wind when she is lying to the tide and rolling to beam swells at anchor. An even more effective means of stabilizing is the use of a flat plate called a *roll control* or "flopper stopper" suspended on a line from the end of a boom on each side of the boat. An at-anchor roll control will be described in Chapter 10. In heavy weather offshore, a small sail aft might be used as a riding sail to help hold the bow up to the seas, or a small sail forward could be used to hold the bow off and the stern up to the seas if the boat is manageable when *scudding* (running off with little or no sail set) and when it is desirable or advisable to make progress to leeward. In using any sail during a blow, however, the skipper must be sure his thirty-seventy has ample stability. Although powerboats are seldom ballasted, motor sailers, regardless of how little sail they carry, should nearly always have at least some deeply located ballast for assurance against capsizing.

The fifty-fifty has sufficient sail for emergency propulsion when the destination lies down or across the wind, but most motor sailers of this type cannot be driven to windward effectively under sail alone. If the engine is operable, however, good progress to windward can be made by *power-sailing*, using the sails and engine simultaneously. A fifty-fifty usually has sufficient engine power to drive her directly upwind against head seas, but many seventy-thirties and sailing auxiliaries cannot make good progress to windward under power alone in strong winds with head seas and a foul current. Under these conditions, power-sailing provides a way of reaching a destination upwind. It is often surprising how close to the wind a boat can point and how much power she has under the combination of sail and power. The engine provides enough speed to prevent the keel from stalling and increases the apparent wind on the sails; the propeller wash gives good rudder control; and the sails augment the engine's thrust and steady the vessel's motion.

The seventy-thirty would be my choice for the best distribution of sail and power in a motor sailer. The sails are of sufficient size and efficiency to allow fast reaching or running and efficient beating to windward in most conditions under sail alone. Furthermore, they are large enough to be effective roll dampers. Yet engine power and fuel capacity are ample for motoring long distances in calm weather or for power-sailing during extended periods of head winds and rough seas.

Most motor sailers are designed somewhat like offshore fishing craft. They are usually seagoing boats of fairly heavy construction, having *displacement* or nonplaning hulls that cannot readily be driven above a speed of 1.35 times the square root of the waterline length. This kind of boat is generally somewhat more roomy and comfortable than a pure sailer, and the helmsman of a typical motor sailer is protected from the spray and weather with a windshield, a *doghouse* (the raised after part of the cabin top), or a pilot house. His visibility is sometimes hampered, however, and in fair weather he might want more exposure to the elements. Draft for this type of boat is not usually great, but the larger the rig, the deeper the keel should be to provide an effective lateral plane for sailing and sufficient depth of keel ballast for ample stability. In general, it would seem that the motor sailer is best suited for long distance passage-making or for living on board for extended periods.

A salty-looking motor sailer, the "Islander 40," has a "great cabin" aft, a taff rail, and a pulpit on the bowsprit.

2

Construction and Safety Features

In shopping for a new or used cruiser, the prospective buyer must look not only for a generally wholesome design of a type and size he can afford but also for a boat that is well built and has specific safety features to assure survival in the worst possible conditions. No one knows when emergencies or extreme weather might be encountered, even in protected waters, so there should be an ample margin of safety and strength.

Construction Features

Sound construction is important not only for safety but also for low-cost maintenance, high resale value, and longevity. This section will not attempt a comprehensive discussion of construction, but it will bring up some major factors of which the prospective buyer should be aware. Since this book concerns primarily stock boats, and since the vast majority of these are built of fiberglass (glass-reinforced plastic), we shall concentrate on this form of construction.

Most stock fiberglass boats are built on the inside of a female mold to assure a smooth hull exterior. The inside of the mold cavity is first coated with a waxy releasing agent to facilitate subsequent lifting of the completed hull from the mold. Building is begun by spraying the outer layer of the hull into the mold. This layer, called the *gel coat*, is composed mostly of pure resin and pigment, and it must be just the right thickness—about fifteen-thousandths of an inch—in order that it will not later wrinkle or crack. Following the gel coat are layers of laminate consisting of various forms of glass filaments imbedded in a plastic—usually polyester resin. The laminate composition may consist of alternate layers of *mat* (loosely bonded glass strands running in random directions), *cloth* (a strong woven fabric of twisted strands), and *woven roving* (a coarse, heavy woven fabric of untwisted strands). In some cases, these preformed reinforcing materials are partially or substantially replaced by random short strands of glass blown into the mold simultaneously with a spray of resin shot from a special tool called a *chopper gun*.

Experts often do not agree on the soundest method of building up the laminate. Many prefer the hand layup method whereby alternating layers of mat, cloth, and roving are laid into the mold by hand, each layer being soaked with resin and carefully squeegeed to remove air bubbles that might become trapped under the fabric. Other experts feel that properly applied chopper gun layup is quite satisfactory. The latter method may be more difficult to control, however, and I believe that hand layup is usually preferable. One well-constructed thirty-footer that successfully completed a rugged circumnavigation was constructed by hand layup of mat, cloth, and seven layers of woven roving in her bilge and keel areas.

In some cases a sandwich construction is used—a core of balsa wood, foamed plastics, or plywood encased by layers of fiberglass. This construction is most appropriate for decks or flat surfaces that must resist flexing from weight or other stress concentrations, but a core is sometimes used in the hull shell. If it is, the outer skin must be amply thick and strong to resist puncture and water penetration, which could damage the core material. It is important that the core be securely bonded to both skins. Solid hard woods and conventional planking generally are not recommended for encasement, because the working of seams or swelling of the wood could crack the laminate.

Vulnerable areas in a fiberglass boat are joints, points of attachment, sharp bends or angles, and areas subjected to flexing. These are spots that should be checked before buying a new or used boat. Since most hulls, except for large ones (or those with pronounced tumble homes), are molded in one piece, while the deck, cabin trunk, and cockpit form another piece, the only connection joint is where the deck joins the hull. This is a very important junction, because the seam runs entirely around the boat and is highly stressed by the tendency of the topsides to be deflected by seas and by rigging strains. The very best builders will often bolt the deck to the hull and bond it with resin. Sometimes pop rivets are used, and these can be satisfactory if used with bonding. On a few boats, however, the connection is made with self-tapping

FIGURE 2-1: HULL-DECK CONNECTIONS

FIGURE 2-2: FITTING ATTACHMENT

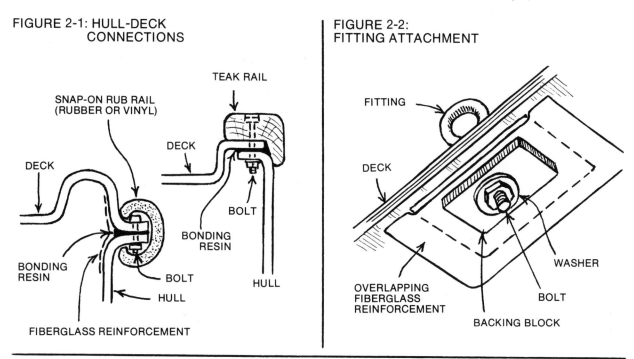

FIGURE 2-3: FIBERGLASS HULL REINFORCEMENT (SUGGESTIVE OF LLOYD'S RECOMMENDATIONS)

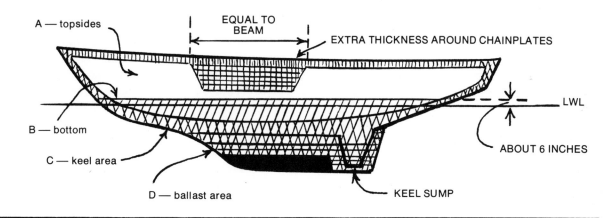

FIGURE 2-4: HARD SPOTS AND TWO POSSIBLE REMEDIES

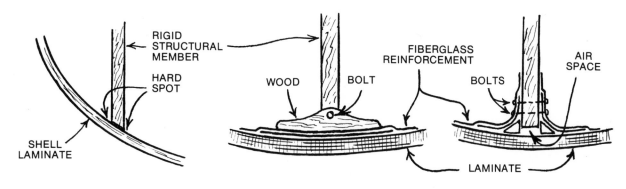

screws and with little or no bonding. In my opinion, this method is less than sturdy to begin with, and the unbonded joint, which usually relies on bedding compound to keep the water out, will often leak after the compound dries out. A couple of acceptable methods of hull-deck attachment are shown in Figure 2-1.

Attachments occur wherever fittings are joined to the hull, and these areas require suitable reinforcement. Fittings such as mooring or anchor cleats, winches, or chainplates that take a lot of strain often need more than a simple backing block for their through bolts. In most cases the laminate shell should gradually be thickened with overlapping layers of laminate as shown in Figure 2-2 so that stress can be distributed over a wide area. Staggering the layers of laminate as illustrated helps prevent stress concentrations and repeated flexing in one spot. If a small section of fiberglass is allowed to flex, or "oilcan," over and over again, there is a possibility of fatigue cracking. Figure 2-3 shows reinforcement layers along the gunwale and topsides in way of the chainplates equal in length to the beam. This is similar to the specifications set forth in Lloyd's Register of Shipping rules for construction, which are among the highest boat-building standards. Lloyd's also specifies that the laminate weight is to be increased at least 25 percent in way of joints, flanges, and fittings.

The principle of gradual reinforcement and wide distribution of stress also applies to areas known as *hard spots*, where bulkheads or other rigid strengthening members attach to the hull shell, especially if the shell is somewhat flexible near the point of attachment. The hull can "work," or move, considerably in a seaway, and it will often vibrate under power; thus it is important that there be a gradual transition from areas of flexibility to those of rigidity. There must be ample hull stiffeners in the form of bulkheads and longitudinal members such as stringers or integrated bunks, shelves, and lockers that are bonded to the hull. Where a stiffener touches the hull, however, there should be gradual, local reinforcement—extra layers of laminate, a flat plate under the stiffener, or some other means to distribute the stress over a wide area (see Figure 2-4).

Corners also take a lot of concentrated stress. Be wary of sharp bends and right angles in fiberglass. These bends can lead to subsequent cracking, and there might be voids or pockets of air under the laminate where it is bent. It is almost always preferable that corners be curved or gently rounded, both in places where flat surfaces change direction (such as where the deck turns into the cabin trunk) and where holes are cut through the fiberglass (such as where a hatchway is cut through the deck). Incidentally, some stock boats offer optional midships hatchways in the cabin top for extra ventilation. If such an opening is cut out close to the mainmast, the step or partners could be weakened, and so compensating structural support might have to be added.

The hull shell should gradually thicken from the topsides down to the keel as suggested in Figure 2-3. Area A, the thinnest laminate, begins slightly below the rail and runs to about six inches above the designed LWL, where it gradually thickens to form area B, which runs to a region somewhat above the *garboards* (where the hull begins to turn into the keel appendage). A further gradual thickening of the laminate forms area C, which runs down to another gradually thickened area, D, just above the ballast. As a rough rule based on Lloyd's *scantlings* (specifications for size or weight of construction materials), the weight per square foot of laminate in area D should be about or almost two and a half times greater than the weight in area A.

Keels are of three general types: the hollow keel integral with the hull and having internal ballast, the hollow integral keel with external ballast bolted to its bottom, and an all-metal fin made separately and then bolted to the hull. The last type usually does not have the inherent strength of the former types, and the hull carrying a bolted-on fin needs special reinforcement—extra layers of laminate and probably transverse frames or floors near the point of attachment. Another drawback of the solid metal fin is that there is no internal space for tanks or a sump for bilge water. The sump, shown in Figure 2-3, is important to keep any water that might collect in the bilge from rolling up under the bunks and possibly wetting lockers when the boat heels. Twin-keel boats with all-metal fins usually need transverse frames linking the keels to prevent hull flexing.

Hollow integral keels with internal ballast are advantageous for racing boats, because the keel can be kept very smooth when there is no seam or irregularity in surface between the ballast and the integral keel. These keels also free you from worry about corroding keel bolts. Occasionally, however, there is a problem with bonding the ballast to the interior of the keel. This bonding is important, because any movement can cause wear and abrasion. Large masses of polyester resin cannot be used for bonding without the risk of generating excessive heat when they set, and this could possibly cause undetectable internal cracks in the fiberglass. It is preferable that the internal ballast be one piece of lead that is exactly shaped to fit snugly into the keel cavity, as this allows the ballast to contribute to the keel's strength, discourages movement of the ballast, and keeps the center of gravity low. The ballast should be tightly covered at its top with a heavy laminate seal to help prevent movement or detachment of the ballast during a severe knockdown and to keep water out of the hull if the keel should be ruptured during a grounding.

There also are advantages to an integral keel with external ballast, especially for a boat that cruises in areas with coral or rocky bottoms. A grounding on a hard bottom can easily damage a keel with internal ballast by rupturing the laminate and allowing water to enter the keel cavity or to penetrate between the layers of laminate. Water trapped in pockets in the bottom of a keel is extremely difficult to remove, and if it is allowed to remain, it can cause delamination and other weaknesses. With external ballast there is far less chance of keel damage during a grounding. External ballast also gives the lowest possible center of gravity for a given weight, providing good stability with minimal draft. The tops of external ballast bolts should be accessible for inspection and tightening. Washers of considerable size are required to prevent crushing the laminate, and Lloyd's recommends that bolts be fitted alternately on opposite sides of the keel's centerline for maximum strength.

The skeg is another area that needs extra support and reinforcement, as this appendage often takes a considerable wringing stress from the rudder. I believe that the top of the cavity of an integral skeg should be tightly sealed so that the hull will not become flooded in the event that the skeg should break off.

Other boat-building materials used much less often than fiberglass for stock boats are wood, aluminum, and ferrocement. Conventional plank-on-frame wood construction is becoming increasingly rare in America because of the high cost of labor and the fact that, compared with newer building methods, this construction, with its many seams that need caulking, is the least watertight. Plywood boats, whether molded or built from sheets, have minimal seams, and the stability of the material often allows the exterior surface to be covered with fiberglass cloth for added protection and water-tightness. Sheet plywood, however, can only be used on boats with flat or simple curved surfaces, usually those with chines and V bottoms. It is extremely important to see that there are no plywood butt ends left uncovered, because they could allow water penetration and subsequent rot or delamination. Of course, all plywood used for boat building should be marine grade of high quality. Another water-tight wood construction is planking of narrow strips that are edge-nailed and glued together. This makes an almost monolithic shell, which does not require the number of structural members (especially trans-verse members) as does conventional plank-on-frame construction. Boats with wide planking and glued seams are best suited to fairly cool climates and those that do not have extremes in temperature and humidity that could possibly crack the planking or split the seams.

The greatest drawback of any wood construction is its vulnerability to rot, but this need not be a problem if the following precautions are taken: (1) See that the wood is suitable for boat building, that it is well seasoned, and that it is treated with preservative such as Cuprinol. (2) Allow no part of the construction to trap pockets of fresh water. This may require extra *limber holes* (drains) or sloping edges to permit drainage, and, of course, all leaks should be stopped if possible. (3) Be sure that every nook and cranny is well ventilated. There should be a circulation of air behind the *ceiling* (liner inside the ribs) from the bilge—perhaps through a grate in the cabin sole—to an opening in the ceiling near the deck. Furthermore, there should be ample ventilation holes in all lockers or closed spaces and a fore-and-aft flow of air through water-tight ventilators at all times. More will be said about this in Chapters 3 and 6.

Aluminum construction is expensive, but it gives an extremely high strength-to-weight ratio, and the hull can be made very smooth when seams are properly welded. The newest alloys are highly resistant to salt-water corrosion, but great care must be taken to use metal fittings and fastenings that are compatible with the aluminum to avoid galvanic corrosion. Stainless steel usually is not very harmful to aluminum, but bronze cannot be used unless it is completely isolated with a barrier such as micarta, neoprene, or rubber. Even antifouling paint containing copper and especially mercury can be very destructive to bare aluminum; thus, paints containing tri-butyl tin oxide (TBTO) are often recommended for the bottoms of aluminum boats.

Steel-reinforced concrete, or *ferrocement*, construction is slowly increasing in popularity, especially with amateur boat builders. Advantages of the material are its great strength, fire resistance, rigidity, durability, resistance to abrasion, and freedom from rot or corrosion (provided, of course, that moisture is kept away from the steel supporting frame). Disadvantages are that boats of conventional ferrocement construction are usually quite heavy, that voids under the cement are often hard to detect, and that a completely smooth and fair hull surface is difficult to obtain. Also, I have heard of one or two ferrocement boats that seem to reject paint, but the builder may have applied the paint before the cement had dried sufficiently. A drying period

of at least three months is recommended, and an undercoating of epoxy is said to be helpful. The future for ferrocement looks quite promising as new building techniques are developed to overcome the problems of weight, smoothness, and voids. Very likely there will be a growth in molded, mass-produced concrete boats in the near future. Although we hear a great deal about the low cost of this construction, I think this aspect has been overrated. There may be a slight saving on the hull shell, but the hull is only a small part of the cost of a completed boat.

It is always important to choose a builder who is well established, reputable, and experienced with the material of which the boat is made. This is especially true with ferrocement boats, which seem to vary in quality. The buyer of any used boat, particularly, should engage the services of a competent marine surveyor to inspect the hull, the rig, and all equipment. It pays to take some trouble in finding a thoroughly dependable surveyor and checking his background and experience with the

The high-silled companionway with bridge deck, seldom found on modern stock boats, is visible on this small Friendship sloop shown off the coast of Maine. Notice the self-tacking headsail.

material of which the boat in question is built. Insurance companies or the National Association of Marine Surveyors might be helpful in suggesting a reliable surveyor in the prospective buyer's area.

Safety Features

Aside from the safety aspects of hull design, such as seaworthy lines, wholesome proportions, and ample stability, the boat buyer should be aware of some important safety features related to the deck, cockpit, and permanently installed equipment. Unfortunately, present standard stock boats often lack many of these features, but some may be ordered as extras, or the owner can add them after he has taken delivery of the boat. Important safety considerations are:

FLOTATION. Capsizable boats (those that lack sufficient stability beyond about 90 degrees heel) or boats lacking watertight integrity (those with open cockpits or other means of admitting water to the bilge) should be fitted with sufficient flotation to buoy up the swamped hull and all the weight carried.

COCKPIT DRAINAGE. If a boat lacks flotation, she must be capable of being made watertight to avoid the risk of sinking in heavy weather. This calls for a self-bailing cockpit well that can drain rapidly. A common fault on many stock boats is undersize cockpit *scuppers* (drains). The American Boat and Yacht Council (ABYC), a body of marine safety experts that sets standards for small craft, presently recommends that drainage for a watertight cockpit should be accomplished with scuppers on the port and starboard sides with the minimum total scupper area in square inches equaling $L \times W \div 15$, where L is the cockpit length in feet and W is the cockpit width in feet. If the boat will be raced in exposed waters, the North American Yacht Racing Union (NAYRU) requires that the combined area of cockpit scuppers be not less than the equivalent of four three-quarter-inch drains.

COCKPIT VOLUME. Another important consideration is the volume of a watertight cockpit, because an extremely large well that becomes filled from a knockdown or a sea breaking aboard can seriously weigh down the stern. For boats sailing in unprotected waters, the NAYRU limits the volume to 6 percent times LOA (length overall) times maximum beam times freeboard aft. The bottom of the cockpit should be at least ten inches above the LWL.

COMPANIONWAY SILL. One of the most common safety faults on stock boats is the low companionway sill. Of course, the feature allows easy access to the cabin, but the low sill is potentially dangerous for any boat that will sail in exposed waters, because a boarding sea or a severe knockdown could flood the cabin. The safest arrangement is to have a bridge deck between the cockpit well and the companionway, as this not only prevents flooding below, but gives extra strength, provides a convenient step for those going below, and reduces the volume of the cockpit. The next best arrangement is to have a low bulkhead beneath the companionway that raises the sill to a height at which water would flow onto the deck before spilling below if the cockpit were flooded (see Figure 2-5). Lacking the bridge deck or raised sill, there should be a vertical slide, stronger than the customary slide, that may be fit securely into the lower half of the companion hatchway in heavy weather.

LATCHES AND DOGS. All deck openings must be capable of being securely closed. Hatches and portholes should be provided with *dogs* similar to the type illustrated in Figure 2-6. The hatch hooks found on some boats are not strong enough for heavy weather in exposed waters. Seat locker lids often lack fasteners, but they could fall open during a knockdown and admit water to the bilge; therefore it is important that they be provided with some means of being secured. An effective device is the simple hasp that can be held shut with a snap hook (see Figure 2-6). Ventilators should be removable, and the holes they cover must be provided with secure plugs or screw-on plates.

WINDOWS AND HATCHES. Port lights and windows must be of shatterproof safety glass or Plexiglas set in strong metal frames, and windows should not be excessively large on any boat that will venture into exposed waters. In addition to the companionway hatch, there ought to be a forward hatch large enough to be used as an alternate exit. If the boat will be taken to sea, I think it is important that the hatches be located near the boat's centerline.

SEACOCKS AND HOSE CLAMPS. All through-hull pipelines anywhere near and especially below the waterline should be fitted with shut-off valves at the point where they penetrate the hull shell. It is highly preferable that these valves be tapered, plug-type seacocks that shut off by turning a lever handle a quarter of a turn as shown in Figure 2-7. Hoses connected to the through-hull fitting should be attached with dependable, screw-type hose clamps

FIGURE 2-5: COCKPIT VOLUME

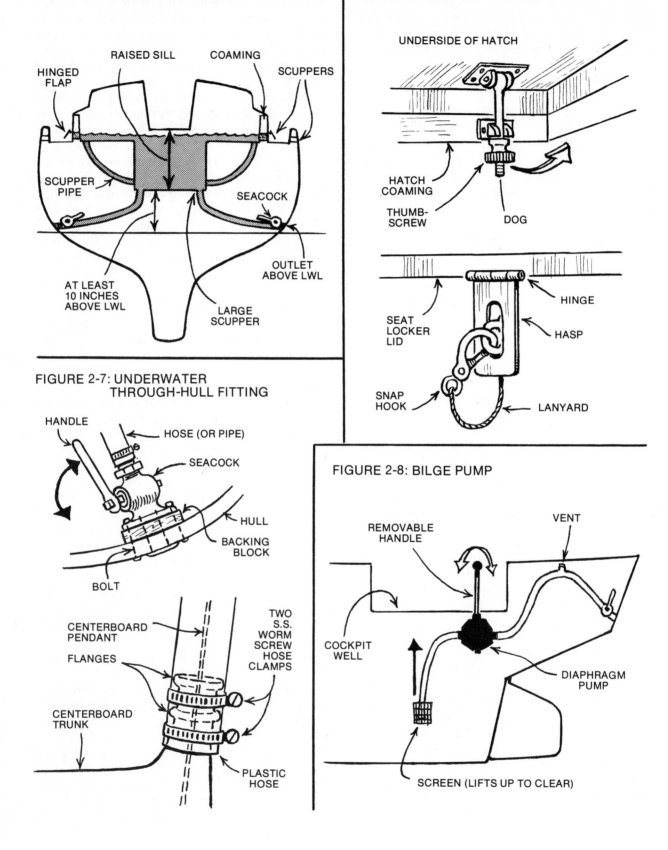

HINGED FLAP

RAISED SILL

COAMING

SCUPPERS

SCUPPER PIPE

SEACOCK

AT LEAST 10 INCHES ABOVE LWL

OUTLET ABOVE LWL

LARGE SCUPPER

FIGURE 2-7: UNDERWATER THROUGH-HULL FITTING

HANDLE

HOSE (OR PIPE)

SEACOCK

HULL

BACKING BLOCK

BOLT

CENTERBOARD PENDANT

FLANGES

TWO S.S. WORM SCREW HOSE CLAMPS

CENTERBOARD TRUNK

PLASTIC HOSE

FIGURE 2-6: HATCH FASTENERS

UNDERSIDE OF HATCH

HATCH COAMING

THUMB-SCREW

DOG

SEAT LOCKER LID

HINGE

HASP

SNAP HOOK

LANYARD

FIGURE 2-8: BILGE PUMP

REMOVABLE HANDLE

VENT

COCKPIT WELL

DIAPHRAGM PUMP

SCREEN (LIFTS UP TO CLEAR)

made of stainless steel. Be sure that the nipple over which the hose fits is flanged to prevent the hose from slipping off. This is especially important at the point where a centerboard pendant penetrates the hull underwater, because a seacock cannot be fitted there. Also, the nipple should be sufficiently long to accept two hose clamps.

ACCESSIBILITY. It is important that all seacocks, the nuts of fitting-attachment bolts, electrical wiring, and piping be accessible for inspection and/or servicing. Many stock boat interiors are of *unitized construction*, a large part of the boat's insides being built as a one-piece molded liner that often seriously blocks accessibility to the hull shell. A boat with this problem should have access ports cut so that vital parts of the hull, bilge, mast step, piping, wiring, fittings, and so on can be reached. On some boats it is surprisingly difficult to reach many parts of the engine, although it should be obvious that these must be periodically inspected and serviced. There also must be easy access to the battery, shaft, *stuffing box* (the fitting where the shaft penetrates the hull), and tanks.

PERMANENT BILGE PUMP. Although a permanently installed bilge pump is one of the most important safety items, it is optional on many stock boats and must be purchased separately. The buyer of a new boat should by all means order a ruggedly built, large-capacity pump installed so that it can be used from the cockpit. It should not be put inside a seat locker, however, because opening the locker lid to operate the pump in heavy weather might admit more water to the bilge than could be removed. The pump's intake hose should reach to the deepest part of the bilge sump and be fitted with a strainer that can be lifted for clearing in the event that it becomes clogged with dirt or wood chips. A boat with no sump and a shallow bilge may need an intake hose on each side of the bilge so that water can be sucked up on either tack. The discharge hose should penetrate the hull high above the LWL, and it should be looped and have an air vent valve at the high point as shown in Figure 2-8 to prevent water from siphoning back into the bilge if the outlet should happen to become submerged through heeling or wave action. Electric pumps are a great convenience, but they are not as reliable as sturdy manual types. Especially recommended is the double-action diaphragm type that pumps an almost continuous flow of water no matter which way the handle is moved (see Figure 2-8).

FIGURE 2-9: MINIMAL LIGHTNING PROTECTION

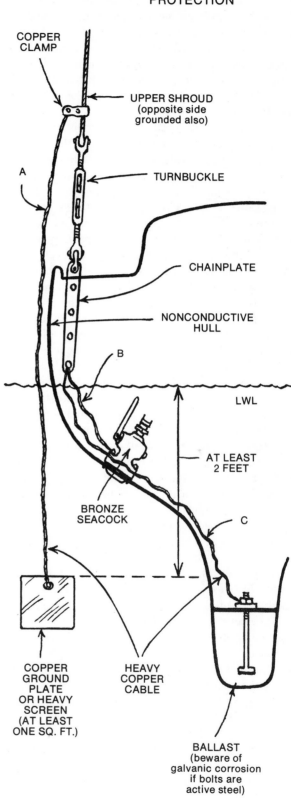

COPPER CLAMP

UPPER SHROUD (opposite side grounded also)

A

TURNBUCKLE

CHAINPLATE

NONCONDUCTIVE HULL

B

LWL

AT LEAST 2 FEET

BRONZE SEACOCK

C

HEAVY COPPER CABLE

COPPER GROUND PLATE OR HEAVY SCREEN (AT LEAST ONE SQ. FT.)

BALLAST (beware of galvanic corrosion if bolts are active steel)

ENGINE CONTROLS. The throttle, gear shift, and ignition switch on many sailboats are exposed in the cockpit and are subject to being bumped inadvertently. Especially vulnerable is the throttle, which can be moved very easily. A sudden accidental speed-up of the engine might not be as dangerous for a large boat that picks up speed slowly as for a small boat that accelerates rapidly, but I think that all throttles should be recessed into the side of the cockpit or otherwise protected unless the handle is removable and the throttle can be operated easily with the handle removed.

LIFE LINES AND GRAB RAILS. On every cruising boat there should be a *bow pulpit* (metal railing at the bow) and at least one wire life line running from the pulpit to the stern on each side of the boat. *Stanchions* (vertical pipes) supporting the life lines should be no further than seven feet apart, and they should be at least twenty-four (but preferably twenty-seven) inches high. Sockets or bases for the stanchions must be bolted through the deck, and it is preferable that there be three rather than two bolts for maximum strength. It is highly advisable to have a stern pulpit also if the boat will be sailed in exposed waters. Sturdy grab rails bolted along each side of the cabin trunk are essential.

NONSLIP SURFACES. Decks must be made skidproof with abrasive paint, rough patterns molded into fiberglass decks, or some other means. A problem with some newer boats is their excessive *crown* or roundness on the cabin tops and foredecks. Such surfaces make it difficult to maintain one's balance on the lee side when the boat is heeled and pitching in a head sea. Install abrasive strips or toe rails on very rounded surfaces and abrasive strips on all varnished or slippery hatch covers and on the companionway ladder.

VISIBILITY. The helmsman's seat must be sufficiently high for good visibility over the cabin trunk and bow. Sails can also obstruct visibility, especially the low-cut "deck-sweeper" jibs carried by many racing boats. I would like to see such jibs banned by racing committees, because they completely cut off the helmsman's view to leeward, while the increase in aerodynamic efficiency seems very slight and only when hard on the wind. Certainly cruising boats should carry high-cut jibs that will neither chafe on the life lines nor blind the helmsman.

LIGHTNING PROTECTION. All boats—especially those made of fiberglass, a relatively poor conductor of electricity—should be provided with some kind of protection against lightning. All stays, shrouds,

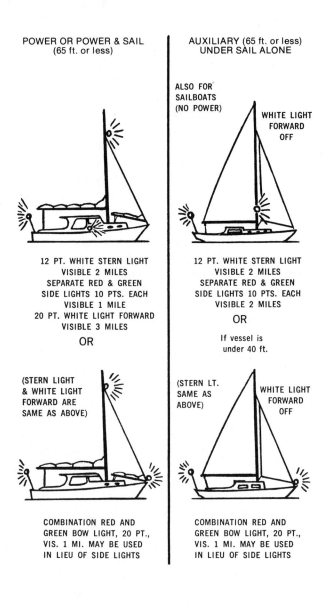

FIGURE 2-10: REQUIRED LIGHTS UNDER INTERNATIONAL RULES required on the high seas and may be shown on U. S. waters

POWER OR POWER & SAIL (65 ft. or less)

AUXILIARY (65 ft. or less) UNDER SAIL ALONE

ALSO FOR SAILBOATS (NO POWER)

WHITE LIGHT FORWARD OFF

12 PT. WHITE STERN LIGHT VISIBLE 2 MILES SEPARATE RED & GREEN SIDE LIGHTS 10 PTS. EACH VISIBLE 1 MILE 20 PT. WHITE LIGHT FORWARD VISIBLE 3 MILES

OR

12 PT. WHITE STERN LIGHT VISIBLE 2 MILES SEPARATE RED & GREEN SIDE LIGHTS 10 PTS. EACH VISIBLE 2 MILES

OR

If vessel is under 40 ft.

(STERN LIGHT & WHITE LIGHT FORWARD ARE SAME AS ABOVE)

(STERN LT. SAME AS ABOVE)

WHITE LIGHT FORWARD OFF

COMBINATION RED AND GREEN BOW LIGHT, 20 PT., VIS. 1 MI. MAY BE USED IN LIEU OF SIDE LIGHTS

COMBINATION RED AND GREEN BOW LIGHT, 20 PT., VIS. 1 MI. MAY BE USED IN LIEU OF SIDE LIGHTS

A RED & GREEN BOW LIGHT MUST BE AT LEAST 3 FEET BELOW 20 POINT WHITE LIGHT FORWARD.

EXCEPTION: WESTERN RIVER RULES. SIDE LIGHTS FOR VESSELS UNDER SAIL MUST BE VISIBLE FOR 3 MILES.

NOTE: There is a permissive clause under International Rules enabling a boat under sail alone to carry (in addition to normal side lights and 12-point stern light) a 20 point red light over a 20 point green light at the masthead, sufficiently separated so as to be clearly distinguished and visible for 2 miles.

sail tracks on wood masts, and the heels of metal masts should be grounded through the hull if it is metal or to external ballast or a ground plate if the hull is nonmetallic. Minimal protection can be obtained by grounding the upper shroud chainplates to seacocks directly below the shrouds or by clamping to a stay or shroud a temporary copper cable supporting a ground plate held at least two feet below the water surface (see Figure 2-9). For maximum protection all large metal objects in the boat should be bonded to the lightning ground system, and there should be a pointed copper rod at least six inches high fastened to the top of the mast.

FUEL AND ELECTRICAL SYSTEMS. Proper installation of the fuel and electrical systems is extremely important not only to prevent loss of power but to prevent fires and explosions. These systems must be installed by competent, experienced marine electricians and mechanics. More will be said on this subject in the next chapter, which includes a brief discussion of galley stoves, and in Chapter 5, which deals with mechanical matters.

SOUND RIGGING. This will be discussed in Chapter 9, which deals with the cruising rig.

LEGAL REQUIREMENTS. All boats should be fitted out to meet Coast Guard standards and requirements for the Rules of the Road. This includes such items as proper lifesaving devices (at least one for each person on board), engine room ventilation, backfire flame arresters on carburetors, fire extinguishers, horn, bell, and proper navigation lights. At present, some lighting options are allowed under the various rules of the road, but in my opinion, lighting should be standardized as much as possible by equipping boats to meet requirements of the International Rules, which are necessary on the high seas and can be used on all U.S. waters (except where controlled by a state that has not given approval). Furthermore, it seems fairly certain that U.S. Inland Rules will be changed in the near future to agree with the International Rules (although there will probably be some lighting exceptions for the Great Lakes). See Figure 2-10 for International Rule lighting and Appendix A for minimum federal equipment requirements.

3

Accommodation, Galley, and Comfort Features

In selecting a boat for cruising, accommodation and comfort features are obviously a major consideration, because considerable time will be spent living on board. Stock boats are offering an increasing variety of standard accommodation plans. A single class may offer a choice of three different arrangements. Most of the basic plans are shown in Figures 3-1, 3-2, and 3-3, but with the dozens of stock classes being produced there are many slight variations on the standard layouts.

Small Cruisers

The most commonly seen accommodation plans for the smallest sailboat cruisers, from about twenty through twenty-six feet, are shown in Figure 3-1. The very smallest and least expensive boats, starting at a price just above $3,000 (at the time of this writing), usually have a relatively large cockpit for day sailing comfort with a *cuddy* (small cabin shelter) forward housing two bunks and a *head* (w.c.) for spending one or two nights aboard (see Figure 3-1, A). Other boats, usually slightly larger, have a greater portion of the cockpit space allocated to the cabin for more room below decks. This type might have an arrangement similar to plan B in Figure 3-1, which has one cabin but four berths and an athwartships curtain to provide privacy for the head located between the forward bunks. The after bunks might be considered *quarter berths,* as their after ends extend under the cockpit seats; their forward ends project quite far into the cabin, however, so they may be used for seats. Notice that there is a shelf above one bunk for a one-burner stove and a small sink. An ice chest might be stowed abaft the companionway steps. Boats slightly larger than B often have two cabins with a bulkhead and doorway at the forward end of the after berths. The door may serve double duty, closing off the head compartment when it is closed

in the fore and aft position but separating the two cabins when it is in the athwartships position. Still larger boats with this arrangement often have room for a small galley aft with a stove on one side of the boat and a sink and perhaps an icebox on the other side.

Accommodation plan C features a small dinette, a table and seating arrangement for two to four people. The table may be lowered to make a wide single berth. On some of the newer boats of this general size, the conventional companionway steps or ladder is replaced by a folding step and a cushioned seat below the companionway hatch to allow extra seating space near the dinette. The galley is conveniently located directly across from the dinette. The arrangement with one quarter berth leaves ample stowage space for sails and other gear in a large cockpit seat locker on the side of the boat opposite the quarter berth.

Boats under about twenty-six feet LOA normally don't have full standing headroom in the cabin, for this would require an excessively high freeboard or cabin trunk. All that is really needed on small boats is adequate sitting headroom or perhaps, if there is no great detraction from the boat's looks, standing headroom for a woman of average height. Many small boats have *raised-deck cabins* (cabin trunks extended athwartships to the sides of the hull as shown in Figure 3-4). This feature may add to stability by delaying immersion of the rail when the cabin extends far aft, and it affords good sitting headroom over the outboard area of the dinette, but many sailors think that raised decks detract from a boat's looks. Also, there may be some safety drawbacks in that without side decking and a coaming placed inboard of the rail, the cockpit is more subject to flooding during a severe knockdown (see Figure 3-4), and open portholes are more likely to admit water. On any boat, of course, ports should be closed when sailing in a fresh breeze, but the skipper of a boat with a raised deck must be especially cautious about watertightness. Another advantage to having a trunk cabin rather than a raised deck is that most sailors feel it is easier to leave the cockpit and go forward in rough weather when there are side decks to walk on and firm handrails to grip on a cabin top.

Some new small boats have adjustable cabin tops—sometimes referred to as "pop-tops" in advertising literature—that allow standing headroom when the top is raised. Curtains are usually provided to fill in the spaces under the edges of the raised

FIGURE 3-1: SMALL CRUISER ACCOMMODATIONS (ABOUT 20′ THROUGH 26′ LOA)

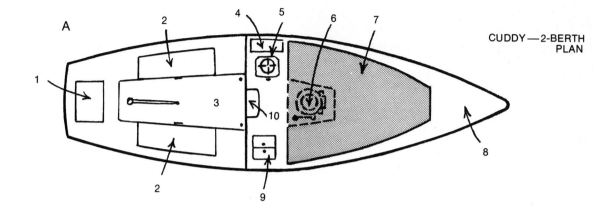

A   CUDDY—2-BERTH PLAN

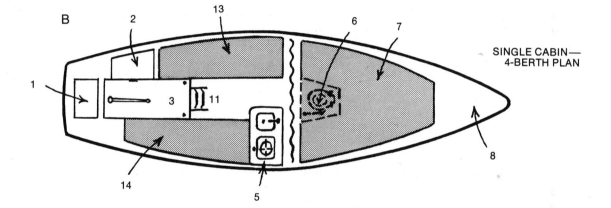

B   SINGLE CABIN—4-BERTH PLAN

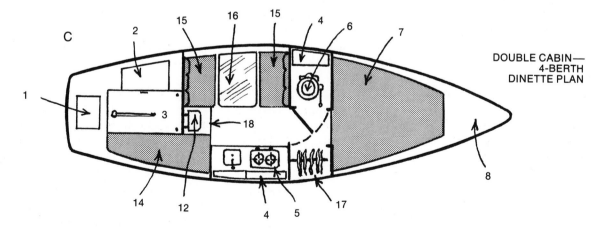

C   DOUBLE CABIN—4-BERTH DINETTE PLAN

1 — LAZARETTE (may contain outboard motor well), 2 — SEAT LOCKER, 3 — COCKPIT WELL, 4 — SHELVES, 5 — STOVE, 6 — WC (under berths on A and B), 7 — DOUBLE BERTH, 8 — FOREPEAK (stowage), 9 — ICE CHEST, 10 — STEPS, 11 — COMPANION LADDER, 12 — FOLDING STEP, 13 — SINGLE BERTH, 14 — QUARTER BERTH, 15 — DINETTE, 16 — TABLE (lowers to convert dinette into a wide berth), 17 — HANGING CLOTHES LOCKER, 18 — REMOVABLE CUSHION.

The "O'Day 23," a trailerable keel-centerboarder, shown with her pop-top up.

top. On some boats with this feature, only a small portion of the top can be raised, but on other craft the entire cabin trunk lifts up. One such arrangement, operated by a single crank, is shown in Figure 3-5. Great care must be taken, of course, to see that a pop-top is securely latched when it is in the down position to assure watertight integrity under all weather conditions.

Many boats having the adjustable top feature are also trailerable, having either twin keels, centerboards, or retractable keels for shallow draft. This is desirable not only for shoal-water cruising, but also for easy stowage on the trailer, easy launching, and accessibility to the boat's accommodations while she is sitting on the trailer so that she can be used as a camper ashore. Such versatile craft, sometimes called *camper-cruisers*, allow coastal or inland cruising to remote and distant areas at a great saving in time, expense, or both. It is very economical to be able to live aboard the boat while she is on the road. To allow trailering on American highways without the need for special permits, the beam of these boats should not exceed eight feet. Overall length for this beam would normally range from twenty-three to twenty-six feet. An essential feature for a camper-cruiser is an easy means of raising and lowering the mast, but this will be discussed in Chapter 7.

Medium-Sized Cruisers

Common interior plans for medium-sized boats, approximately twenty-seven through thirty-six feet, are shown in Figure 3-2. Although all three plans show six-berth arrangements, it would be miserably crowded to cruise with six people aboard the smaller boats in this size range. The larger boats, however,

can accommodate six in reasonable comfort on short inland cruises or on lengthy passages when, for a great deal of the time, half the crew are on deck while the other half are off watch below. All the boats illustrated have double cabin arrangements with a stateroom forward that may be closed off with a swinging or sliding door, a *saloon* (main cabin) aft, and an enclosed head compartment and clothes locker separating the two cabins.

Plan A is the standard plan, especially for many of the older boats of medium size. There are several variations on the arrangement, but basically it features an athwartships after galley on both sides of the companionway that is partially separated from the saloon by low partitions on both sides. The main cabin has bunks on both sides and a dining table more or less on the boat's centerline. The table in A is a double drop-leaf type. The dashed lines in the illustration show the table with leaves up, while the solid lines show it with leaves down. One problem with this arrangement is that the table partially blocks the passageway even when the leaves are lowered; thus it is often necessary to remove the table and keep it stowed when it is not needed. The berths shown in the main cabin of boat A are the *transom seat-pilot berth* arrangement with an elevated pilot berth near the side of the hull connecting with a lower, inboard transom seat that may be slid out or extended toward the boat's centerline to form a reasonably wide lower berth (see Figure 3-6). Although plan A of Figure 3-2 shows a pilot berth on each side of the cabin, some boats have only one pilot berth and a single bunk or sliding transom berth alone on the cabin's opposite side. This latter arrangement may allow the table to be set to one side of the boat's centerline in order to allow more room in the central passageway.

Plan B in Figure 3-2 or some variation on the arrangement is probably used most often on the newer American cruisers. It has some drawbacks for ocean racing, but it is a practical and very popular plan for inland cruising and living aboard with a small family. As illustrated, there is a quarter berth on each side of the boat aft, and a full size dinette with a galley laid out in the fore and aft direction on the opposite side of the main cabin. Such an arrangement offers a very comfortable sitting arrangement below decks, and it keeps the central passageway clear without the need of removing the table. The dinette is convertible to a double bunk by lowering the table to fill in the open space inside the U-shaped seating

FIGURE 3-2: MEDIUM-SIZED CRUISER—6-BERTH ACCOMMODATIONS (ABOUT 27′ THROUGH 36′ LOA)

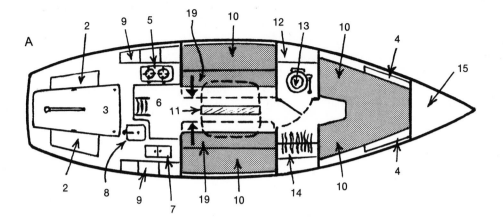

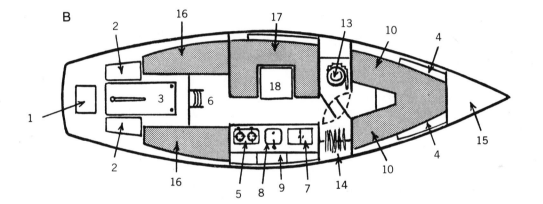

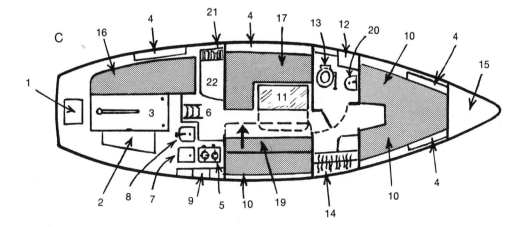

1—LAZARETTE (stowage), 2—COCKPIT SEAT LOCKERS, 3—COCKPIT, 4—SHELVES, 5—STOVE, 6—COMPANION LADDER, 7—ICEBOX, 8—SINK, 9—CUPBOARD, 10—SINGLE BERTH, 11—DROP-LEAF TABLE, 12—LOCKER, 13—WC, 14—HANGING CLOTHES LOCKER, 15—FOREPEAK (stowage), 16—QUARTER BERTH, 17—DINETTE, 18—TABLE (lowers to make double berth), 19—TRANSOM EXTENSION BERTH (slides out), 20—BASIN, 21—BOOK SHELF, 22—CHART TABLE.

area. Of course, if only four people are living aboard, they can use the quarter berths and the two berths in the forward cabin, and they need not bother with converting the dinette. Such a sleeping arrangement affords reasonable privacy for two couples. The dinette plan is especially good in port when the party includes young children, who can often be entertained for a considerable time when there is a convenient table on which to play games. In addition, a dinette table that can be left up while under sail is often valuable for the navigator, as he can plot courses and leave his charts spread open.

The arrangement shown in plan C of Figure 3-2 might be considered a blend of plans A and B. The galley is aft, but it is on only one side of the boat, and it is L-shaped, running both athwartships and fore and aft. The dinette is also L-shaped instead of being U-shaped as in plan B, and the table is a single drop-leaf type that allows a large table area, although it blocks the passageway when the leaf is up.

The particular dinette shown does not convert to a double berth, but the fore and aft seat is sufficiently wide for a single berth, and there is a transom seat-pilot berth arrangement on the opposite side of the cabin. Plan C has a slightly smaller dinette than plan B, and there is only one quarter berth, but C has a chart table and navigator's niche just forward of the quarter berth. This bunk is usually extra long so that the navigator can use its forward end as a seat without interfering with a person stretched out on the berth.

Large Cruisers

Boats larger than the size already discussed have a volume that allows a further dimension in accommodation comfort and privacy. In small and even medium-sized boats, partitioning and bulkheading is somewhat limited for claustrophobic and ventilation reasons, but in the larger sizes, vessels can be divided into a number of different compartments or cabins. Figure 3-3 shows three popular tri-cabin arrangements, the kind that are often found on sailing cruisers from approximately thirty-six to fifty feet long.

The layout illustrated in Figure 3-3, A, which has two staterooms forward and the saloon aft in a pilot house, is closely related to a plan often found on medium-sized motor sailers, but the scheme is also used on some auxiliary cruising sailers. In the latter case, the aftermost cabin may not be a true pilot house, because often there is no steering position there, but that particular cabin is usually raised considerably higher than the other cabins, and the engine is generally located under the after cabin sole; thus in some respects the cabin resembles a pilot house. This plan is not unlike those found on the "Newporter," the "Cruising Cal 36," and others. Although the scheme gives a commodious interior, there are some drawbacks—cockpit space usually must be compromised, the helmsman may have difficulty seeing over the raised after cabin house, and the sleeping and head arrangement does not allow the privacy of plans B and C in Figure 3-3. A true pilot house with a steering wheel must, of course, have reasonably large windows forward for good visibility, and there should be an alternate steering position aft in the cockpit.

Another arrangement of three cabins is shown in plan B (Figure 3-3). In this case, the two staterooms are separated by the main cabin, but the plan usually requires two companionways for easy access to both the saloon and the after stateroom. One companionway is conventional, going through an after hatch, usually with a sliding cover, at the forward end of the cockpit leading into the after cabin. The saloon companionway is slightly farther

The 40-foot "Rhodes Reliant" has a tri-cabin, double companionway arrangement.

FIGURE 3-3: BASIC TRI-CABIN PLANS (ABOUT 36′ TO 50′ LOA)

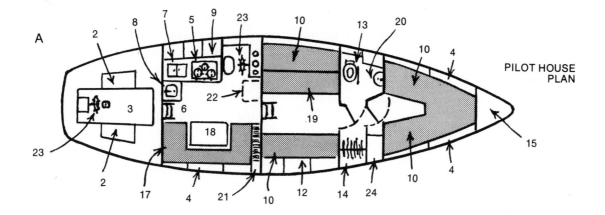

PILOT HOUSE PLAN

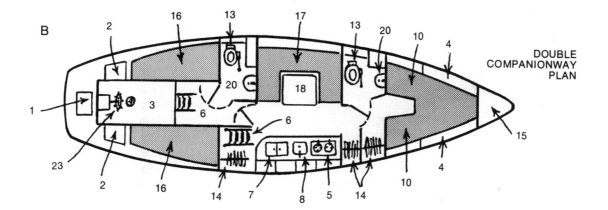

DOUBLE COMPANIONWAY PLAN

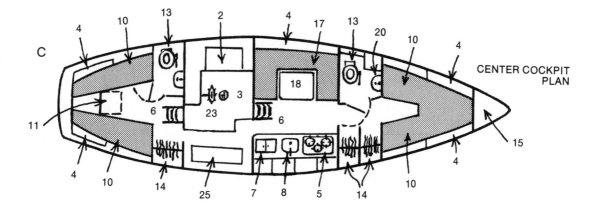

CENTER COCKPIT PLAN

1 — LAZARETTE (stowage), 2 — COCKPIT SEAT LOCKERS, 3 — COCKPIT, 4 — SHELVES, 5 — STOVE, 6 — COMPANION LADDER, 7 — ICEBOX, 8 — SINK, 9 — CUPBOARD, 10 — SINGLE BERTH, 11 — DROP-LEAF TABLE, 12 — LOCKER, 13 — WC, 14 — HANGING CLOTHES LOCKER, 15 — FOREPEAK (stowage), 16 — QUARTER BERTH, 17 — DINETTE, 18 — TABLE (lowers to make double berth), 19 — TRANSOM EXTENSION BERTH (slides out), 20 — BASIN, 21 — BOOK SHELF, 22 — FOLDING CHART TABLE, 23 — HELM, 24 — BUREAU, 25 — WORK BENCH.

forward, located near the side of the cabin trunk. In some boats, such as the "Rhodes Reliant," the cabin house is indented so that the bridge deck extends to the forward companion hatch in order that the saloon can be entered with a minimum of inconvenience (see Figure 3-7). For offshore sailing in the heaviest weather, however, I don't approve of any hatches or companionways being very far from the boat's centerline, because a severe knock-down could cause flooding below decks; for sailing in normal, semiprotected water, however, the off-center companionway is usually safe enough. If a boat with this feature is taken offshore, a high cockpit coaming should be extended to the forward companionway as shown in Figure 3-7. Furthermore, in heavy weather, off-center hatches should be kept securely closed. Vertical companionway slides should be very heavy and perhaps provided with a means of bolting or dogging them to the after end of the cabin trunk in extremely heavy weather.

The "Allied Mistress," a tri-cabin, center cockpit cruiser, has a long, shallow keel.

Many cruising sailors prefer a center cockpit arrangement similar to the one illustrated in Figure 3-3, C. This plan affords maximum privacy for two couples on a fairly large boat, but it does not always work well on small craft. Although a few boats as small as twenty-four feet have after cabins abaft the cockpit, the main reason for splitting the accommodations with a central cockpit is to provide privacy, and unless the boat is large enough to have two enclosed heads, one for the forward and one for the after stateroom, there is not sufficient privacy to justify the disadvantages of the arrangement. Some drawbacks of the plan for small boats are detraction from the boat's appearance because of the high cabin trunk aft, sacrifice of fore and aft cockpit length, lack of privacy in the after cabin from the cockpit due to the need for a companionway in the forward end of the after cabin, and perhaps cramped accommodations because the cabins are located in the relatively narrow ends of the boat instead of near her point of maximum beam.

On the other hand, large boats with this arrangement can have a lower cabin trunk aft, a completely enclosed head in the after cabin, a sufficiently large cockpit, ample beam for comfortable accommodations abaft and forward of the cockpit, and complete privacy from the cockpit for those in the after cabin, as its companionway can be located at its after end. The latter point is somewhat controversial, because many sailors prefer the companionway at the forward end of the after cabin. Advantages of the forward location are that it affords easy access to the after cabin, provides good ventilation when the boat is lying head to wind, and it is protected from the elements when the boat is running off in heavy weather. On the other hand, this location allows spray and rain to blow down below when the boat is headed into the wind if the hatch is opened, in addition to reducing privacy. Furthermore, if the forward-facing companionway is located on the boat's centerline, it is sometimes difficult to put the helm in a convenient location. Occasionally the helm is placed quite far off center, a practice I don't like on a sailboat unless there are two identical helms—one on each side of the boat.

In my opinion, there should be a passageway under one side of the cockpit connecting the after cabin with those forward. This passageway not only provides an alternate means of entrance and exit from the after cabin (especially desirable in rainy weather), but it allows easy access to the engine,

FIGURE 3-4: RAISED DECKS

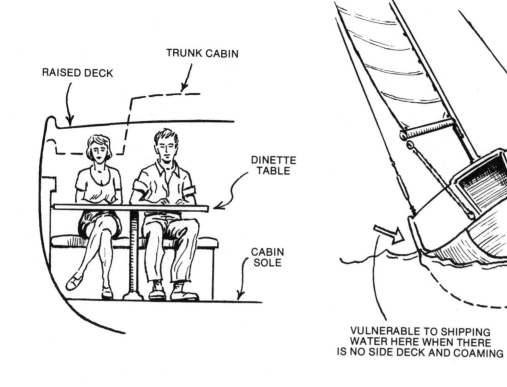

RAISED DECK

TRUNK CABIN

DINETTE TABLE

CABIN SOLE

VULNERABLE TO SHIPPING
WATER HERE WHEN THERE
IS NO SIDE DECK AND COAMING

FIGURE 3-5: POP-TOP (one method of raising cabin top)

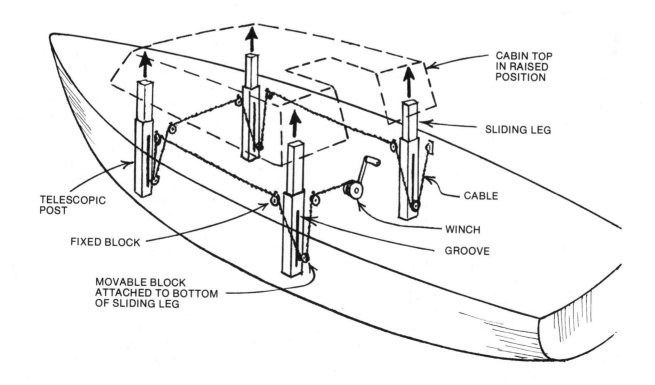

CABIN TOP
IN RAISED
POSITION

SLIDING LEG

CABLE

WINCH

GROOVE

TELESCOPIC
POST

FIXED BLOCK

MOVABLE BLOCK
ATTACHED TO BOTTOM
OF SLIDING LEG

which is nearly always located under the cockpit sole. On large boats the passageway, being located near the point of maximum beam, is sufficiently wide to allow an extra bunk or work bench near the side of the hull. If the passageway is located under a cockpit seat, the seat lid can be lifted in fair weather to provide light and air down below. This lid, like all seat locker lids, should be provided with a secure dog for heavy weather. Forward accommodation on a center cockpit boat usually follows a normal two-cabin plan with the saloon aft, a stateroom forward, and an enclosed head and clothes-hanging locker between the two cabins.

On very large center-cockpit boats, those near or over fifty feet long, the after cabin can take the form of a *great cabin* (a trunkless, raised-deck type with windows in the stern). It is great fun to be inside such a cabin, as it reminds one of a bygone era of square-riggers with stern castles. For the sake of safety in heavy weather, however, windows in the topsides or transom should be of heavy, unbreakable glass or Plexiglas, adequately braced and set in heavy metal frames. It is also wise to carry strong emergency shutters when going offshore.

Berths and Seats

Quite often advertising literature puts too much emphasis on the number of people a boat can sleep. A small boat might be physically capable of berthing six people, but they would be uncomfortably cramped when on board for any length of time. Furthermore, an extra bunk might deprive the boat of adequate stowage space or might necessitate a compromise in the length of the other berths. Bunks should be at least 6 feet, 4 inches long. Their width will depend to some extent on whether the boat will be used extensively for night sailing offshore. If so, the bunks should not be too wide, perhaps not much more than 24 inches, in order that a sleeper can wedge himself in. On the other hand, if the boat will seldom be sailed at night, it is desirable that a bunk be at least 30 inches at its widest part.

Another consideration is the correct width for comfortable seating. For women, children, and men with fairly short legs an 18- to 20-inch seat seems to be a good width for the normal sitting position with one's back against a backrest. Sliding transom berths, of course, provide one means of obtaining the combination of proper sleeping and seating width. On sailboats, this type of berth should be provided with hooks or drop pins (see Figure 3-6)

to hold the bunk securely so that it will not slide in or out accidentally when the boat is heeled.

Another means of achieving proper width for seating without sacrificing sleeping comfort is to use fairly long, rigid back cushions, which may be set against one or two removable or hinged supports that hold the cushions a foot or so away from the back edge of the bunk as shown in Figure 3-6. With the cushions and supports removed or swung up when hinged (see Figure 3-6), the bunk is full width, but with the cushions serving as a backrest, the bunk is a proper width for sitting comfort, and the space behind the cushions can be used as a handy stowage compartment for bedding.

Still another arrangement for bunk width variation is with the use of the old-fashioned pipe berth, also illustrated in Figure 3-6. The pipe berth, consisting of a piece of canvas (or preferably Dacron) lashed tightly inside a pipe frame, is hinged so that it can fold up to serve as a backrest or fold down to serve as a full-width bunk. When down, the berth overlaps the seat, and the pipe frame fits into some sort of removable or hinged crutch support similar to the one in Figure 3-6. These berths with a suitably thick foam mattress can be quite comfortable when the Dacron is properly lashed so that it is stretched very tight, and the beauty of the arrangement is that the bunk can be left made up and simply folded back out of the way when a seat rather than a berth is desired.

For those who don't like pipe berths, a sturdy piece of plywood with foam padding or cushions on the underside for backrest comfort could be substituted for the canvas and pipe frame. A further advantage of this type of berth is that its outer edge can be raised higher than its hinged inner edge with an adjustable crutch or straps to facilitate sleeping when the boat is heeled.

Fore and aft fixed bunks (those that do not hinge) should be fitted with some sort of *bunk boards* (removable sides) to keep the occupants from rolling out when there is a considerable angle of heel. This is especially true for lofty pilot berths, for some serious injuries have resulted from crew being rolled out of high bunks during knockdowns at sea. As a matter of fact, I would even suggest safety belts similar to car seat belts for very rough weather offshore. Bunk boards can be removable or hinged as shown in Figure 3-6. The type illustrated should be hooked to the bulkhead or partitions at the head and foot of the bunk to assure sturdiness. As a substitute for a bunkboard, a cloth side screen

FIGURE 3-6: BERTH DETAILS

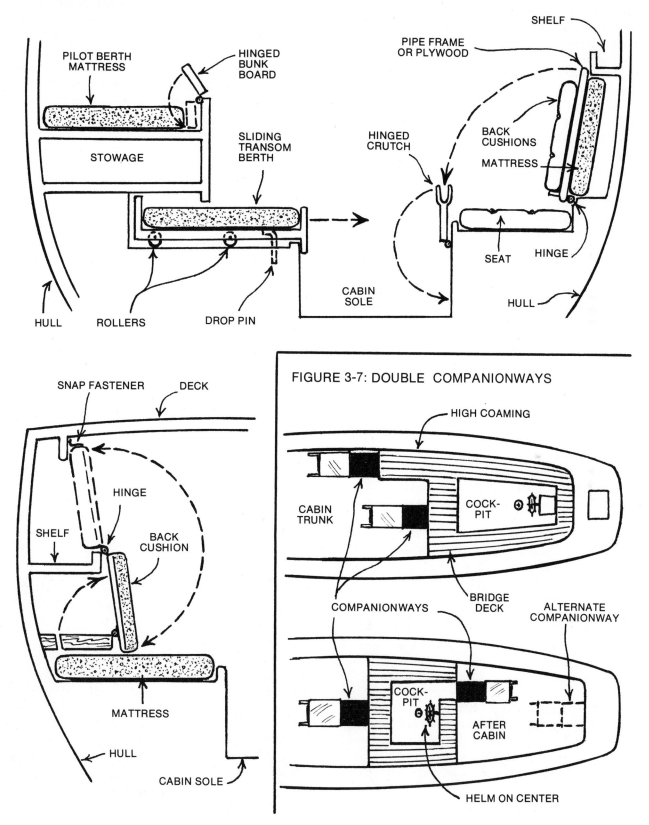

FIGURE 3-7: DOUBLE COMPANIONWAYS

of canvas or Dacron can be secured to the bulkhead at each end of the bunk or to the overhead with lanyards and snaphooks. The bottom edge of the side screen can be secured with snaps or a batten to the bunk's edge under the mattress.

Forward stateroom berths are usually quite narrow at their forward ends because they are in the vicinity of the bow where the topsides converge. Many small boats have one double V berth forward in lieu of two singles. In some cases a rigid, wedge-shaped cushion can be used to fill in the space between the after ends of single bunks in order to convert them to one large double berth. This arrangement affords good width for sleeping yet provides a small standing space between the bunks when the cushion is removed. The forward ends of V berths on some stock boats are excessively narrow for good footroom.

Some sailors dislike quarter berths, but they have many advantages when well designed. They make use of some space that is partially wasted under the cockpit seats, and they are very suitable for sleeping when the boat is underway, because of their location near the boat's transverse turning axis, at the point of minimal motion caused by pitching. And the sides of a quarter berth prevent its occupant from being rolled out at high angles of heel. Furthermore, these bunks are handy for the skipper or navigator, who can rest near the chart table (normally located aft) and the companionway so that he can get on deck in a hurry. Disadvantages of quarter berths are that they may be difficult to make up, and, if located far under the cockpit seats, they can be hot and difficult to crawl into and out of. If the forward ends of the bunks extend out into the cabin, however, most of these drawbacks are minimized. In my opinion, the after ends of quarter berths should be provided with ventilation ports that open into cockpit seat lockers so that in fair weather at anchor the seat locker lids can be opened to create a draft over the bunks. In some cases opening portholes of heavy glass with strong dogs can be put in the sides of the cockpit seats, but care must be taken to keep the ports closed when under sail.

Dinettes that convert to single or double bunks should be carefully checked by the prospective boat buyer to see that the table and seats are a comfortable height for sitting and to see that there is sufficient sitting headroom under the side decks. Some tables are too high for people of short stature, but very often table legs can be shortened quite easily. A typical kind of table has a single sturdy leg that is removable or that telescopes when the table top is lowered to convert the dinette into a wide berth. Back cushions are generally removed to fill in the area on top of the lowered table to provide a flush, cushioned sleeping surface. If the dinette is opposite a galley that runs fore and aft on the opposite side of the boat, it is very important for the dinette to be large and to have ample space to seat the greatest number of crew the boat will carry. If there is a seat or bunk opposite the dinette in lieu of the galley, then obviously the dinette can be smaller.

The principal drawback of the convertible dinette

The dinette arrangement of the "Balboa 26," with berth opposite, affords a large sitting area.

The main saloon and galley of this "International 600" show the dining area on a large cruiser.

FIGURE 3-8: DINETTE WITH SAFETY RAIL

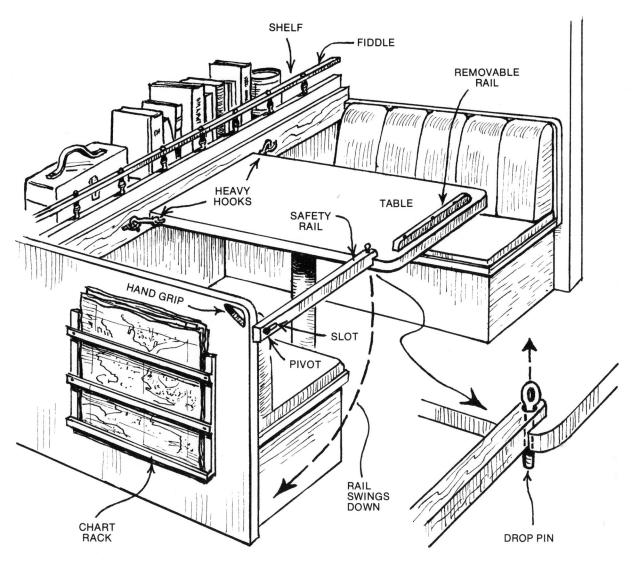

arrangement is that the athwartships seats, those facing forward and aft, are almost impossible to use when the boat is heeled. One possible means of preventing a person from falling or sliding off these seats is with the use of safety rails or pivoting arms. One is shown in Figure 3-8. The arm is attached with a pivot pin to the edge of the partition or bulkhead that forms the back of the athwartships seat. The arm hangs down when not in use, but it may be swung up and secured to the corner of the table if someone sits in the seat when the boat is heeled. The arm will hold the person in his seat when the athwartships dinette is on the high side of the boat, and on the opposite tack the occupant can lean against the lockers or shelves at the side

of the boat. A simple means of securing the arm to the corner of the table is with a pin that drops through a hole as illustrated. A cloth belt with a snaphook also may be used as a safety rail, but it will lack rigidity. Whatever kind of safety rail is used, the table must be rigidly secured to support the seat occupants when they are thrown against the rails in a seaway.

On large boats with great cabins aft, a single or double bunk may run athwartships. This is the arrangement that veteran offshore sailor Irving Johnson has used on his famous ketch *Yankee*. The advantage of such a berth is that the occupant cannot roll out when the vessel heels. Naturally (unless one practices yoga, perhaps) the sleeper rests with his head on the high side. One drawback of an athwartships double berth and also a dinette double is that it is difficult for the occupant on the inside to climb out of the bunk without disturbing the other occupant. To avoid this problem, double berths should be open at the head end whenever possible. Adequate hand grips are a help for hauling oneself in and out of a bunk that lacks easy accessibility.

Mattresses and bedding will be mentioned in Chapter 6.

Heads

On most modern small cruisers, heads are located forward to afford maximum privacy from the cockpit. Curtains are often used to hide the w.c. on very small boats, but swinging, folding, or sliding doors are preferable. Small boats with forward cabins usually have the w.c. located between the V berths, and the curtain or door separates the forward and after cabins as in Figure 3-1, B. Larger boats usually have the head located between the forward and after cabins with doors arranged so that both cabins can be closed off as shown by B in Figure 3-2. This arrangement allows ample room in the head because, with the doors closed athwartships (closing off both cabins), the head extends across the entire width of the boat.

Still larger boats have a separate head compartment on one side of the boat, usually between the forward and after cabins, which affords complete privacy without blocking the passageway between the two cabins (see Figure 3-2, C). With the latter arrangement, however, there must be sufficient boat size to allow ample room for one person inside the closed head compartment. It is highly desirable to have enough room for a wash basin, a small standing area, and a bulkhead mirror of sufficient length to be used by a man for shaving or by a woman for putting on makeup. Very often the standing floor space can be somewhat dish-shaped with a drain at the low point to catch shower water. The shower can be operated from a water pressure system activated by an electric pump that is energized by the boat's 12-volt battery, or the shower spray can be hand operated with the wash basin pump. The latter system conserves the boat's fresh water supply as well as her electricity. Wash basins should be as close as possible to the boat's centerline to allow drainage when the boat is heeled on either tack. If this is not possible, a shut-off on the outlet line must be closed when the basin is on the low side

of the boat to prevent the possibility of sea water backing up in the basin and overflowing. In some cases the basin water drains into the w.c., from which it can be pumped quite easily.

At present, heads on most boats are operated with a hand pump that forces sea water through an intake pipe or hose into the toilet bowl, which empties through an outlet pipe or hose that leads overboard through the hull. Some details of operation and installation will be mentioned in Chapter 5. Several states, including New York and Michigan, presently restrict the use of flow-through toilets—those that discharge overboard—whether or not the sewage is treated, and this necessitates the use of a holding tank, which must be pumped into shore sewage systems at marinas or elsewhere. This waste disposal system has been far from satisfactory, partly because of the lack of adequate shore pumping facilities in many areas. In the near future federal regulations set forth by the Environmental Protection Agency will establish performance standards for marine toilets. Preliminary EPA effluent standards require the use of holding tanks in new boats, but flow-through chemical toilets (certified by the Coast Guard as meeting EPA standards) will probably be allowed on existing boats. A workable flow-through system is the macerator-chlorinator toilet that grinds up and chemically disinfects the waste and discharges it overboard. Some of the newer toilets of this type use tablets of sodium hypochlorite, a disinfectant said to be safer and more effective than the common chlorine bleach often used in early models. For maximum sanitation, I would prefer that a macerator-chlorinator be installed even if the boat has a holding tank when there is room for such a system. Needless to say, the latest applicable federal and state laws should be checked before installing a marine toilet, and the appropriate kind of system should be used.

An important point regarding any head compartment is that it should be provided with an adequate means of ventilation. Some stock boats lack this feature. Sometimes ventilation is provided merely with an opening at the top and bottom of the head door. I think the door should fit tightly in its doorway except possibly for a port at the door's bottom capable of being easily opened and closed (perhaps with a sliding panel). Overhead there should be a ventilator that will not admit water (see Figure 6-5) and, if possible, a head compartment porthole that will let in light and air with a snap-on hood that will keep out rainwater.

Stowage and Tanks

With the present emphasis on putting the greatest possible number of bunks into a boat's interior, stowage space is often neglected on modern stock cruisers. If there is any choice in accommodation arrangements, I would choose the plan with the most stowage space even if it means the sacrifice of one berth.

One of the greatest stowage problems is the sails. If one quarter berth is given up, the space under one of the cockpit seats can be used for sail stowage. In other cases a pipe berth can be installed in the forward cabin so that the space under the bunk forms a sail bin when the berth is folded up. Of course, there should be sail covers for mainsails and mizzens so that those sails can be left bent to their booms, and when cruising, the jib can be bagged (without removing its hanks from the stay) and left on deck to allow more room below. Soft sails, which lack plastic filler between the woven fibers, are perfectly satisfactory for cruising boats, and they take up much less space when stowed.

Every cruising boat except perhaps the very smallest should have at least one hanging locker in which coats, trousers, dresses, and so on can be hung from coat hangers. Medium- to large-sized boats ideally should have a small hanging locker or space for foul weather gear near the companionway so that the rain- or spray-soaked crew coming below during wet weather can stow their gear without getting the cabin unduly wet.

Each bunk should have some kind of shelf above it and, if possible, a drawer or bin for clothes and bedding under it. Be sure, however, that bilge water cannot get into stowage areas under bunks when the boat is heeled and rolling in a seaway. And be sure that articles will be secure on shelves. Surprisingly, most stock boats I've seen lack sufficiently high fiddles to prevent articles from falling off at moderately high angles of heel. One or two catch-all shelves near the companionway are convenient for frequently needed items such as sunglasses, sunburn lotion, lubricating oil, a ball of marline (twine), and basic tools such as a screwdriver and pliers. A container or shelf for binoculars and a loud horn should be within easy reach from the cockpit. Spare canned goods and heavy gear such as large tools that will not often be used should be stowed as low as possible—perhaps under the seats and bunks or in a completely dry portion of the bilge—so that they will contribute to the

boat's stability. There should be one or two drawers or lockers with compartments that can be used for extra small fittings and spare parts.

In or near the head, a fairly large cabinet will be needed for toilet articles, medical supplies, towels, linens, and so forth. In the galley area, a space is needed for a trash and garbage container. All the way forward, there should be a fairly large forepeak containing a chain locker for anchor chain or rope. Abaft the chain locker, the forepeak is handy for stowing such items as sails, blankets, and spare lines. It will be helpful if the opening to the forepeak is sufficiently wide and high to accept the ends of long objects such as the boat hook or awning poles when they are placed on or secured to the shelves over the forward bunks. Usually, of course, those long objects will be carried on deck, but there will be times when they should be stowed below. There must be a few easily accessible bins or spaces enclosed with battens for life jackets distributed throughout the boat's interior. If there is no navigator's compartment, there should be stowage space for rolled or preferably folded charts, perhaps under a bunk or behind slats secured to a partition or bulkhead as shown in Figure 3-8. Charts should be kept near the cabin table (or the chart table, if there is one), as should a radio, navigation instruments, and books. Deck gear is usually stowed in lockers on deck, but it may be convenient to keep a few items of such gear in shelves or hanging from hooks just inside the companionway or forward hatch. Stowage areas on deck are normally located under the cockpit seats and in a stern lazarette. To minimize pitching and changing the hull trim, however, the heaviest gear should be kept out of the lazarette.

Most stock boats lack adequate fuel and especially water tank capacity for long cruises. As a very approximate rule of thumb, small cruising boats should carry at least twenty-five gallons of water, while medium-sized and large cruisers should carry a minimum of fifty and seventy-five gallons respectively. I think it is desirable to carry enough engine fuel for a minimum of twenty hours of running the auxiliary at moderate speeds regardless of the boat size. Obviously motor sailers and offshore passage-makers should carry considerable fuel, at least fifty gallons on the smaller boats. If it is necessary to add tanks, they should be placed low, fairly close to amidships, and near the boat's centerline whenever possible. In most cases tanks will have to go under bunks or in the bilge. Take care not to have a tank capacity on one side or end of the boat so large that it would adversely affect her trim or cause a list when the tanks are filled. Tanks that will fit down into a hollow keel are very helpful to stability not only because they lower the hull's center of gravity, but because their deep, narrow shape minimizes the free surface effect of the liquid (in a partially filled tank) shifting to one side when the boat heels or rolls. In my opinion, tanks should not be built in permanently but should be removable for cleaning or repairs. More will be said about tank materials and piping in Chapter 5.

Cockpit Comfort

The last chapter covered safety aspects of the cockpit, but its comfort aspects are nearly as important, since the crew will spend most of their time here. A primary consideration is cockpit length. The cockpit should be sufficiently long to seat comfortably the largest number of crew that will normally be carried, although its volume should not be so great that it weighs the boat down in the event of an accidental flooding. The seats should be sufficiently long and wide to permit sleeping on deck in hot weather, and they should be high enough to allow good visibility over the cabin trunk. The cockpit well should be wide enough for ample knee room but narrow enough for people to brace their legs against the opposite side when the boat is heeled. High coamings that are raked

The saddle seat provides a horizontal surface regardless of heel in this unique cockpit.

outboard slightly provide not only spray protection but backrest comfort for those seated.

Seat locker lids should have wide, deep gutters around their edges to prevent rainwater or spray from leaking into the lockers. These gutters must be sloped or provided with scupper pipes so that they will drain into the bottom of the cockpit. If the seat lids are not hinged near the coamings, the corners where the coamings meet the seats should also be provided with drains so that water will not lie in the corners when the boat is heeled (see Figure 2-5).

Some boats are provided with small stowage compartments under the winch bases that are accessible by way of handholes cut through the cockpit coamings. These compartments are handy not only for the stowage of winch handles but also for the temporary placement of sail stops, beer cans, drinking glasses, or anything else that needs to be put down momentarily in a protected, convenient place while the boat is tacked or otherwise maneuvered. Be sure there are adequate scupper drains in the bottom of these compartments, as they can become partially filled with rainwater and spray.

The helm on a cruising boat should be as unobtrusive as possible. Wheels often are positioned at the extreme forward end of the cockpit where the helmsman can be close to the companionway, but this helm position usually blocks the way of those going below or coming on deck. In my opinion, the wheel usually should be located fairly far aft. Tillers can be hinged to fold back out of the way when they are not in use. If the rudder stock comes through the cockpit sole it is often desirable to have the head of the stock raised or the tiller S-curved to minimize the tiller's interference with the legs of seated crew members when underway.

A most annoying feature of many stock boats is the raking of the after end of the cabin trunk so that the top of the end is forward of its bottom. Presumably this is done for aesthetic reasons, to give the boat a modern look, but the rake allows water to enter the cabin in rainy weather unless slides are inserted in the after end of the hatchway. This fault might be partially corrected by repositioning the stops for the runners of the horizontal sliding hatch on the companionway so that, when slid all the way aft, it will slightly overhang the cabin trunk. A more effective solution is to rig a simple cloth cover or *dodger* (a folding hatchway hood). More will be said about this in Chapter 6.

The Galley

An efficient, well-planned galley is of paramount importance on a cruising boat. In fact, the difference between a good and a bad galley could very well determine whether or not a sailor's wife likes cruising. It is normally desirable that the galley be aft, near the main companionway, because this location provides good light and air, accessibility to the cockpit, maximum room near the boat's point of maximum beam, and minimal motion in a seaway. Furthermore, on small boats the location provides maximum headroom, and quite often a cover or lid over the top of the stove can convert the area to a chart table, which should always be near the cockpit. Some boats with dinette arrangements have side galleys opposite the dinette, of course, and this means that only the after end of the galley can be near the companionway. Such an arrangement has advantages for harbor cooking, because the galley is convenient to the dinette and there is ample room for counter space, but underway, when heeled, the cook may lack security. The L- or U-shaped galley usually affords better accessibility of utensils and a better means of bracing or holding oneself when under sail, but usually at some sacrifice of counter and locker space. If much cooking in rough weather is anticipated, the galley should be equipped with a snap-on strap that will hold the cook securely when he or she leans against it.

Whenever possible, sinks should be located close to the boat's centerline to allow gravity drainage on either tack. A sink on the boat's low side will very likely flood and perhaps overflow if the angle of heel is substantial. If side sinks are unavoidable, they should be fitted with easily accessible shut-off valves or seacocks on their outlet lines. Most sinks are made of stainless steel, a very practical material. If there is any choice, I would choose a sink of ample depth that does not have an absolutely flat bottom. A slope or dip in the bottom lets water drain out at frequently encountered angles of list or hull trim. Many sinks on stock boats not only fail to drain entirely, but they are often too small and located too close to bulkheads or are placed under bridge decks where they lack adequate accessibility. Sinks should be large enough to hold a large dinner plate, and there should be room around the sink to allow easy washing of the largest pots and pans carried. Water is generally supplied to the sink from a fresh water tank with a hand pump or with a pressure system activated by an electric pump. In my opinion, there should be a hand pump on any boat in case the battery goes dead. To conserve fresh water, some offshore boats have an auxiliary sea-water pump on the sink for washing dishes.

Most American cruisers have large and well-insulated iceboxes. Many foreign boats that are attractive and very well built lack some practical features that are considered important by American yachtsmen unless they are designed for the U.S. market. The most common of these deficiencies are adequate ventilation and the size and insulation of the icebox. Small cruisers should be able to carry at least fifty pounds of ice that will keep for four days or longer in hot weather. Furthermore, there should be sufficient room for all the fresh food and drinks needed inside the box when it is loaded with ice. A common difficulty with many iceboxes is that they are placed next to the engine compartment, which heats up considerably after the boat has been under power for any length of time. If such an arrangement is necessary, a great deal of extra insulation should be placed between the icebox and the engine compartment. An advantage of the side galley is that it allows the icebox to be placed far from the engine. Recommended insulation for hot climates is at least four inches of styrofoam or urethane foam. Fiberglass icebox liners are usually considered better than stainless steel liners, because the latter material more rapidly conducts heat into the box.

It is generally best for an icebox to open on its top rather than its side, because cold air sinks, and there is less loss of cold air when the top is opened to put food in or to take it out. To prevent contents from spilling when the boat is heeled, it is preferable that doors on side-opening boxes run athwartships, not fore-and-aft. On some boats the icebox may be loaded through a hatch in the bridge deck. This is very convenient, but the ice is likely to melt, especially when the sun beats directly on the hatch and when a thirsty crew is continually opening the lid for cold drinks.

Although iceboxes normally drain into the bilge on stock boats, it is preferable for them to drain into sumps that can be lifted out and emptied or pumped out. In fact, it is possible to fit a two-way valve to the sink pump so that in addition to its normal function of supplying the sink with fresh water, it can be used to pump out the icebox or its sump through the sink. With this system, however,

FIGURE 3-9: SOME GALLEY DETAILS

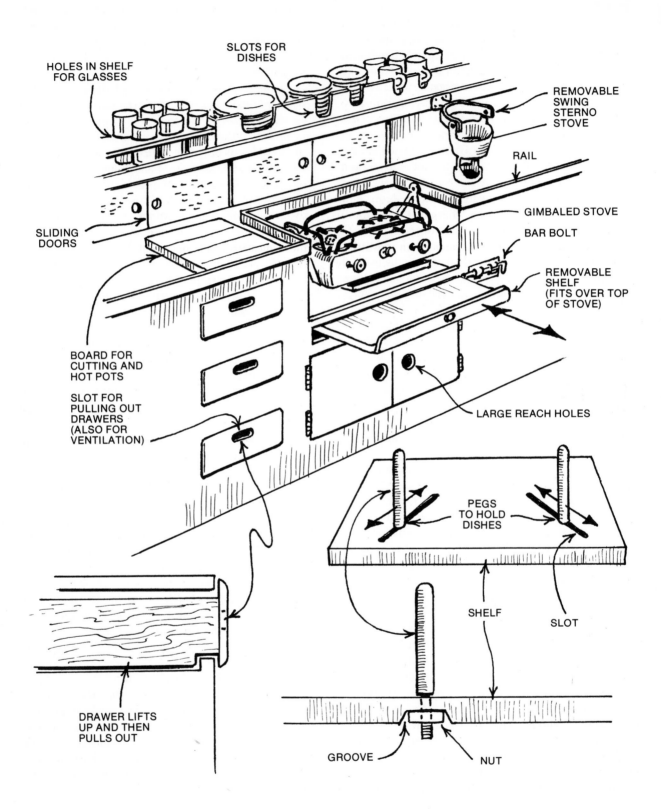

it is mandatory to keep the bottom of the icebox or the sump clean. Even if the melted ice drains into the bilge it should be kept reasonably clean, because bits of decayed food or spilled milk can be extremely difficult to remove from the bilge, and the odor can become sickening. Although clean ice water probably will do little harm to the bilge of a fiberglass boat, it could cause rot in a wood boat, and so the latter should very definitely be fitted with a sump or means of pumping the water directly from the box. Mechanical refrigeration can be used when shore power is available at a dock or marina slip, but when under sail, refrigerators or freezers drain the batteries to such an extent that the engine or generator must be run quite frequently to keep up the charge. Kerosene- or gas-operated refrigerators can be obtained, but for safety reasons, I don't like the idea of an unwatched flame burning below decks in case of a leak in the fuel line and the possible accumulation of explosive fumes in the bilge. More will be said about refrigeration in Chapter 5.

Most cooking stoves on U.S. boats are the kind that burn vaporized alcohol. Although somewhat inconvenient to get started, they are easy to install, efficient, quite odorless, and about as safe as a flame-producing stove with adjustable heat can be. Before starting one of these stoves it is necessary to *prime* or preheat a section of tubing at the burner in order that the liquid alcohol fed to the burner will vaporize. Although the priming is normally done by burning the raw liquid, the actual cooking heat comes from burning vapor. The fuel is stored in a capped tank from which it is fed to the burners by pressure that is built up with an air pump attached to the tank. Normally, there is a gauge to indicate the proper operating pressure, perhaps between five and twelve pounds (use no more pressure than is needed), but on some smaller, cheaper stoves there is no gauge, and pressure must be estimated by feeling the force against the pump plunger. When pumping begins to require a little muscle, after perhaps fifteen to twenty strokes (depending on the particular stove and the fullness of its fuel tank), pressure should be sufficient. Of course, operating instructions for the individual stove should be followed closely.

The stove should have a fairly deep and securely attached priming cup under each burner. The normal procedure for priming is to pump up pressure in the tank as described, open the burner control momentarily to let a small amount of fuel run into the priming cup, then immediately shut off the control when the cup is about three-quarters full, light the alcohol in the cup and allow it to burn out, and, finally, open the burner control again slowly while lighting the burner.

Serious fires from these stoves are rare, because alcohol will not explode, and an alcohol fire can be extinguished with water. A flare-up—a high burst of flame above a burner—may occur every so often, usually if the burner is insufficiently heated to vaporize the fuel and raw alcohol is ignited at the burner. When a flare-up takes place, shut off the burner control immediately. This should cause the flame to subside, but if it does not, let the pressure off the fuel tank. If the tank is some distance from the stove and there is a shut-off valve on the fuel line, shut this valve at once. If these measures fail, pour water on the fire, but be sure to pour plenty, because burning alcohol that has been diluted with a little water tends to smolder. Obviously, if the fire seems out of control, don't hesitate to use your fire extinguishers—dry chemical or carbon dioxide types are recommended.

To avoid galley fires take the following precautions:

1. See that all piping connections are tight.

2. Be careful not to overflow the priming cup or spill fuel when filling the tank, and wipe up any fuel that does get spilled.

3. See that priming cups are sturdy and that there is a steel tray under the stove to catch drips or spills; be sure the tray is kept clean.

4. See that there is adequate fireproof insulation around and under the stove.

5. Do not hang curtains or towels near the stove.

6. Don't leave a lighted stove, lest the flame should go out and allow raw alcohol to drip out of the burner.

7. See that the fuel tank shut-off valve can be reached during an emergency (quite often it is behind the stove where it could only be shut off by reaching across the top of the flaming stove).

8. Keep a large pot of water handy when lighting the stove, and be sure that a fire extinguisher is mounted in the galley area.

9. If the fuel tank is higher than the burner so that the fuel is gravity-fed, be certain there is a tank shut-off valve with the "off" position plainly marked, and see that the valve is always kept shut except when the stove is in use. Be especially wary of fuel leaking from top burners when there is a lighted oven beneath the stove.

Less frequently seen on U.S. boats are pressure kerosene stoves that work on the same principle as the alcohol types. A kerosene stove of this kind, similar to the famous Primus stove, is economical and produces a very hot, adjustable flame that is usually much cleaner than one produced by a wick burner; furthermore, kerosene is available in remote cruising areas. Kerosene does have a slight odor, however, and priming still must be done with alcohol, so one must carry two kinds of fuel. Some alcohol stoves can be fitted with kerosene burners.

A particularly handy stove for very small boats and for a coffee or soup warmer on larger craft, is the one-burner, bulkhead-mounted "swing" stove that burns a solid canned fuel such as Sterno. These stoves hold a pot securely and they are gimbaled in both the fore-and-aft and athwartships directions so they always remain level. Thus they are ideal for cooking underway in rough waters. They are easily removable from the bulkhead, usually with the twist of a thumb screw, so they can be stowed out of the way when not in use. The solid fuel also may have a safety advantage when cooking in a seaway. Although Sterno heat is not adjustable, it can be regulated by securing a standard shielding device over the top of the flaming can.

Many foreign and some U.S. boats have stoves that burn bottled LP-gas (liquefied petroleum gas). These stoves are very convenient, because they do not need priming, but they have a serious safety disadvantage in that LP-gas fumes can be highly explosive. Although such stoves are used with little worry when camping on shore, the hull of a boat naturally catches escaping gas fumes which, being heavier than air, sink into the bilge, where they are subject to explosion by a spark from the boat's electrical system or from static electricity. For this reason, gas bottles or cylinders should be stored on deck in a ventilated box that is fitted at the very bottom with a drain that leads overboard. Great care must be taken to see that tubes leading from the cylinders to the stove have no leaks. The fuel system should be fitted with a pressure gauge so that leaks can be looked for periodically (at least biweekly) in the following manner: With the burner control valve shut but the master shut-off valve and cylinder valve open, read the pressure on the gauge. After shutting off the cylinder valve, wait for ten minutes and see whether the pressure remains constant. A drop in pressure indicates a leak that may be located by applying liquid soap to all connections or other parts of the fuel line. *Never look for leaks*

with a flame! Other rules for safe use of LP-gas are: Always keep cylinder valves closed when the boat is unattended and close them at once in any emergency; be sure control valves on the stove are shut before opening the cylinder valves; always apply flame to a burner before opening its control valve, and be sure there is a master cut-off valve and that it is kept closed when the stove is not in use.

Electric stoves are clean, easy to use, and safe. Like electric refrigerators, they are fine for living aboard while tied up at a marina slip or dock that is adequately wired, but underway or at anchor these stoves require considerable running of a generator. If a moderate amount of time will be spent in the marina, you might have a nonelectrical primary stove but carry in addition a small, one- or two-burner Calrod (noncoil) electric stove, which operates on 115-volt current for secondary use when alongside the dock.

All stoves on monohull sailboats should be gimbaled to swing in the transverse direction so that they will remain level when the boat heels. Pot clamps or sea rails around the edge of the stove are needed to hold pots and pans on the burners when underway. Many small- to medium-sized boats have a stove well that is large enough to accept a three-burner stove with an oven. Think it over carefully before you decide on the oven, because it may not be needed on short summertime cruises. An oven will heat up the cabin in hot weather and take up valuable stowage space, and there is the flare-up danger mentioned earlier if fuel leaks from a burner above a hot oven. Remember that there are Dutch ovens, bun warmers, and toasters intended for cooking on the top of the stove that will take care of many simple oven needs. Elaborate oven dishes, such as baked bread or large roasts, can be brought aboard after having been cooked ashore when the cruise is to last for no longer than a few days or a week. If you insist on having an oven, be sure there is ample stowage space near the stove for all pots and pans used frequently. We decided against having an oven on our boat and converted the bottom of the stove well (which was intended to house an oven) into a roomy locker for pots and pans similar to that shown in Figure 3-9. We also installed a sliding shelf just above the locker that can be slid all the way in when not in use, slid halfway out (as illustrated) for use as a temporary shelf, or slid all the way out so that it can be removed and fitted securely above the stove for extra counter space and to protect the stove when it is not being used. This arrangement is particularly good on small boats that are short on counter space.

Most counters on stock boats are covered with Formica—a hard, durable material, but one that can blister if a really hot pan is put on it. It is wise to have a hardwood section of the counter near the stove that can accept hot pans and can be used as a cutting board. If there is no permanent board of this kind on the counter, a portable asbestos pad or a lightweight wood grate can be used.

The galley should have plenty of shelves, lockers, or bins for cups, plates, glasses, condiments, and utensils. Some people hang cups and other utensils with handles from hooks, but they rattle and may break in a seaway. Drinking mugs with wide bottoms that don't require saucers are generally easier to stow and are more practical than conventional cups. Plates, dishes, and bowls are often kept on shelves with high rails that are slotted, as shown in Figure 3-9, for easy removal of the utensils. A clever method of stowing plates is to use slotted shelves with movable pegs that can be adjusted to hold plates of any size. This is also shown in Figure 3-9. Notice that the pegs are threaded at the bottom and can be moved by unscrewing them from nuts in grooves under the shelf. Several drawers are needed for silverware, cooking spoons, knives, can openers, and so forth. These drawers must be self-locking so that they will not slide open. The usual method of keeping them closed is by means of runners at the bottom of the drawers, which are notched to fit over lips when the drawers are pushed closed (see Figure 3-9). To open, the drawers are lifted up slightly before they are slid out. Locker doors on many stock boats are fitted with magnetic or friction catches, but these are seldom satisfactory in really rough weather. Better latching methods are sliding bar bolts or metal spring catches, some of which are mounted flush with the door surface so that they can't be accidentally tripped or present any obstruction. Very often the catches are mounted inside the locker, and reach holes (shown in Figure 3-9) are provided. These holes should be considerably larger than the size of a finger, however, because a finger could be broken in a small hole if the person opening the locker lost his balance in rough seas. If nylon friction catches are used, be sure to carry spares, as they can break quite easily.

An important safety feature in the galley and other areas below decks is liberal placement of hand grips and grab rails. These are important not only for cruising in unprotected waters but for inland waters as well, because the wake from a passing power boat can cause a severe roll that may take a person below by surprise and throw him off balance. A related safety feature, often neglected on stock boats, is that all table, counter, and partition corners should be rounded so that no one can be injured by being thrown against them in a seaway.

4

Inspecting and Testing a New Boat

Many prospective buyers of new or used boats do not know how to go about inspecting and testing the craft they are considering for purchase. Certainly the buyer need not have the knowledge of a marine surveyor, but there are a few simple checks he can make that could influence his decision to buy and that might save regrets later. It is also possible for the buyer ordering a new boat to request certain changes from the stock model. It is surprising to see the hasty once-over that some prospective buyers give the boat they are seriously considering for purchase; even if they take a trial sail, they will often sit like bumps on logs, enjoying the sail but not really attempting to investigate the boat's handling and performance characteristics. Even stock craft above the smallest sizes represent a considerable investment, and if seriously defective (most are not, fortunately) they can cause their new owners no end of troubles and disappointments.

Inspection

Before getting down to the fine points of inspection, a few generalities on the choice of boat are in order. To begin with, beware of super bargains. As with most products, a very inexpensive boat is apt to be poorly constructed and lacking in good workmanship and attention to details. Sales gimmicks also can be misleading. Very often a boat that offers color-coordinated wall-to-wall carpeting or dinner plates with the boat's picture on them will have cheap fittings or other serious deficiencies. Broadly speaking, to minimize the risk of buying an unsatisfactory boat, choose one of moderate or higher price designed by a recognized naval architect and built by a well-known, reputable company. Before buying a stock boat, try to talk with the owner of a sister vessel. His opinions and experience with her can be most valuable. Have a used boat thoroughly surveyed.

DOCKSIDE INSPECTION. Before stepping aboard the boat to be inspected, take a good look at her from a short distance away. Is she aesthetically pleasing? Study her hull lines and proportions to see that they are suited to her intended purpose (as discussed in Chapter 1). Observe her flotation to see that she floats level on her lines without *listing* (having a slight angle of heel) or trimming down by the bow or stern. See that she has enough fullness aft to support a full crew in the cockpit. Move in closer to the boat and examine her topsides. Are they regular and smooth? Sight along the topsides, looking forward and then aft to see that there is no slight unevenness. Examine reflections in the topsides. Distorted reflections, similar to but less exaggerated than those seen in amusement park fun-house mirrors, indicate irregularities in the hull that not only will decrease speed but may indicate poor production in general. If the hull is of fiberglass, examine the gel coat to see that it is smooth, hard, shiny, and free of blisters or cracks. A very slight transparency that allows the barely discernible pattern of woven roving to show through the gel coat is not necessarily bad; in fact, it may be superior in that it indicates the gel coat is sufficiently thin to resist cracking under impact or deflection of the laminate.

ON DECK. When boarding the boat, step on her rail and notice how much she heels. This will give some indication of the initial stability of a small- to medium-sized boat. Grab the life line stanchions to test their security and sturdiness. Walk heavily, bouncing up and down, on the deck and hatch covers to see that they are rigid and do not make undue creaking or cracking sounds. You can expect some flexibility in most fiberglass hatch covers. Look at the fittings such as the Genoa track, mainsheet traveler, cleats, chocks, and grab rails to see that they are heavy and well secured. Note the electronic instruments (these will be discussed in the next chapter). Check the navigation lights, noting their quality, water resistance, visibility, and legality. See if the deck is skidproof and that it does not have an excessive crown. The decks should be light enough in color to keep the cabin cool, but not so light as to cause serious glare. Check the cockpit to see that it is comfortable, is unobstructed by the helm, and has seats long enough for sleeping and for seating a reasonably large crew. Also, of course, check the cockpit safety features mentioned in Chapter 2, especially the volume of the well, the height of the companionway sill, and the scupper sizes. Examine the deck, cabin trunk, and coamings. If they are fiberglass, look for blisters or cracks, especially at corners, angles, or sharp bends. Tap suspicious-looking areas with a coin; a blister or air pocket under the gel coat or laminate will produce a somewhat hollow sound. The discovery of a few concealed voids is not necessarily a serious enough fault to kill the boat's sale, but it is indicative of questionable workmanship, and repairs should be made. Look also at the wood trim, such as rails and coamings, to determine the quality of the wood and joiner work.

Look over the rig, and sight up the mast to see that it is straight. A hook, bow, or S curve will most likely indicate poor tuning that can be corrected with adjustment of stays or shrouds, but occasionally a spar may take a permanent set; before purchasing the boat, the buyer should be sure that a faulty mast can be straightened. Important rigging features will be discussed in the Trouble-Free Rigging section of Chapter 9.

Another consideration is stowage space on deck. See if there are large seat lockers and a sizable lazarette for stowing sails, lines, fenders, swimming ladders, buckets, ground tackle, and the numerous other items of equipment a cruiser will carry. Check the lids to see if they can be secured and if the lazarette hatch can be opened without its striking the permanent backstay. Also check the water-tightness of the lockers. Is there a large enough space on the cabin trunk or elsewhere to stow a dinghy or a rubber boat? See if there are stowage compartments in the winch bases for stowing winch handles, sail stops, a horn, or other gear that should be readily available.

BELOW DECKS. After the deck inspection, it is time to look below. Perhaps the first question to ask oneself concerns the ease and safety of entering the cabin. Is the companionway ladder well secured and the steps properly spaced and skidproofed? There should be conveniently located hand grips. Do you have to step over the galley sink or a counter on which cooking utensils will be placed? Once below, take note of the headroom, and see whether it will meet your requirements, especially in the all-important galley area. If there is not full standing headroom, it is desirable that there be hatches or liftup tops over key areas. Is there ample sitting headroom and enough space in the cabin? Is it reasonably open, uncramped, and uncluttered?

Next check the general accommodation plan. Obviously, there should be the right number of bunks for your requirements. It is important that berths be comfortable and sufficiently long. See if there is enough seating space. Does the table block the central aisle in the main cabin? Try sitting on the seats to see whether they are comfortable and whether the table is the correct height. Check the galley to see if it is well located and properly planned. Is there sufficient counter space and enough stowage shelves, compartments, and drawers? Be sure the icebox is large enough, and check its insulation and drainage. Is the sink large enough and conveniently located near the boat's centerline? Check the sink pump to see that it works easily and doesn't leak. It should not be a cheap plastic type but a strong metal one that can be disassembled easily for repairs. Inspect the stove. Is it safe, gimbaled, convenient, and sufficiently large? The stove, shelves, and counters should have sea rails or fiddles to keep objects from falling to the cabin sole during a knockdown.

After looking over the main cabin and galley, check the head and the forward stateroom. Is the head out of sight and adequately private? Try pumping the w.c. to see if it works easily, and look over its installation. (This subject will be discussed briefly in Chapter 5.) Is the w.c. a type that is approved by the laws that govern your area? Does the head compartment have a wash basin, medicine cabinet, mirror, proper light, and especially ample ventilation? How about the forward cabin? Is there standing space for changing clothes, good ventilation, and sufficiently large bunks with ample footroom forward? By all means, check stowage space throughout the accommodations. There should be sufficient bins or drawers for clothes, lockers for galley supplies, a shelf over each bunk, a clothes-hanging locker, and an oilskin locker or hanging space for wet clothes near the companionway. It is also important that there be a stowage place for navigation equipment and a surface near the companionway where charts can be spread. Check the electric power. Is the boat rigged for shore power? Are there enough electric lights—one over each bunk, the galley, the dining table, and the chart table, and in the head? Windows should be large enough to admit ample light in the daytime but not so large as to detract from the boat's appearance or be vulnerable to breakage. Ample ventilation with hatches, opening portholes, and ventilators is also important. On a fiberglass, metal, or ferrocement boat, there should probably be enough natural woodwork below to give the cabin a warm, elegant look but not so much dark paneling as to make the cabin dark and depressing. Try to visualize the cabin with your family or guests cooped up in it on a rainy day.

CONSTRUCTION DETAILS. After sizing up the accommodations, the prospective buyer should begin a more careful examination of the boat's interior. Check the joiner work; see how drawers and locker doors work; and peer into nooks and crannies to examine details of workmanship that are hidden from view. Jagged spikes of fiberglass or careless fitting together of wood trim or cabinets in hidden places can be indicative of the workmanship of the hull. Puddles of sticky resin and a strong odor may indicate lack of workmanship or proper curing. Extremely splotched or discolored areas may indicate too much or too little resin or even water migration into the laminate on boats that have been afloat for a long time. Some sunlight seen through the hull is not necessarily the sign of a thin laminate. If the semitransparent shell is unsplotched or fairly evenly illuminated, this is indicative of a healthy laminate.

Look at the junctions of bulkheads and stiffening members to the hull. They should be attached with continuous strips of fiberglass on both sides. See that the strips are not peeling up anywhere. Are there any hard spots where the stiffening members press against the hull? Examine the connection of the deck to the hull. Is it bonded with resin and secured with rivets or bolts? See if there is any bedding compound in the joint that would indicate a lack of bonding and possible future leakage. Look for any evidence of leaks at the hull-deck joint, under stanchions, under Genoa track bolts, and around chainplates. Do there appear to be adequate structural stiffening members in the boat? Look under a deck-stepped mast and see if there is a pipe or post there to support the downward thrust of the mast. Examine all attachments. See if fittings are through-bolted. Are the washers large, and is there ample reinforcement or proper backing blocks where the fittings are secured? Examine the chainplates to see that they are well secured. Be sure that unitized construction does not limit accessibility to important parts on the inside of the hull shell. Can bolts, wiring, piping, and all parts of the engine be reached? It is important that there be accessible seacocks on all through-hull fittings. If the prospective buyer should have doubts about any of these things or other aspects of the construction, it would be wise for him to call in a competent marine surveyor to look the boat over.

The buyer of a new boat can order changes that improve on the stock model. For example, he might specify that his particular boat have bolts instead of self-tapping screws in the hull-deck connection, that she have access ports installed, that she have seacocks and a proper bilge pump fitted, and so forth. Basic inspection of electric wiring, piping, tankage, the engine, and certain instruments will be discussed in Chapter 5, which deals with mechanical matters.

OUT-OF-WATER INSPECTION. If there is a chance to look at the boat out of water as well as afloat, by all means do so. Observe her lines; look for rough or uneven areas that cause unnecessary drag; see if the fairing around the keel, skeg, and rudder is smooth; see that appendages are streamlined and that through-hull fittings are reasonably flush; see that seams are as smooth as can be expected; and check the bottom of the keel for roughness. Even if the boat will never be raced, a reasonably smooth bottom will make a tremendous difference in her sailing performance. As compared with a boat that has a dirty, rough, and uneven bottom, the boat with a smooth, clean bottom is faster, more responsive, more maneuverable, safer in some respects, and far more fun to sail.

Don't fail to inspect the rudder to see that it is not warped, that it does not bind or strike the propeller in the hard-over position, and that it is securely attached. Inspect the propeller and shaft. Are they corroded or loose? See if the blades move easily when the prop is a *folding* or *feathering* type (having movable blades that either fold back or twist to minimize drag). Also check the *sacrificial zincs* (small pieces of zinc fastened to underwater metal fittings to protect the fittings from galvanic corrosion). The zincs should be streamlined and properly attached to the fittings they are to protect. Badly eaten protectors indicate considerable galvanic action, and the zincs will need frequent renewing.

If the boat is fiberglass, check for peeling or chipping paint on her bottom, and for small blisters. Antifouling bottom paint may not adhere to the smooth gel coat surface of a new boat, often because of incomplete removal of the waxy releasing agent that clings to the exterior surface of the hull. The agent is used to facilitate removal of the hull from the mold, but all traces of the wax must be removed with a solvent such as acetone before paint is applied to the gel coat. It is also important to sand the gel coat lightly but thoroughly to give it some "tooth" or a slightly rough surface for better adherence of the paint.

The blister problem, which rarely appears above the waterline, sometimes occurs on new boats after they have been afloat for several weeks. This problem, although not uncommon, is seldom mentioned, and it can be quite troublesome. Fiberglass manufacturers and paint chemists do not seem to know a great deal about the ailment, but it appears to be related to the curing of the resin. According to one theory, styrene or perhaps other chemicals in the fiberglass bleed through the gel coat and combine with water, penetrating the antifouling paint to cause a hydrolysis that forms the blisters. The problem can be lived with, and in time it may rectify itself after the fiberglass has adequately cured. Speaking from personal experience, however, there is an immediate corrective measure that is not cheap but can be quite successful. First the bottom paint is removed with a paint remover that will not attack the gel coat; then the bottom is thoroughly sanded and painted with at least two coats of clear epoxy resin. It is a good idea to tint the coats of epoxy with color to assure complete coverage. After this, of course, antifouling bottom paint is applied over the epoxy. This treatment creates a barrier between the water and the chemicals and forms a hard, waterproof coating that helps prevent water migration into the laminate. I won't guarantee that the treatment will solve all blister or gel coat problems, but it has worked very well on our boat.

A Trial Sail

If possible, it is desirable to take a trial sail in a boat that you are seriously considering for purchase. If the sales agent or producer of the stock boat cannot arrange a trial, the prospective buyer should make every effort to go out on a sister boat in his area. Most proud owners are willing to show off their boats, and sales agents often have demonstrator models for trial sails by serious customers. In some cases the customer must pay a small insurance fee to cover possible damage to the boat and to show evidence of his earnest intentions.

SAILS AND RIGGING. Before getting underway on the trial sail, the prospective buyer should check all the rigging, sail fittings, and gear to see that these items are of suitable design and are in good working order. He should examine the sails and the tautness of the rigging. The jib stay especially should be sufficiently taut to prevent a considerable curve from side pressure on the jib, as this hinders windward performance. Later, when under sail, the rigging should be checked again to see that the stays keep their tension within reason and that the shrouds hold the mast straight. Serious slacking off of the rigging under sail can indicate that the hull lacks rigidity and is flexing or bending. (See the exaggerated example in Figure 4-1.) Some slackness in the lee shrouds caused by the mast leaning to leeward as a result of heeling can be expected, but the shrouds should not be so slack as to flop around excessively. Look for evidence of chafe where lines and sails are rubbed, and check for chafe when under sail.

UNDER POWER. If the boat leaves her mooring area under power, the engine performance should be carefully noted. Does the engine start easily and is it quiet? See if it can be idled down without stalling and note whether there is undue vibration at high rpm's. Is the exhaust smoke-free? Does the boat handle well under power? Check her speed, maneuverability, and turning radius, and try backing. The average auxiliary sailboat is difficult to back when there is any kind of wind blowing, because her bow blows off due to the fact that her center of effort (windage of the hull and rig) is considerably farther forward of her center of lateral resistance (the geometric center of the underwater lateral plane). There are a few boats, however, that have the rudder forward of the propeller. These craft often have superior steering control when backing, because wash from the propeller is thrown against the rudder, but they lose considerable maneuverability when going ahead. Check, too, for rudder vibration. If the tiller quivers excessively on a boat with a keel-hung rudder and a centerline propeller, the vibration might possibly be caused by the propeller aperture being too small. A very small aperture may be desirable to minimize drag on a racing boat, but it is unnecessary on a cruiser.

Some boats have a strong propeller *torque* (tendency to turn as a result of the rotating propeller pushing the stern sidewise). A *right-hand propeller* (turning clockwise when viewed from aft) driving the boat ahead will move her stern to starboard and thus cause her to turn to port. The extent of the torque with a single two-bladed screw will depend primarily on four factors: (1) the length of the keel, (2) whether or not the propeller is on center, (3) whether or not the shaft is angled to the boat's centerline, and (4) the angle of the shaft with the load waterline. A long keel will encourage directional stability, while a shaft correctly angled to the centerline will act against the torque. Offsetting a right-

FIGURE 4-1: SAILING STRESSES & RIGGING TENSION

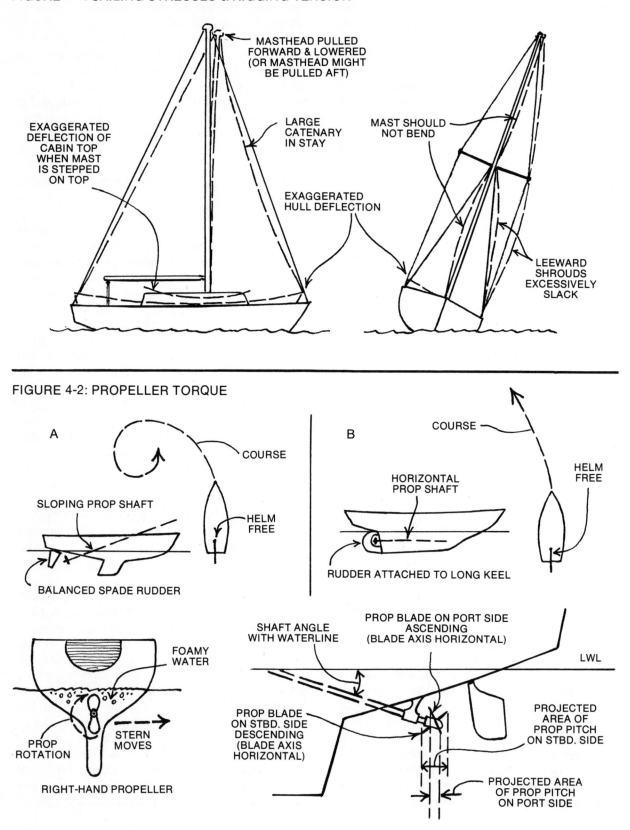

MASTHEAD PULLED
FORWARD & LOWERED
(OR MASTHEAD MIGHT
BE PULLED AFT)

EXAGGERATED
DEFLECTION OF
CABIN TOP WHEN MAST
IS STEPPED
ON TOP

LARGE
CATENARY
IN STAY

EXAGGERATED
HULL DEFLECTION

MAST SHOULD
NOT BEND

LEEWARD
SHROUDS
EXCESSIVELY
SLACK

FIGURE 4-2: PROPELLER TORQUE

A

COURSE

SLOPING PROP SHAFT

HELM
FREE

BALANCED SPADE RUDDER

B

COURSE

HORIZONTAL
PROP SHAFT

HELM
FREE

RUDDER ATTACHED TO LONG KEEL

FOAMY
WATER

PROP
ROTATION

STERN
MOVES

RIGHT-HAND PROPELLER

SHAFT ANGLE
WITH WATERLINE

PROP BLADE ON PORT SIDE
ASCENDING
(BLADE AXIS HORIZONTAL)

LWL

PROP BLADE
ON STBD. SIDE
DESCENDING
(BLADE AXIS
HORIZONTAL)

PROJECTED
AREA OF
PROP PITCH
ON STBD. SIDE

PROJECTED AREA
OF PROP PITCH
ON PORT SIDE

hand screw to port of the centerline will also counteract the torque, but such an arrangement might cause a fair amount of drag when under sail. To some extent torque is caused by the fact that the lower blade is immersed in solid water while the upper blade is in less solid, more aerated, water, but probably the major cause of this inadvertent turning is the pronounced angling of the shaft with the load waterline. The reason for this is that the *propeller pitch* (blade angle, defined as the distance the propeller advances without slipping in one revolution) is greater in projected area on the starboard side where the blades are descending than on the port where they are ascending when the shaft slopes downward. See Figure 4-2 for an explanation.

A strong torque in combination with a balanced spade rudder will probably result in excessively quick turning if the helm is left momentarily. Notice in Figure 4-2 that boat A, having a short fin keel with a sloping, centered propeller shaft and a balanced rudder, veers to the left and then spins into a tight turn when her helm is abandoned; whereas boat B, with a longer keel, an almost level shaft, and a rudder hinged to the keel, simply turns very slowly to port. The behavior of the latter is far more desirable in a cruising boat, of course, especially if she is to be sailed short-handed. The behavior of A could be improved if her propeller were off-center, but this would be detrimental to her sailing performance. Extra drag would even be caused by transversely angling the shaft because of its considerable exposed length. When you test a boat for her turning characteristics with helm freed, take care to see that she is in an isolated spot away from boat traffic.

BALANCE UNDER SAIL. After sail is hoisted and the engine is shut off, one of the first and most important characteristics to check is helm balance. Ideally, the boat should have an almost perfectly balanced helm in very light airs and a little weather helm when the wind increases. In strong winds the weather helm will usually increase, especially on a beam reach and when the boat is heeled. At normal fresh wind heeling angles with normal sail trim, however, the helm should never be so strong that the tiller must be held with most of the helmsman's strength to an angle beyond approximately 7 degrees to the centerline to keep the boat on her course. Also, a free-standing spade rudder should not begin to lose its bite on the water until the boat is knocked down beyond at least 30 degrees angle of heel. You can get a good indication of the rudder's drag by looking over the windward side of the stern above the rudder to observe the turbulence, which can produce a considerable amount of foam when the blade is badly stalled.

A mild weather helm is desirable as a built-in safety device, because it causes the boat to round up into the wind during a knockdown if the helmsman loses his grip on the tiller or wheel. In addition, the helmsman should find it easier to steer and feel the boat's response to the wind and waves when there is a slight weather helm to pull against. A few boats have lee helms, and a few others change from weather to lee helm as they change their angle of heel. In my opinion such boats are not only annoying to steer but possibly dangerous, because they might bear off during a knockdown or steer unpredictably in crowded waters. I have even sailed a couple of boats that had a lee helm on one tack and a weather helm on the other. This is most likely caused by very poor tuning, but it could indicate something far more serious, such as misalignment of the keel. Fortunately, the vast majority of boats do not have major helm faults and do not behave very erratically.

When testing the helm balance, be sure that the boat has a balanced sail combination—that she has approximately the same area of sail forward of the total center of effort (TCE, the geometric center of the sail area) as abaft the center. The actual location of the center can be obtained only from the boat's sail plan, but as a general rule on the average modern sloop, the TCE will be just forward or slightly abaft the mainmast. On a modern yawl it might be slightly farther abaft the mainmast, and on a ketch about one-third of the length of the main boom abaft the mainmast. On a cruising boat in light airs I would test for balance under a high-cut 150 to 170 percent Genoa jib. This means that the jib's *LP* (a perpendicular from the luff to the clew) is between 150 to 170 percent of the *foretriangle base* (the distance from the base of the forestay to the fore side of the mainmast at the deck). In medium to fresh breezes, testing should be done with a *number three Genoa* (a small overlapping jib) or a *working jib* (a nonoverlapping jib with a fairly long luff). If the breeze is too light to cause much heel, put all crew weight on the leeward rail to get an indication of the boat's helm tendencies when heeled.

PERFORMANCE UNDER REDUCED SAIL. When sail is handed before returning to port, experiment with sailing the boat under mainsail alone before it is lowered. Under the mainsail alone, a sloop should have a fairly strong weather helm, but she should be manageable and have reasonable speed for maneuverability. It is desirable to be able to sail up to one's mooring or to jockey around before the start of a race without a headsail being hoisted. Next, try sailing her under jib alone. Does the jib alone produce excessive lee helm? Can the boat be sailed to windward with only the jib hoisted? The greater the jib's overlap, of course, the better a sloop's balance should be when her mainsail is furled. If the boat is a yawl or a ketch, she should be tried not only with the mainsail lowered, but also with the mizzen lowered while the main is hoisted. In a sloop, try heaving to with the jib backed, the main luffing slightly, and the helm down. Most modern boats will not stop headway and lie to under full sail, but the test might give some indication of how a boat will behave under shortened sail, with a deeply reefed main or storm trysail with a backed storm jib.

SAILING SPEED. Speed and responsiveness usually can be felt, but you can get an objective measure of your relative speed if you can arrange a *brush* or informal race with other boats sailing in your area. In a medium to fresh breeze a boat's resistance to forward movement can often be estimated by examining her *quarter wave*, the wave and turbulence under her stern, especially under the weather quarter. A large quarter wave and foamy turbulence fairly far forward of the quarter will indicate a high degree of resistance. Take into account, of course, that a deep-bodied, heavy-displacement boat will pull a deeper quarter wave than a light-displacement hull. When the region of concentrated foam, called the *breakaway point*, is well forward of the quarter, however, this may be an indication of early *flow separation* (the water flow failing to remain close to the hull and breaking away into eddies), and consequently, there is probably considerable drag (see Figure 4-3).

Note whether or not the stern squats at high speeds. On some boats that lack buoyancy aft or when the hull shape encourages a particularly deep wave near the stern, the stern will sink or seem to be sucked down as speed increases. If there is not enough wind to produce sufficient speed for stern squat or a sizable quarter wave, observe them while the boat is under power. Although some propellers might tend to suck the stern down at high speeds, this might be counteracted to some extent by the upward thrust component of a sloped shaft. It is best

that the breakaway point be observed while the boat is heeled under sail, since this turbulent area may be influenced to some extent by the crossflow of water passing behind the keel from the leeward to the windward side of the boat.

STABILITY AND MOTION. You will obviously check the boat's tenderness. Bear off with the sheets trimmed in to see how far the boat heels, and if the wind is light, move all the crew weight to leeward. A boat initially might heel quite easily, but she should stiffen before the rail gets close to the water. In a fresh breeze, check the boat's motion in a seaway. Sail her into shallow water, and, if possible, into short and choppy seas. Is she excessively wet, throwing a lot of spray back into the cockpit? Does she pound or hobbyhorse? Does she have the power to drive through a sloppy sea? Steer the boat to head into the waves and also to take them on the beam and the stern. If the day is calm, check the boat's behavior in power boat wakes or steamer swells. One word of caution, however—don't approach steamers too closely, as they are difficult to maneuver, and it is against the law to hamper them in a narrow channel. In one or two cases, too, crew members have been washed overboard from small yachts that were too close to fast-moving ships.

Another important consideration is the boat's steering tendencies, especially downwind in rough seas. Does she tend to yaw badly in following seas or in power boat waves from the stern or quarter? Is the helm easy to manage, or is it heavy and hard to turn? If the boat has a steering wheel, do you have to turn it a great distance before the rudder takes hold? And, incidentally, is the main sheet located within easy reach of the helmsman? This is a very important requirement for a cruiser.

CLOSEWINDEDNESS. Test the boat's windward ability by seeing how close to the wind she can point. Note her course on the compass on the port tack and compare it with her course on the starboard tack. For a reasonably closewinded cruiser, the difference should be about 90 degrees. Try tacking for a buoy or another stationary object that lies exactly abeam and then try to fetch the object. This should give an approximation of the boat's pointing ability and leeway when the effects of current are taken into consideration. Consider the state of the sea in making your judgments, for a boat will be less closewinded and make more leeway when the water is rough.

If the boat has reasonably accurate electronic

FIGURE 4-3: THE QUARTER WAVE

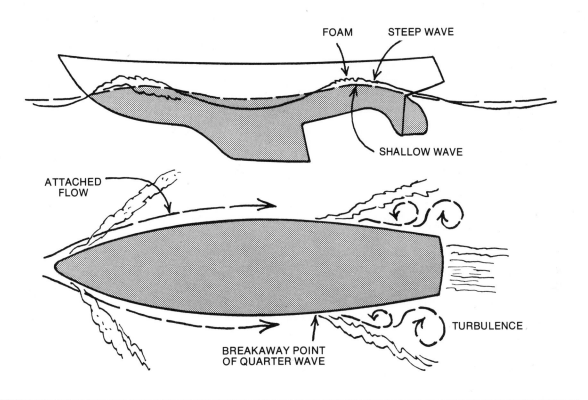

FOAM STEEP WAVE

SHALLOW WAVE

ATTACHED FLOW

TURBULENCE

BREAKAWAY POINT OF QUARTER WAVE

FIGURE 4-4: SPEED MADE GOOD (Vmg)

(for greatest accuracy scale should be at least ½ inch to each knot of speed)

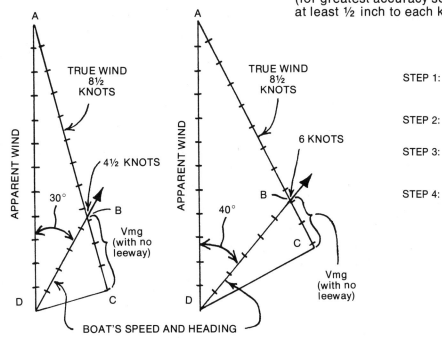

A

TRUE WIND 8½ KNOTS

APPARENT WIND

4½ KNOTS

30°

B

Vmg (with no leeway)

D   C

A

TRUE WIND 8½ KNOTS

APPARENT WIND

6 KNOTS

40°

B

C

Vmg (with no leeway)

D

BOAT'S SPEED AND HEADING

STEP 1: Draw apparent wind speed as vertical line.

STEP 2: Draw boat's heading angle.

STEP 3: Extend heading line to correspond with boat's speed.

STEP 4: Draw line from A to B and extend to C (where the angle between B and D becomes a right angle).

wind instruments, an approximate appraisal of her pointing ability may be obtained by drawing *speed made good* to windward (Vmg) vectors. What is needed is a speedometer, an *anemometer* (to tell the velocity of the apparent wind) and an apparent wind indicator to record the boat's angular heading to the apparent wind. Two vector examples are illustrated in Figure 4-4. In both cases the true wind is blowing at 8½ knots. When the boat heads 30 degrees to the apparent wind, on a heading that makes her closehauled sails begin to luff, her speed is 4½ knots and her Vmg is very slightly over 3. When she bears off to 40 degrees from the apparent wind, her speed picks up to 6 knots, but she makes less distance to windward, and her Vmg is only slightly over 2. Thus it appears that the boat being tested is a good performer to windward for a cruiser, and it pays to sail her fairly close to the wind. You should realize, however, that the boat's heading will not be the same as her course because of her leeway, which might be in the neighborhood of 4 degrees in smooth water, depending on the boat's draft and the shape of her keel. Leeway can be estimated roughly by holding a steady compass heading directly toward a buoy and then noting the buoy's apparent movement against a distant shoreline in the background when there is no lateral current.

TACKING AND JIBING. Although cruising boats need not be as quick in stays as racers, you will want to be sure the boat will come about smartly. A few cruisers in rough seas cannot be tacked without backing the jib. Needless to say, this characteristic is hardly commendable. Inspect her jib sheet winches. Are they powerful enough for a woman to handle in a moderate breeze? See if the jib will come around by itself without fouling on the spreaders or shrouds. Incidentally, there should be correctly positioned leads for all sizes of headsails. Try several rapid tacks to see whether the boat gets in stays, and tack while the boat is moving very slowly to see whether she can be brought about when making little headway. If she gets in irons, attempt bringing her around by backing the jib or reversing the rudder when she gains sternway. Then try turning her by gently *sculling* with the rudder (putting the rudder hard over slowly and then quickly turning it the opposite way to force the stern sidewise). Sculling should be done gently lest one strain the rudder or its attachments.

Next try jibing the boat. Is the main sheet easy to handle, or can it foul during a jibe? Lift the end of the boom up several feet above its normal position to see if it is well clear of the permanent backstay. Are there any running backstays that need adjusting, and if so, are they really necessary in light to moderate winds? Notice whether the battens bend against the shrouds when the boom is broad off. See whether the topping lift can possibly foul the spreaders. This happened on a boat I was skippering just before we were to jibe around a turning mark during a race. See if the boom vang can be released instantly. Can a jibing preventer be rigged? Notice whether the boat has a very strong tendency to round up immediately after jibing.

INSPECTION BELOW WHILE UNDERWAY. At some point during the trial sail, it is very important to go below and look things over. Check to see that objects are not spilling out of shelves and that locker doors are staying shut. Are grab rails conveniently placed? Are there any sharp corners you could fall against? Look for leaks through the decks, around bolts for fittings, and through ports or hatches. See if any sinks or the head is filling up. Listen for creaks and groans. There will probably be some, but excessive noise may indicate that the hull, bulkheads, or stiffeners are straining. Look for hull movement, especially forward in the vicinity of the bow wave when the boat smashes into a sea. On a rough day some flexing might be expected, but not a great deal; there should be no hard spots where the flexing occurs, of course. If the day is calm, watch and feel the area around the chainplates while someone on deck yanks on the shrouds. Some slight movement can be expected, but not too much. In a rough sea or when the boat is being rolled by power boat swells, listen carefully for any shifting of ballast in the keel. If the boat is a centerboarder, listen for excessive thumping of the board in its well. Also listen to the water and fuel tanks. Any significant sloshing of liquid can indicate a lack of sufficient baffles. This is not only annoying, but it can be dangerous in a gas tank. I was once on a boat that split open her gas tank from excessive surging in a seaway.

Check the movement of the mast. It should be held reasonably still and straight by its rigging. When down below, check the mast step and the area directly below the step when the mast sits on top of the cabin house. If there is a beam supporting the mast step, lay a straightedge along the underside of the beam to see whether there is any bending. Quite often a simple check is opening and closing the door to the head. If the beam is bending due to the downward thrust of the mast, the head door will usually jam at the top. Do not tolerate this characteristic. See whether a vertical pipe can be installed directly under the step.

DRIFT ATTITUDE. Before starting the engine to return to the mooring area after a sailing trial, lower all sails (while well clear of shore or boat traffic) and check the boat's drift tendency. Most boats will lie almost beam-on to the wind and seas, making a knot or more of leeway, depending on the strength of the wind. A few boats, however, will lie with their quarter toward the wind and forereach slowly, even moderately fast in a strong wind. Boats that have a stern-up tendency might be brought beam-on to the wind and their forereaching slowed by lashing the helm down or, on a yawl, by hoisting the mizzen alone. Knowledge of a boat's drift tendency is important, because it gives a clue to how she should be managed in extremely heavy weather. Many boats with a beam-on drift tendency will behave well when *lying ahull* (lying with all sails down-beam to the wind and seas) in bad storms in open water, but boats with a more stern-up tendency may behave well running off under bare poles, perhaps towing drags. The latter tactic, of course, presupposes that there is plenty of sea room to leeward.

FINAL CHECKS. When the engine is started, notice whether there is any unusual vibration. On some boats with folding propellers, one blade will occasionally "hang up" or fail to open fully. This will cause a considerable vibration that could damage the *stern tube* or *shaft log* (the areas where the shaft passes through the hull). If this has happened frequently it would be well to have the stern tube thoroughly inspected, especially on a fiberglass boat. The chances are, however, that if the area has already been damaged, the boat will be leaking noticeably. The usual cure for a hung-up blade is to momentarily put the gear in reverse at once as soon as the vibration is noticed. The next time the boat is hauled out of the water, the prop should be cleaned of marine growth, barnacles, or any buildup of antifouling paint that could be contributing to the failure of the blade to open, and the blade hinge should be well lubricated. Prop cleaning and lubrication sometimes can be done underwater without hauling the boat.

Returning to the mooring area can afford a further opportunity to study the boat's handling characteristics under power. Observe how far she *shoots*—how much way she carries when turned into the wind with the gear in neutral—and how quickly she can

be stopped when the engine is reversed. Observe her steering control when backing if she is moored in a slip with her stern facing inward. Can she be turned by alternately backing and then going ahead? Finally, see if securing procedures such as covering sails and closing valves can be carried out quickly and easily.

It may not be possible to make all the observations and perform all the tests suggested in this chapter, but the prospective buyer obviously should do his best to check the really important characteristics, which should be apparent after a careful reading of the chapter. There is no such thing as a perfect boat; boat design always involves compromises. Thus, any boat being considered for purchase will not pass *all* the suggested requirements and tests with flying colors, but she should meet the basic needs and be as safe as possible. Remember, too, that if the boat has certain minor deficiencies, they can be corrected. Taking the time and making the effort to inspect and test a boat thoroughly before purchase may save many future disappointments and help assure that she will give her new master many years of satisfaction and pleasure.

Summary Inspection List

Dockside Inspection
- Size, proportions, lines, and rig (suitability for intended purpose)
- Appearance (aesthetic considerations)
- Level flotation
- Condition of topsides (evenness, condition of gel coat, etc.)

On Deck
- Initial stability
- Sturdiness of stanchions, rails, deck, and hatch covers
- Condition of fittings and instruments
- Visibility, water resistance, and legality of navigation lights
- Slipperiness and glare of deck and cabin top
- Cockpit comfort and safety features
- Workmanship (cracks, blisters, joiner work, etc.)
- Condition of mast and rigging (also see Chapter 9)
- Adequacy of deck gear and stowage areas

Below Decks
- Accessibility and security of companionway
- Headroom
- Size of cabin and general accommodation plan
- Number and size of bunks

- Table and seating arrangements
- Galley features (size, stowage and counter space, sink, icebox, stove, etc.)
- Safety features (hand grips, rounded corners, stove installation, etc.)
- Head features (privacy, w.c. installation, ventilation, sink, stowage space, etc.)
- Adequacy of lockers for clothes and foul weather gear; general stowage space
- Forward stateroom features (standing space, size and shape of bunks, shelves, and stowage space)
- Features of navigator's area (galley conversion on small boat)
- General ventilation below decks
- Light (from windows, ports, and electric lights)
- Woodwork (quality and aesthetic considerations)

Construction Details
- Quality of joiner work
- Fiberglass workmanship
- Adequacy of bulkheads and stiffeners and soundness of their junctions to hull
- Security of hull-to-deck connection and fastenings
- Proper through-bolting of fittings
- Adequacy of mast support and chainplates
- Accessibility of wiring, piping, tanks, and engine
- Adequacy of seacocks and bilge pump and soundness of piping
- Safe installation of fuel tanks and engine (also see Chapter 5)
- Lack of odor (no strong smell of resin, mold, or rot)
- No evidence of leaking

Out-of-Water Inspection
- Design aspects (keel length, skeg, type of rudder, etc.)
- Smoothness, fairing, and streamlining
- Rudder condition (strength, attachment, and freedom of movement)
- Condition of propeller and shaft (corrosion, security, and blade movement)
- Condition of keel ballast and underwater fittings
- Condition of bottom paint and gel coat

Trial Sail Checklist
Sails and Rigging
- Condition and design of sails and rigging
- Quality of fittings and gear
- Efficiency of operation (also see Chapter 9)
- Ability of mast to remain straight and rigging to stay taut
- Absence of chafe

Under Power
- Engine performance (ability to start quickly, smoothness, power, ability to idle down, lack of smoke and fumes)
- Maneuverability under power (turning radius, reverse steering control)
- Propeller torque
- Extent of vibration

Balance under Sail
- Existence of weather or lee helm under different sails and points of sailing
- Rudder drag
- Feel and consistency of helm
- Effect on balance by heeling and changing trim

Performance under Reduced Sail
- Ability to sail under mainsail alone
- Ability to sail under headsail alone
- Ease of reefing (also see Chapter 9)
- Sail reduction with a divided rig (also see Chapter 9)
- Performance when heaving to

Sailing Speed
- Responsiveness and acceleration
- Observation of quarter wave and bow wave
- Stern squat and the effect of heeling on speed
- Comparison of speed with another boat or observation of speedometer

Stability and Motion
- Tenderness
- Hobbyhorsing or pounding tendencies
- Directional stability and tendency to yaw
- Rolling motion in beam seas

Closewindedness
- Pointing ability (under a variety of conditions if possible)
- Leeway
- Speed made good

Tacking and Jibing
- Speed in stays
- Winch power
- Fouling tendencies of sheets, lifts, sails, or booms
- Response to gentle sculling and backed jib
- Boom clearance when jibing
- Operation of boom vang and jibing preventer
- Tendency of boat to round up after jibing
- Filling away after being in irons

Inspection Below While Underway
- Security of objects on shelves and in lockers
- Location of grab rails

- Lack of sharp corners
- Leaks
- Hull flexing
- Sounds (creaks and groans, shifting of ballast, sloshing in tanks, thumping of centerboard)
- Mast movement and straightness of beam holding the mast
- Sink and head drainage while heeled

Drift Attitude

- Drift attitude with all sails down

Final Checks

- Engagement of folding propeller
- Way carried (extent of "shoot" with no power)
- Performance when backing down under power
- Ease of securing

5

Mechanical Matters and
Basic Instruments

Most small boats these days are becoming increasingly loaded—and overloaded—with mechanical and electronic equipment. A lot of this gear is useful, is fun to play with, and makes certain aspects of boating easier. Bear in mind, however, that much of the mechanical gadgetry found on yachts is by no means essential. Some of it is very expensive, and it is subject to breaking down. Certain instruments, such as electronic *apparent wind indicators* (instruments that show the direction of the apparent wind on a dial mounted near the helmsman) and *wind sensors* (electrically powered sensing devices that measure pressure on the sails), are of far greater value on racing boats than on cruisers. Although speed indicators, too, are more useful on racers, they are handy for navigation on any kind of boat, so they will be discussed briefly. I believe the novice sailor should equip his boat with only the most essential mechanical equipment to begin with. Not only will he save money, but he will learn the basics of boating without becoming overly dependent on sophisticated equipment that might fail him and leave him vulnerable. After he has acquired more knowledge and has mastered the fundamentals of boat handling, he can add what equipment he can afford and thinks will be useful.

Batteries

Much mechanical and, of course, electronic equipment uses electricity. Power is usually supplied by lead-acid storage batteries when a boat is away from a dock that has shore current. For those who know very little about electro-mechanical matters, shore power is nearly always 115-volt AC (alternating current), while boat power, for the typical small- to medium-sized sailing cruiser, is generally 12-volt DC (direct current). Most marine equipment is designed to operate on the battery power of the boat, so when she is alongside the dock using shore current, it must be converted, usually with a rectifier. When away from shore, the batteries must be kept charged with a generator or alternator. If the engine is run periodically, even at slow speeds, a suitable engine-driven alternator will keep the batteries up, but when there is a lot of electro-mechanical equipment aboard and the engine is seldom run, an auxiliary gasoline- or diesel-powered generator probably will be needed. Very generally speaking, the average small- to medium-sized cruiser with a moderate amount of equipment—perhaps electric running lights, a few low-wattage lights below, a pressure water system, a low-powered radiotelephone, and a depth sounder—should require only a 30- to 40-ampere alternator, provided there are proper batteries and the engine is run periodically.

Many new boats are fitted with undersized batteries for the amount of equipment just listed. Such gear should probably be powered with at least two 12-volt, 120-ampere batteries. It is important to have two batteries and save one for the engine, which is normally considered the most essential piece of equipment, for its starting motor draws a lot of current. Customarily, a three-way master switch is installed so that either battery or both can be used by the engine and charged with the alternator (see Figure 5-1). One word of warning, however: Don't turn the switch through the "off" position to change from one battery to the other when the engine is running, because this may destroy the regulator and do major damage to the alternator. Electric motors can require a lot of current, but normally they are run for very short periods, and some motors, such as those used to power water pressure systems or shower sump pumps, are very small, probably less than one-eighth horsepower.

Batteries should be well secured in acidproof battery boxes that have nonconductive covers with holes for ventilation. Lead-acid batteries generate hydrogen gas, which is explosive; thus it is important to ventilate the battery and the compartment in which it is housed. I once saw a man blown from an engine room to the cockpit deck by an explosion from a bank of tightly sealed batteries. Furthermore, batteries should be located outside the engine compartment if possible (but near the starting motor) and away from fuel tanks or any place where gas fumes might accumulate. Some racing boats carry their batteries deep in the bilge, but this is not sound

FIGURE 5-1: ELECTRICAL SYSTEM (on a 30-ft. LWL cruising sailboat)

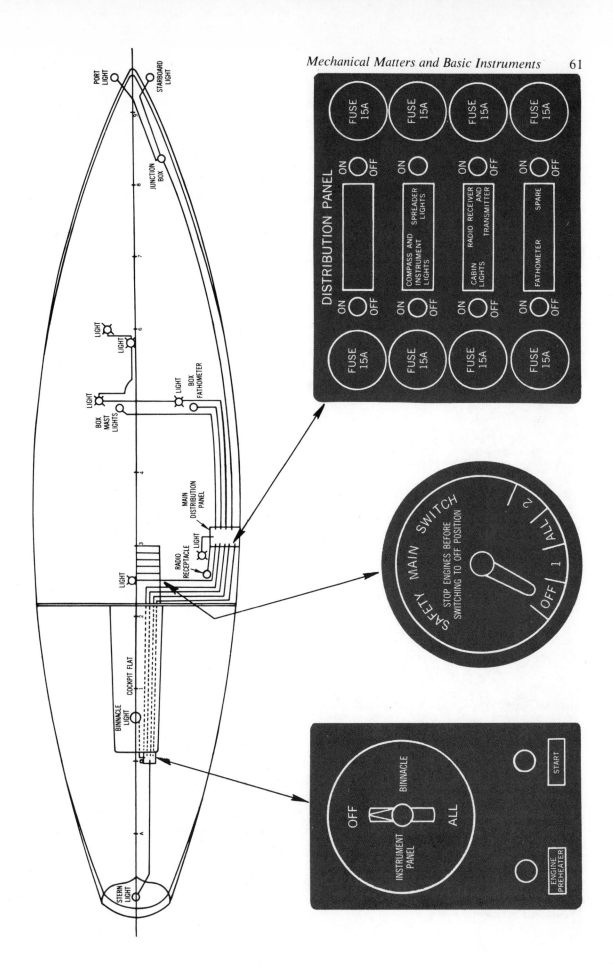

practice, in my opinion, because of the possible accumulation of water and fumes and the lack of ventilation in the normal bilge. Wiring should be kept high, where there is little chance of its becoming wet. Electrical circuits should be protected by fuses or non-self-resetting circuit breakers, and there should be a master cut-off switch on the ungrounded conductor close to the battery. Be sure that all switches are sparkproof. Figure 5-1 shows the electrical system for a diesel-powered cruising sailboat with a waterline length of approximately thirty feet.

Engines

The auxiliary engine comes as close to being essential as any piece of mechanical equipment found on board a cruising sailboat. Although it is possible to do without mechanical propulsion, and there are still a few sailing purists around who refuse to fit their craft with auxiliary power, engines provide the ability to move in calm weather, maneuverability and control when docking, the capability of power-sailing (as described in Chapter 1) in heavy weather or against a strong current, and the ability to lower all sail and yet maintain headway to windward in short-lived squalls. Then, too, when shore power is not available, the engine can provide a means of keeping the batteries charged without hefting them ashore for periodic charging or running a noisy generator.

At a time like this, an auxiliary engine is almost essential. The becalmed boat is an "International 500," a 31-footer designed by Robert G. Henry.

The new boat buyer will be confronted with several basic decisions in the choice of an engine. The first of these will be the choice between outboard or inboard power, and the principal determining factor may be the boat's size. The smallest trailerable cruisers generally have outboards, because these motors are removable (for easy servicing and winter storing), and they are lighter, occupy less space, and are less expensive than inboard engines. Larger boats, those with an overall length greater than approximately thirty feet, may be better served by inboard power. An inboard engine needs no outboard bracket mounted on the transom or an outboard well in the boat's counter; more efficient power is provided in rough seas, against strong currents, and on long engine runs; batteries may be kept charged more easily; and there is no need to lift a heavy outboard on or off its mount.

If inboard power is used, the next basic choice will be between a gasoline and a diesel engine. A strong argument for diesels is their safety, because the fumes from diesel fuel oil will not explode easily, whereas gasoline fumes are highly explosive. A gasoline engine is perfectly safe, however, so long as every part of its fuel system is properly installed and gasoline is never allowed to escape from that system inside the boat. Then, too, a leak in any kind of fuel system—gas or oil—creates a fire hazard, because all fuels burn. Furthermore, diesel oil escaping into the bilge of a wooden boat can, in time, deeply penetrate the wood. I have seen a boat in which this penetration was so severe that oil had permeated the bottom planking and anti-fouling paint could not be made to stick to the bottom. Don't forget that a gasoline engine can also leak lubricating oil; thus drip pans under engines should be large and deep so that oil cannot spill into the bilge when the boat is heeled.

Aside from the safety factor, other considerations affecting the choice between diesel and gas engines are initial cost, economy of operation, noise, odor, engine weight, availability of fuel, and reliability. Usually diesels are considerably more expensive than gas engines, but they consume less fuel, and the fuel is cheaper. A very general rule of thumb is that gasoline engines consume about one gallon of fuel per hour for each 9 to 12 horsepower being developed, while a diesel will burn about one gallon an hour for each 15 to 18 horsepower developed. Diesels are often more expensive to service, but they may not need as much servicing as gas engines. Considering all factors of economy, it might be

said that gasoline power is less costly if the engine is not often used and/or if the boat is not kept for a long period of time, but a diesel will be less costly in the long run if considerable use is made of the auxiliary power and if the boat is kept for many years.

As compared with gas engines, diesels are generally somewhat noisier; at least they have a "heavier" sound. Well-installed and carefully maintained engines should not be unduly malodorous, but diesel fuel in the bilge can create a very unpleasant smell, and diesel exhaust fumes can be annoying when under power with a fair wind. Gasoline fumes have an odor, of course, but this is very fortunate, because it gives warning of a potential explosion below decks. If a definite odor of gas fumes is ever apparent in the cabin or engine compartment, the space should be aired out, the mechanical ventilating blower should be turned on, and the entire fuel system should be examined carefully for leaks. Needless to say, no flame or spark should ever be produced in the cabin when fumes from gasoline or odorized LP-gas are present.

Diesel engines are being made increasingly smaller and lighter in weight, but they still are heavier than normal gasoline engines of equal horsepower. Weight is a significant factor in a racing boat, but usually it is not important in a cruising boat unless the trim of the boat is adversely affected. A simple rule of thumb for determining the power needed to push an auxiliary sailboat is one horsepower per 500 pounds of boat weight.

Another important consideration is the availability of fuel. In most parts of this country both diesel oil and gasoline are readily available, but there are a few remote areas where either fuel might be somewhat more difficult to obtain than the other. Diesel oil is usually easier to buy than high-grade gasoline outside of this country; thus it seems, in this respect, that diesel power is more advantageous for extensive foreign cruising.

The diesel engine is generally considered to be somewhat superior in reliability, too, because, unlike the gasoline engine, it has no electrical ignition system that can be troubled by a damp marine environment. Unfortunately, though, a diesel is sometimes hard to start in cold weather (usually when compression is lower than it should be), and its starting motor can drain a battery rather quickly. One means of overcoming this problem without electric heating is with the use of a starting booster fuel (generally containing ether), which is sprayed with an aerosol can into the air intake. On rare occasions, improperly operating diesels are hard to stop, even with the fuel cut off, as it is possible for some engines to cannibalize their lube oil, but the difficulty usually can be overcome by holding a rag over the air intake. Some diesels have air dampeners that close off the air supply if the engine speed should become excessive. The air intake, by the way, must be located where water can never enter it, as this might cause a hydraulic lock in the combustion chamber that could possibly explode the engine. One of the greatest sources of unreliability in any kind of boat engine comes from dirt or water in the fuel. The water problem is more prevalent with diesel engines, because carburetors are more tolerant of water than injectors, and some of the diesel fuel is often used to cool the injectors, which may tend to heat the entire tank of fuel on long runs and thus contribute to condensation. Tanks should be kept reasonably full to minimize condensation; air vents must be well protected from spray or rainwater; fill pipes must have watertight caps; and there should be one or preferably two accessible marine-type filters on the fuel lines. An advantage in having two filters is that, with a spur in the line, cutoff valves, and the filters arranged abreast of each other (rather than in tandem), each can be cleared, one at a time, without stopping the engine.

A further decision regarding engines is the choice of cooling. Most sailboat auxiliary engines are water-cooled, but some are cooled with sea water and others with a closed fresh-water system. The major consideration affecting the choice of cooling systems is the salinity and purity of the waters on which the boat will be operating. In most cases, boats used on reasonably pure fresh or slightly brackish water can use sea-water cooling without much risk to the engine's longevity. On the other hand, it is advisable that boats operating in salt water (and in areas where there is considerable water pollution from chemicals and acids) be fitted with closed, fresh-water cooling in order to minimize corrosion inside the engines' water jackets. Such a system can use a keel cooler or a heat exchanger on the inside of the hull. Except perhaps in extremely dirty water, I prefer the latter method, because the keel cooler, which is located on the exterior of the hull, can cause a good deal of drag unless it can be recessed so that it is flush with the hull, and, even though the cooler may be of copper and its temperature somewhat discouraging to marine life, it can become

fouled with growth, which might very well cause overheating of the engine. These problems are overcome with an arrangement that uses an open sea-water line leading to an interior heat exchanger that cools the closed fresh-water system inside the engine's water jackets. Another advantage of a closed cooling system is that with antifreeze added to the cooling water, engine operation in cold weather is greatly simplified.

There are a few points that should be made about exhaust systems also. Surprising numbers of boats have less than ideal exhaust arrangements, presumably because boat manufacturers or engine installers occasionally do not realize what extreme motions a boat can go through in very heavy weather. I know this from personal experience, for our boat had water forced up the exhaust pipe and into the engine manifold during a bad storm. To avoid a repeat experience that could severely damage the engine, we had the whole exhaust system rebuilt. Some essential or at least highly desirable features for the sailboat's usual wet exhaust are as follows: a slight upward slope of the exhaust pipe from the outlet toward the engine; a *swan neck* (a high bend in the line) or a vertical muffler as far as possible above the load waterline (illustrated in Figure 5-2); water injection at least four inches below the underside of the pipe at the top of the swan neck in such a way that no cooling water can flow back into the manifold; water jacketing or preferably insulation on the exhaust pipe prior to water injection (where water does not flow through the pipe); a condensation trap and drain in the low part of the line (also a drain in the water jackets, if any); a heavy flexible hose well clamped to prevent fatiguing of metal pipe from vibration; and a shut-off valve at the exhaust outlet. These points are illustrated in Figure 5-2. Of course, the swan neck or vertical muffler is essential if the exhaust manifold is located below the load waterline, but even when the manifold is considerably higher, allowance must be made for extreme heeling, pitching, stern squat, and seas slamming against the exhaust outlet.

Perhaps the most common fault with stock sailboat engine installations is lack of accessibility for servicing, inspection, and repairs. The engine should be located where every part can be reached even if this requires the installation of removable compartment panels or bulkheads. Of course, one should have easy accessibility to parts that need regular inspection or servicing—the oil dipstick, oil fill and filter,

FIGURE 5-2: A SAILBOAT'S WET EXHAUST INSTALLATION

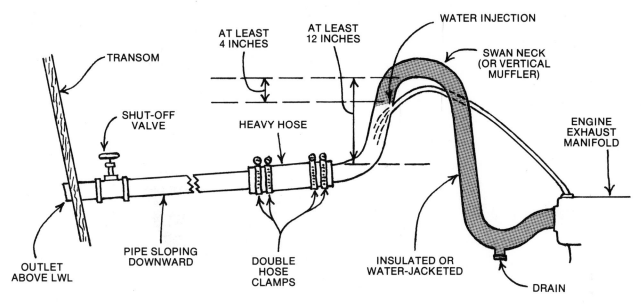

fuel filter, carburetor, distributor, spark plugs, air intake, all fuel and water shut-off valves, grease fittings, and sea-water cooling pump and impeller. In addition, the batteries and propeller shaft and engine shaft coupling must be within easy reach.

The shaft must be reached quite often and rotated by hand to bring the propeller into the position where it causes the least amount of drag when the boat is under sail. On most cruising sailboats with solid, two-bladed propellers, this position would be vertical, where the propeller blades can hide behind the keel deadwood. The position should be marked with a line of paint on the shaft. A more important reason for reaching the shaft is for the inspection and servicing of the stuffing box, the bronze packing gland that prevents sea water from leaking into the boat where the shaft penetrates the hull. A fast drip from the stuffing box is usually rectified with a gentle turn on the packing nut, but occasionally repacking is necessary. At any rate, care must be taken not to tighten the nut too much, as this could result in binding the packing on the shaft. A very slow drip while the engine is running is perfectly tolerable.

Tanks and Piping

At the time of this writing, the Coast Guard is drawing up new regulations for engine and fuel systems under authorization of the Federal Boat Safety Act of 1971. It seems highly probable that these regulations will follow very closely the safety standards and recommendations developed by the American Boat and Yacht Council (ABYC) and the Boating Industry Association published in the book *Safety Standards for Small Craft*. Some desirable or essential features for the fuel system are listed below:

• The fill pipe should be securely attached to deck plates.

• The fill pipe should be located on the side deck rather than in the bottom of the cockpit, if possible, to minimize water leakage through the cap and accumulation of fumes in the bottom of the cockpit.

• The fill pipe should be straight if possible to facilitate measuring the amount of fuel with a stick.

• There should be an accessible flexible section near the top of the fill pipe to prevent fatigue of the metal pipe from vibration.

• The fill pipe and fuel tank should be grounded to prevent buildup of static electricity (flexible hose in the fill pipe must be jumped with a heavy copper wire).

• The fill pipe should extend to near the bottom of the fuel tank and preferably terminate in a well so that there is a liquid seal to safeguard against a possible tank explosion from an ignited fill pipe.

• A screened air vent to the tank should be

FIGURE 5-3: TANKS & PIPING

(on a 30-ft. LWL cruising sailboat)

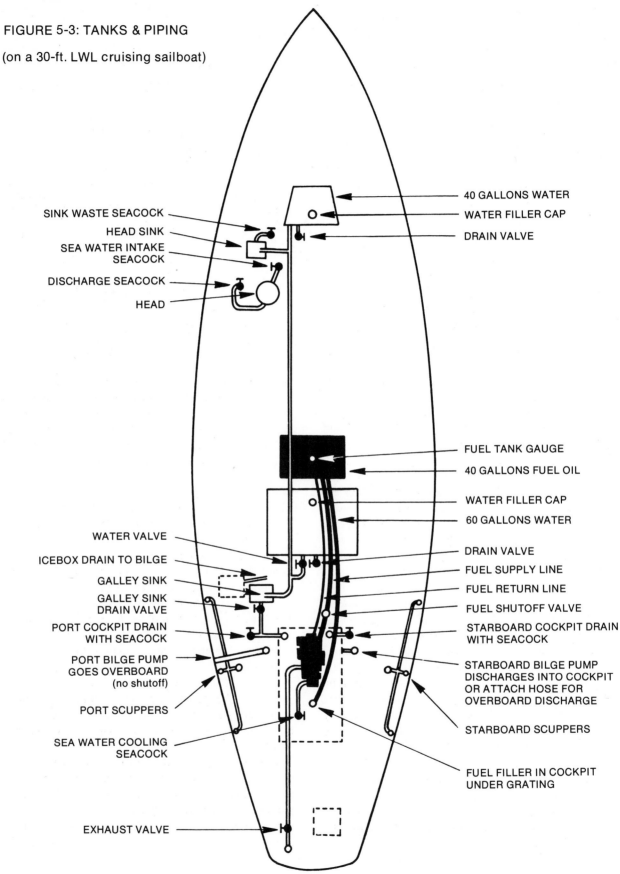

SINK WASTE SEACOCK

HEAD SINK

SEA WATER INTAKE SEACOCK

DISCHARGE SEACOCK

HEAD

40 GALLONS WATER

WATER FILLER CAP

DRAIN VALVE

FUEL TANK GAUGE

40 GALLONS FUEL OIL

WATER FILLER CAP

60 GALLONS WATER

WATER VALVE

ICEBOX DRAIN TO BILGE

GALLEY SINK

GALLEY SINK DRAIN VALVE

PORT COCKPIT DRAIN WITH SEACOCK

PORT BILGE PUMP GOES OVERBOARD (no shutoff)

PORT SCUPPERS

SEA WATER COOLING SEACOCK

DRAIN VALVE

FUEL SUPPLY LINE

FUEL RETURN LINE

FUEL SHUTOFF VALVE

STARBOARD COCKPIT DRAIN WITH SEACOCK

STARBOARD BILGE PUMP DISCHARGES INTO COCKPIT OR ATTACH HOSE FOR OVERBOARD DISCHARGE

STARBOARD SCUPPERS

FUEL FILLER IN COCKPIT UNDER GRATING

EXHAUST VALVE

located on a side deck where fumes will go overboard, and the vent should be swan-necked so that it cannot admit water.

• All tanks should be well secured to prevent shifting or breaking loose in any kind of seaway or severe knockdown (special attention should be paid to securing bow tanks, as they are subject to violent motion).

• Tanks should be adequately baffled to minimize the surging of liquid contents.

• The fuel line should run from the top of the tank (recommended by the ABYC).

• There should be shut-off valves on the fuel line to permit servicing the engine without spilling fuel, and a shut-off valve at the tank.

• There should be a flexible section (approved for marine use) in the fuel line near the engine to avoid fatigue from vibration.

• The carburetor should be fitted with an approved backfire flame arrester and a drip collector that will return drips to the intake manifold.

• There should be adequate ventilation of engine and fuel tank compartments (meeting Coast Guard requirements) having intake and exhaust vents and hoses, and the air exhaust hose should lead to the deepest part of the bilge.

• A sparkproof mechanical blower should be installed high in the air exhaust line.

Preferably, tanks should not be permanently built into the boat in order that they can be removed periodically for inspection and cleaning. They can be made of such materials as copper-silicon (Everdure), fire-retardant fiberglass, Monel, or galvanized iron or steel. The last three materials are recommended for diesel fuel, but the inside of tanks containing diesel oil should not be galvanized. The use of stainless steel for tanks seems to be somewhat controversial, especially for gasoline tanks. Some insurance companies frown on stainless tanks because some types are subject to "shielding corrosion" behind holding straps or elsewhere. This corrosion can result when air does not reach the stainless steel surface and form a protective oxide film that prevents corrosion. Water tanks should be fitted with large handholes having screw plate covers for easy cleaning. Some boats have fiberglass water tanks, but these may give the water a bad taste.

As said earlier, there should be seacocks on all through-hull fittings, especially those below the waterline. Plastic hoses may be used for water piping, but where the hose is clamped on a plastic through-hull fitting, it is advisable that the seacock be kept closed when no one is on board, for the connection can be slippery. Hose clamps should be stainless steel with worm screws for tightening. Spring-type clamps are not to be trusted. Piping should always be installed so that sea water cannot possibly siphon back into the boat in the event that a check valve should fail. Back-siphoning is best prevented with a high loop in an outlet pipe (similar to the swan neck in the engine's exhaust line) and a siphon-breaking air vent valve at the high point in the loop. Permanent bilge pumps should be installed in this manner and so should flow-through toilets on sailboats (even if the bowl is above the waterline) in order to allow for heeling. When plumbing installations use rigid metal pipes, consider the possibility of hull flexing in heavy weather. Pipes in any region where the hull can bend should be joined to the hull with flexible hoses. Marine toilets can cause trouble when they are abused. Don't throw anything in the bowl except a minimum of toilet paper, and never pump the toilet unless the outlet valve is open. Be sure to post operating instructions where they can easily be seen.

Figure 5-3 shows the tanks and piping on a diesel-powered cruising sailboat with a waterline length of approximately thirty feet. It is preferable that the side deck scupper pipes and port bilge pump be fitted with seacocks at the through-hull fittings.

Radiotelephones

The Federal Communications Commission (FCC) presently is phasing out of existence DSB-AM (double sideband-amplitude modulation) radiotelephones on boats. New installations of this equipment have not been allowed since January 1, 1972, but existing DSB sets installed before that date may be used until January 1, 1977, provided their licenses are renewed before expiration. The new replacement for double sideband is VHF-FM (very high frequency-frequency modulation), or, when long distance transmission is needed, single sideband radiotelephones must supplement the VHF equipment.

For short-range communications, VHF has many advantages—less congestion and interference; quicker and more versatile communications; cheaper equipment; less drain on the batteries with transistorized sets; smaller, lightweight antennas; and no need for ground plates. The greatest drawback for

VHF is its lack of range, which is somewhat more than line of sight. This distance depends on the height of your antenna, the power of your set, and the height of the transmitting station. The range could be as much as fifty miles from a very high shore station to a boat, but it is seldom more than fifteen miles between boats, even those with mast antennas. Of course, the range of VHF transmissions might be sufficient for most gunkhole and coastal cruisers, but for communications fairly far offshore (up to perhaps several hundred miles beyond VHF range) medium frequency (2-3 MHz) single sideband equipment will be needed, and it can be installed legally only if there is already a licensed VHF set aboard.

These 2-3 MHz radiotelephones are presently quite expensive and relatively complicated to install. A ground plate—normally a large sheet of copper at least twelve square feet in size—secured to the boat's bottom and a sizable antenna are required for best results. With ground plates, great care must be taken to avoid *electrolysis* (electrolytic corrosion) due to electric current flowing between the radio ground plate and the propeller shaft (which usually serves as the engine's ground). Be sure that the entire radiotelephone system is installed by a competent marine technician. As a matter of fact, a licensed FCC technician will be required at least to align the transmitter and receiver. On many boats the backstay is used very effectively for the antenna, but care must be taken to use proper "egg" insulators, which are designed to take great strain and which allow the part of the stay above and below each insulator to remain connected even if the insulator should happen to break. It is wisest to use flexible wire for the backstay when it is to serve as an antenna. Actually, from a safety standpoint, it may be advisable to use a stern-mounted loaded whip antenna on an offshore boat, even though it is less efficient, because the loss of a mast would incapacitate the radiotelephone when it would be needed most urgently.

An alternative for sailors who want a cheap means of communication over short distances is a *citizen's band* (CB) radiophone, a very low-powered set (less than 5 watts) operating on a frequency of about 27 MHz. However, this is not true marine communication, and it lacks a distress frequency and direct contact with the Coast Guard. With CB it is possible to talk only to private citizens with similar equipment over a very short range.

When ordinary conversation is not needed and safety is the only consideration, emergency *locator beacons* may be carried. These small, relatively inexpensive transmitting radios contain their own batteries and send out distress signals on certain emergency frequencies, usually 121.5 MHz and 243 MHz, but some kinds can send on 2182 kHz, the international distress frequency. It is safest for a boat venturing any distance offshore to carry at least one beacon, whether or not she is equipped with a radiophone, in case the batteries of the latter should be down or drowned out during an emergency.

Information on FCC regulations and license requirements should be obtained from your radiotelephone dealer; from the FCC, Gettysburg, Pennsylvania 17325; or from the Superintendent of Documents, Government Printing Office, Washington, D.C. 20402.

Depth Sounders

Although lead lines afford a reliable means of measuring water depth, electronic depth sounders, sometimes called *fathometers*, have several advantages. They give more continuous soundings with little effort, and they can reach beyond the depth range of an easily manageable lead line. Depth sounders send down high-frequency sound waves, which strike the sea bed and are reflected back to the boat. A transmitter sends pulses of electrical energy to a transducer, normally located at the bottom of the boat, which converts the energy into inaudible sound waves directed downward. Their travel time to the sea bed and back to the transducer is measured and displayed visually on an indicator or recording device.

Depth recorders show the soundings in a permanent way as lines inscribed by a stylus on paper that is moved by a motor at a constant rate. Such a system is especially handy for navigating with the use of soundings, and more will be said about this in Chapter 8. Nonpermanent indicators come in a variety of styles, including one that shows the depth in digital numbers and another called the flashing lamp type. On the latter, an arm with a neon lamp at its end rotates around a circular scale. The lamp flashes at zero depth and then again at the depth of the sea bed or at the depth of any intervening object such as a school of fish that will cause a reflection of the sound waves. Some interpretation is required in reading this kind of indicator. A hard rocky bottom

FIGURE 5-4: DEPTH SOUNDER

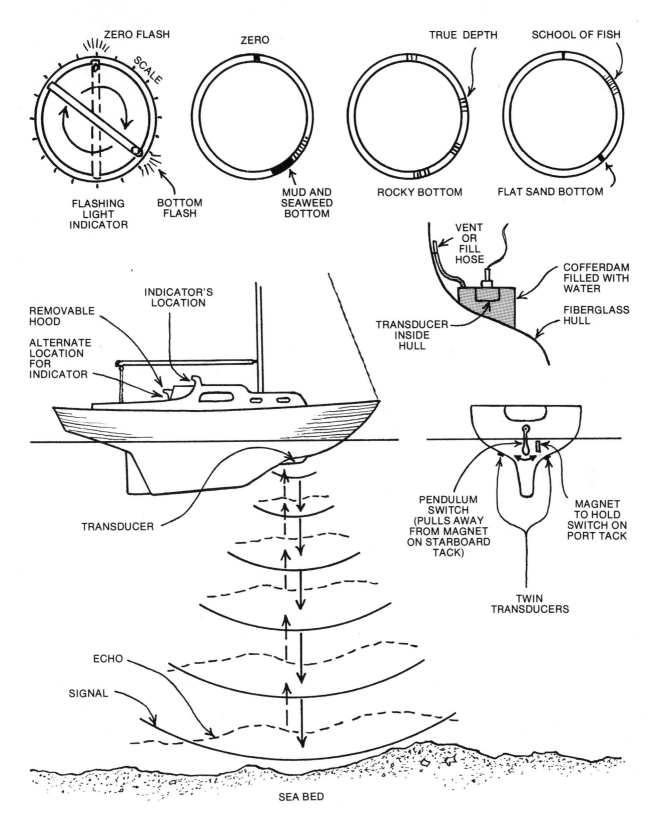

ZERO FLASH

SCALE

ZERO

TRUE DEPTH

SCHOOL OF FISH

FLASHING LIGHT INDICATOR

BOTTOM FLASH

MUD AND SEAWEED BOTTOM

ROCKY BOTTOM

FLAT SAND BOTTOM

REMOVABLE HOOD

ALTERNATE LOCATION FOR INDICATOR

INDICATOR'S LOCATION

VENT OR FILL HOSE

COFFERDAM FILLED WITH WATER

FIBERGLASS HULL

TRANSDUCER INSIDE HULL

TRANSDUCER

PENDULUM SWITCH (PULLS AWAY FROM MAGNET ON STARBOARD TACK)

MAGNET TO HOLD SWITCH ON PORT TACK

TWIN TRANSDUCERS

ECHO

SIGNAL

SEA BED

in shallow water may cause multiple flashes due to *reverberation* (the sound waves bouncing back and forth many times). Quite often the reading can be clarified by retarding the instrument's sensitivity control, but if not, consider that the depth is the flash nearest the zero mark. A soft mud bottom will generally produce a broader, slightly weaker flash, and a sloping bottom also will show a broad flash. A school of fish usually will show up as weak, temporary flashes. Some of these points are illustrated in Figure 5-4. Quite often unidentifiable flashes will occur when the engine is running if the depth sounder is connected to the engine's battery. Ignition interference from the engine can be minimized, however, if separate dry cell batteries are used for the depth sounder.

Transducers often are mounted on the boat's centerline just forward of the keel, but sometimes twin transducers are used farther aft, one on each side of the boat. The leeward one is used when the boat is heeled. Some depth sounders of this type are equipped with automatic gravity-activated switches that change transducers when tacks are changed. On a fiberglass racer, the transducer sometimes is mounted in a *water box* or *cofferdam* attached to the bottom of the hull inside the boat in order to eliminate any drag that can slow the boat (see Figure 5-4). The box is usually filled with water or sometimes a light oil. Quite often this arrangement works reasonably well, but it can be very unsatisfactory if the hull shell or bottom paint interferes with the sound waves or if the transducer is mounted the wrong distance from the hull. When performance is less than desirable, experiment by raising or lowering the transducer (but keeping it level) or by changing bottom paints on the area directly under the transducer. On a cruising boat that will never be raced, where a slight amount of drag is no consideration, an exterior transducer may be preferable.

The location of the indicator also can be a problem. It should be visible to the helmsmen but out of the way. A flashing lamp indicator should be fitted with a hood or shade to reduce the sun's glare. One alternative is to mount the indicator in the after end of the cabin trunk and to have a removable shade that can be stowed when the depth sounder is not in use, or the indicator may be mounted just forward of the companionway hatch. Another alternative is to mount the indicator on a hinged plank that may be swung out into the companionway entrance when the sounder is in use, but swung back out of the way into the cabin when not in use. Of course, with such an arrangement, the companionway will be partially blocked when the helmsman reads the soundings, but he has the option of leaving the indicator retracted inside the cabin and having a crew member stationed in the companionway to read the indicator and call out the soundings when in shoal water.

A depth sounder is well worth its price, which starts at slightly over one hundred dollars, for it not only helps prevent running aground, but also is a great help in selecting a spot to anchor. The instrument also is useful as a navigational aid to help find one's location, and it can be very helpful in choosing a course through shoal waters to avoid strong adverse currents.

Speedometers and Logs

Strictly speaking, a *log* is either a speedometer or a device to record distance, but in general usage an instrument indicating speed is usually called a *speedometer*, while the term *log* is reserved for the instrument that shows distance traveled or distance and speed both. The main value of a speedometer or log for a cruising boat is as a navigational aid to show how far a boat has traveled in a given direction. For a racing boat, of course, the instrument is valuable as an aid in selecting the fastest sail combination and optimal sheet trim.

There are many different kinds of speedometers and logs. Some are operated by water pressure against a movable wand sensor or within a Pitot tube, while others use a rotating impeller (propeller) or a small paddle wheel. There is even a new kind that uses a sensor flush with the hull and works on the principle of measuring the electric current necessary to hold the sensor probe at a fixed temperature. Of course, there is also the old-fashioned but reliable taff rail log, which consists of a rotator streamed overboard from the end of a long line attached to a dial at the boat's stern. This type is ideal for long coastal passages, but it has the drawbacks that it might be fouled by other boats in crowded waters, it may sink to the bottom in very light airs in shoal water, and it is troublesome to haul in when coming to anchor and stream again after getting underway.

A generally well-regarded, reliable speedometer or log that can be effective even at very slow speeds is the kind having an impeller or paddle wheel sensor, but it should be kept in mind that most sensors, except perhaps the heat-sensing kind, will be affected to some extent by high angles of heel and rough water. Heeling changes the sensor's immersion depth and alters the water flow along the hull, and this can cause a slight instrument error. Greater errors can be caused by a heavy accumulation of marine growth on the sensor, so it should be cleaned frequently. To facilitate cleaning, it is preferable that the sensor be removable through a skin fitting having a valve, cap, or plug to allow withdrawal of the sensor into the interior while the boat is afloat. It is also advisable to have a weed defector mounted just forward of the sensor to prevent it from becoming fouled with seaweed or being struck by submerged flotsam.

Refrigeration

In regions where ice is hard to get, mechanical refrigeration is a great boon, but it is not entirely without drawbacks for boats that spend a great deal of time under sail or at anchor, because it requires the running of an auxiliary generator or the engine with an alternator to prevent draining the batteries. Some refrigerators are designed to run on 115-volt AC, while others run directly from the boat's battery power (usually 12-volt DC). Of course, one can connect the former type directly to shore power when this is available at dockside, but at sea, one will need a 115-volt AC generator. A very limited amount of current can be produced by an inverter, which converts battery power to 115-volt AC. On the other hand, the DC "fridge" that operates directly from the boat's batteries will need a battery-charging rectifier alongside the dock, and at sea will require a DC generator or engine-driven alternator to keep the batteries up.

A practical kind of refrigeration for cruising sailboats that don't spend much time at the dock uses *eutectic holding plates*. These are flat, sealed containers that hold a eutectic solution, which is frozen with the use of a compressor. A refrigerant such as freon is compressed into a liquid outside of the cold box (where the food is kept). Then the liquid refrigerant is allowed to expand and evaporate, turning into freon gas inside coils in the eutectic solution and thus absorbing heat from the solution. The compressor is sometimes driven by an electric motor powered by the boat's batteries, which, with the proper alternator, can be charged by periodically running the engine. It is generally far more efficient, however, if the compressor can be directly connected to the engine with a belt drive. Such a system may require that the engine be run for only about an hour every day or two, depending, of course, on the cold box size and the coldness required. If the engine cannot be run each day, or every other day, the holding plates should keep the box sufficiently cool to necessitate running the engine only every three days, perhaps for two hours at a time.

Another form of refrigeration that needs no electricity or moving parts utilizes a small flame to boil ammonia, turning it from a liquid to a vapor and absorbing heat through evaporation. This method usually does not work well on a sailboat, however, because of her heeling angle; furthermore, a constantly burning open flame placed low in a boat carrying gasoline or LP-gas could involve some risk of explosion if there should happen to be any fumes from leaking storage tanks or feed lines or from some other source.

Regardless of the type of refrigeration chosen to suit your needs, adequate cold box insulation is needed. Foamed urethane or styrofoam four inches thick should be effective.

6

Fitting Out for Cruising

When it comes to estimating the cost of fitting out a new boat for cruising, one rule of thumb is that the minimum equipment needed will amount to at least one-fifth of the base price of the boat. In other words, an average new boat having a price tag of $15,000 with no extras or optional equipment will cost at least $18,000 when she is fitted out for simple cruising in protected waters. Actually, this rule may underestimate the cost, because some base prices do not even include the auxiliary engine, galley stove, or sails. A more realistic estimate might be that all necessary and desirable equipment will cost closer to one-third of the base price. Expensive luxury items will run the cost considerably higher.

Safety Equipment

Permanently installed safety equipment such as life lines and permanent bilge pumps were discussed in Chapter 2, and legal requirements were mentioned. (Also see Appendix A for federal equipment requirements.) This section will consider safety gear that is not permanently installed and is not legally required.

As most sailors know, Coast Guard regulations require that boats carry at least one approved personal flotation device (PFD) for each person aboard, but remember that this is merely a minimum requirement. If you are sailing short-handed, there should be more than one PFD per person; a wide choice of equipment should be distributed throughout the boat for maximum accessibility under all conditions. Buoyant cushions kept in the cockpit will be instantly available for the crew and can be thrown easily to a man overboard. Incidentally, I think a buoyant cushion should be at least twenty-two inches long so that it can be worn easily on the chest (never on the back) by inserting a leg through one handle strap and the opposite arm or the head through

the other. It is also desirable that every cruising boat, regardless of her size, carry at least one horse-shoe buoy that is easily accessible from the cockpit. The buoy should have a small drogue attached to it (see Figure 6-1) to prevent it from being blown away from a man in the water.

A water light attached to the buoy is essential for night sailing. A water light is extinguished when it is hung upside down, but when thrown overboard, it rights and turns on automatically. Xenon strobe water lights are so brilliant that they are highly visible during the day and in fog. A man-overboard pole eight feet high (above the water) with a flag as shown in Figure 6-1 also should be attached to the buoy if the boat is going offshore where waves are large enough to hide the buoy from view. In addition, it is advisable to fit the buoy with a loud whistle and a package of dye marker.

Other safety items are:

1. *Safety belts* (strong chest belts with shoulder straps, each belt fitted with a stout lanyard and snap hook to snap onto the rigging or life lines in heavy weather or at night).

2. Distress flares (these can be obtained in kit form from any large chandler).

3. A *radar reflector* (a geometrically shaped object of light metal, as shown in Figure 6-1, that is hung in the rigging to warn radar-equipped vessels of your presence in fog or at night).

4. An inflatable rubber life raft or dinghy or both (dinghies will be discussed in some detail later in this chapter).

5. Navigation equipment, including the all-important compass (these will be discussed in detail in Chapter 8).

6. Anchors and adequate anchor lines (these will be discussed in Chapter 10).

7. A reliable riding light (a 360-degree light to be displayed forward at night when the boat is at anchor).

8. A powerful, waterproof, portable searchlight and several flashlights with spare batteries.

9. A spare portable bilge pump and a sturdy bucket.

10. A fifty-foot buoyant heaving line with a *quoit* (a small rubber heaving ring) readily available from the cockpit.

11. A bosun's chair for making repairs aloft.

12. A portable receiving radio for weather reports and radio direction finding (see Chapter 8).

13. A barometer.

FIGURE 6-1: SAFETY EQUIPMENT

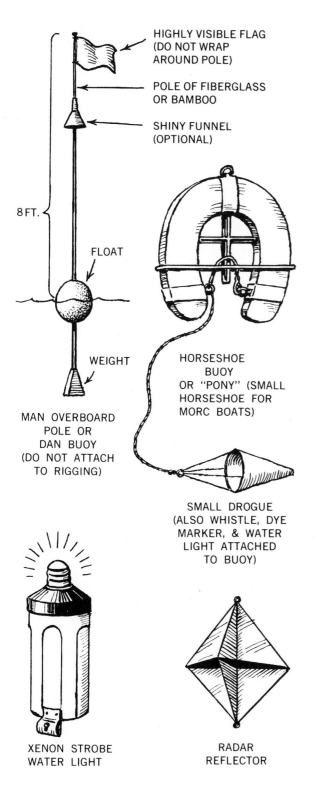

HIGHLY VISIBLE FLAG
(DO NOT WRAP
AROUND POLE)

POLE OF FIBERGLASS
OR BAMBOO

SHINY FUNNEL
(OPTIONAL)

8 FT.

FLOAT

WEIGHT

MAN OVERBOARD
POLE OR
DAN BUOY
(DO NOT ATTACH
TO RIGGING)

HORSESHOE
BUOY
OR "PONY" (SMALL
HORSESHOE FOR
MORC BOATS)

SMALL DROGUE
(ALSO WHISTLE, DYE
MARKER, & WATER
LIGHT ATTACHED
TO BUOY)

XENON STROBE
WATER LIGHT

RADAR
REFLECTOR

14. A lead line or depth sounder (refer to the previous chapter).

15. A first aid kit and instruction book (see the list of medical supplies under the section "Stocking Up" at the end of Chapter 7).

16. Heavy-weather sails (these will be discussed in Chapter 9).

17. Binoculars.

18. An underwater face mask.

19. Basic tools (pliers, screwdrivers, wrenches [one large enough to fit the stuffing box], marline-spike, knife, oilcan [with oil], file, hacksaw, drill, hatchet, spark plug wrench, sail needles and thread, waterproof tape, tapered wooden plugs that can be driven into any through-hull orifice, bedding or seam compound, etc.).

20. Spare parts (extra lines, blocks, shackles, turnbuckles, cotter pins, sail slides, hanks, twine, binding wire, toggles, battens, winch handles, bulbs, fuses, screws, nails, washers, nuts, bolts, hose clamps, etc.).

For offshore work or cruising in areas that are somewhat remote, you should have a few more items:

1. One or more emergency radio beacons or a long-range radiotelephone (see Chapter 5).

2. Extra heavy companionway slides and storm shutters to protect large vulnerable windows.

3. A sea anchor or drogue.

4. An inflatable life raft large enough to hold the entire crew and having at least two buoyancy compartments (the raft should be carried instead of or in addition to a dinghy).

5. Double life lines to prevent a crew member from being washed overboard under the topmost line.

6. *Weather cloths* secured to the life lines to protect occupants of the cockpit.

7. A stern pulpit or life lines around the stern.

8. A *collision mat* (a piece of canvas, usually weighted, with lashings that can be hauled under the boat to stop a serious leak).

9. A spare or emergency tiller and rudder head fitting.

10. Heavy-duty wire cutters (for cutting away rigging in case of dismasting).

11. A hand clamping tool for installing compression sleeves on wire cables.

12. A spare stay and spare spreader.

13. Optional masthead running lights allowed under the International Rules of the Road (see note under Figure 2-8).

14. An adequate fuel line filter (see Chapter 5).

15. Ample sails.

16. Repair kits for the engine and toilets (pre-assembled kits containing necessary spare parts can be obtained from most manufacturers).

Deck Gear

Although the cruising sailboat may not require quite as much extra deck gear as a racing boat, she will need certain optional equipment such as more or different cleats, winches, blocks, fairleads, anchor chocks, and so forth.

Low- to medium-priced standard boats (those without optional equipment) nearly always need more and larger winches. At the very minimum there should be a jib halyard winch and two powerful jib sheet winches, and it is highly desirable that there be a main halyard and main sheet winch. If a spinnaker is carried (and I would certainly recommend it, even on a boat that will never be raced), two more winches for the spinnaker sheet and guy, normally located near the after end of the cockpit, will be helpful. When funds are limited, however, I would put the money into two powerful jib sheet winches rather than spinnaker winches and smaller jib sheet winches, for the spinnaker is carried a relatively small amount of the time on the average cruiser, and children or wives often are expected to tend the jib sheets when cruising. Furthermore, unless the boat is quite large, there is no great problem in using the jib sheet winches for the spinnaker sheet and guy; in wind conditions suitable for setting the spinnaker, the jib sheets can be removed from their winches while broad reaching or running when there is hardly ever a great deal of wind pressure on the jib. For boats over about thirty feet LOA, geared two-speed winches are highly recommended. Boats up to thirty-five feet might use winches similar to the Barient number 22's, boats up to forty-five feet should find number 28's satisfactory, and larger cruisers might use number 35's. These two-speed winches provide a *direct drive* (one-to-one ratio) when the handle is turned clockwise for quick trimming, but when the handle is turned in the opposite direction the winches operate in low gear to obtain power at the sacrifice of speed. Handles are available with switches that allow ratcheting no matter which direction the winch is rotated.

There are seldom sufficient cleats on standard boats. Several cleats usually will have to be added to the mainmast and in the cockpit area, either on the cockpit coaming or on the after end of the cabin top or in both locations. For a cruising boat that often will be sailed short-handed, it is wise to lead the spinnaker halyard and pole lift halyard aft to cabin-top cleats, and, of course, this will require the installation of two fairlead blocks at the base of the mainmast. Extra cleats on the coamings will be needed for the spinnaker sheet and guy or other headsail sheets. If a winch is added for the main sheet, another cleat may be needed or the standard cleat might have to be moved. It is especially important that the main sheet cleat be within easy reach of the helmsman.

Standard mooring cleats are seldom all that they should be on stock boats. Quite often they are too small and are installed so that they are subject to lateral strain. They should be positioned so that the strain is nearly (but not quite) parallel to their axes, and, of course, they should be bolted through large, solid backing blocks under the deck. It is preferable that bow and stern mooring cleats or bitts be on or near the boat's centerline, that the bow mooring chocks be as far forward as possible, and that there be three stern chocks, one on each side for docking lines and one on the centerline for towing. A roller chock at the stem head is handy for the anchor line, and, incidentally, it may be desirable to install a through-the-deck *hawsepipe* so that the anchor line or chain can be stowed below in the forepeak and can be fed up through the pipe. Of course, large boats with heavy ground tackle will need a *windlass* (a kind of winch for handling the anchor line or chain). Windlasses can be operated manually or with electric power. The latter method is quite practical, for with a proper alternator and the engine running while the anchor is being weighed, there is seldom any serious drain on the boat's batteries.

Before leaving the subject of cleats, I would like to warn against relying only on quick-release jam cleats. Although they definitely have their place aboard racers, a more reliable cleat aboard a cruiser is the conventional anvil type with two horns around which the line is wrapped in a criss-cross fashion. The end of the cleat facing the direction in which the line pulls may have a narrow space under the horn for jamming purposes, but be sure the cleat is large enough for ample wraps and a hitch so that the line may be cleated with extra security when this is necessary. Sheets of natural fiber should rarely ever be hitched on a cleat, because they may swell and jam too securely when wet. Jamming is seldom a problem with Dacron sheets, however.

An expensive piece of gear that is optional on most small- to medium-sized cruisers is the steering wheel. The standard helm usually is a tiller, which is generally the most desirable means of steering smaller boats. A tiller usually provides greater sensitivity and "feel" of the boat when she is under sail; it gives quicker response with less movement of the helmsman's arm; there are fewer mechanical parts that need servicing or repair; self-steering devices usually are more simply attached to tillers than to wheels; and at anchor there is often more room in the cockpit when the tiller is hinged to fold back out of the way. On the other hand, wheel steering provides a mechanical advantage and thus requires less physical strength of the helmsman; when the wheel is mounted on a pedestal, the top of the latter provides an excellent location for the compass (see Chapter 8); a wheel does not interfere with the legs of those sitting in the cockpit when underway; and in most cases wheel steering allows greater choice in the helm's location. Weighing all the pros and cons of both steering systems, it would seem that tiller steering is the more desirable on small cruisers, especially those that will be raced occasionally, but wheels should be installed on larger, nonracing cruisers. It is difficult to draw the line on boat size, but very generally speaking, a light to moderately light displacement cruiser with a fairly short keel and good helm balance with a length as great as forty feet overall might be steered very easily with a tiller, but cruisers above that size, especially heavy ones with long keels, usually should have wheel steering. As mentioned before, many cruisers have the wheel located at the forward end of the cockpit, but this position nearly always blocks the companionway, and so I would recommend an after location whenever possible.

Other permanently installed deck gear might include winch handle holders (those made of PVC—polyvinyl chloride—are very satisfactory); extra fairleads on the side decks for storm jibs, staysails, etc.; a main sheet traveler (important on a cruiser that will be raced but also desirable on a nonracer for better trim and to hold the boom steady at times); anchor chocks to hold the anchor securely and protect the deck (they may be mounted on the foredeck or cabin top); spinnaker pole chocks to hold the pole securely on deck; dinghy chocks in which to lash the dinghy, generally in the upside-down position on top of the cabin trunk; a boom crutch or, on large cruisers, a *gallows frame* (a boom

support having two uprights and a horizontal cross piece with boom positions on both sides as well as amidships); and perhaps a watertight deck box located in the cockpit or on the cabin top for stowing loose gear.

Nonpermanent deck gear will include such items as a boathook, a deck mop, a scrub brush, a *handy billy* (small tackle), several short pieces of line (to be used for lashings), *snatch blocks* (side opening blocks for sheet leads and other purposes), docking lines and fenders (see Chapter 10), sail stops, a compass cover, cloth covers for wheel and winches perhaps, a yacht ensign and staff, measuring sticks (for fuel and water tanks), a garden hose (to fill the water tank or hose off decks at docks where there are no hoses), chafe guards (rubber hose types

Long items of deck gear can be lashed to handrails atop the cabin for storage.

are very satisfactory for preventing chafe to lines), and a foghorn. Except for very long items such as the boathook, most loose deck gear will be stowed in cockpit seat lockers, the stern lazarette, or a deck box.

Comfort Equipment

One of the most important pieces of comfort equipment is a good awning. In fact, this should be considered essential in hot climates. Many awnings are made of lightweight white Dacron, and they cover the cockpit and after end of the cabin trunk, stretching from the forward to the after end of the main boom on most boats having long booms. The forward end usually secures to the mainmast shrouds. On a yawl its after end secures to the mizzen shrouds, but a single-masted boat requires an athwartships pole or "spreader" at the after end of the awning that rests on the main boom and is lashed down to the life lines or deck on both sides. In fact, many awnings carry three aluminum poles sewn into the cloth: one forward, one aft, and one in the middle (see Figure 6-2). When the awning is taken down, it is simply rolled up on the poles. Some veteran sailors who cruise in the tropics insist that a proper awning should be made of cotton canvas (Vivetex, a mildew-proofed cotton, is recommended), because this material is very soft, protects most effectively against sun penetration, and does not flap as violently in the wind as lightweight synthetic materials. Judging from my own experiences in hot weather, however, I have found medium-weight, soft Dacron awnings quite satisfactory, and they have the advantage of high resistance to mildew and rot. It is desirable that the awning have a removable side flap or curtain held in place with snap fasteners as shown in Figure 6-2. This flap, which can be shifted to either side of the awning, is used to provide shade when the sun is low.

In very hot climates, small cockpit covers, often called *Bimini tops*, can be set under the main boom on a folding or removable metal frame to provide shade while the boat is under full sail. Of course, the large, regular awning can be carried under sail when the mainsail is furled. Quite often, when the wind is aft in hot weather, a fine cruising rig is the spinnaker and awning. More will be said about this rig in Chapter 9.

Another valuable cover is a companionway dodger. This cloth cover, illustrated in Figure 6-3, is primarily to keep rain and spray out of the companionway in foul weather, and it also provides some protection for the helmsman or crew members at the forward end of the cockpit. As the illustration shows, the dodger is a kind of hood set on a metal frame that is hinged to fold forward (similarly to the hood on a baby carriage) so that it is out of the way when not in use. Dodgers are probably most needed on boats having considerable forward rake to the after ends of their cabin trunks, because this rake can allow rainwater to enter the cabin even when the horizontal sliding hatch cover is completely closed. There should be ample windows in a dodger in order to allow the best possible visibility when underway. Windows in dodgers are usually made of Mylar, a soft, clear plastic that will not crack when it is bent. A well-made dodger is not cheap, and you can make a reasonably effective substitute for a rainy day at anchor with a small triangular awning —lashing two corners to the handrails on the sides of the companionway and the other corner aft as shown in Figure 6-4.

In all but the most northerly of U.S. cruising grounds, adequate ventilation is extremely important to comfort below decks. It is preferable that there be several *Dorade* vents, cowl ventilators mounted on water trap boxes (similar to the type shown in Figure 6-5) in order that air without water can be admitted below on rainy days or when the spray is flying in rough weather. Of course, there are some areas on the deck where water trap boxes will be in the way and an ordinary removable cowl is more desirable. When such a cowl is turned aft to keep out water, however, it will not scoop up air. One solution to this problem is to use a detachable water trap box like the one illustrated in Figure 6-5. In fair weather the cowl is detached from the box and is screwed directly into the deck hole, but in mild rainy weather, the box is used in addition to the cowl vent. Notice that the box is held in place with a wood toggle on a short length of shock cord (elastic cord) that is run through the deck hole. Of course, this rig is not intended for heavy weather when solid water comes aboard, and so the device should be removed and the deck hole plugged with a screw plate when underway in rough waters or in a bad storm. A permanent *Dorade* box should have two cowl positions, one directly over the deck hole for fair weather and maximum ventilation, and the other well abaft the deck hole for rainy weather when some ventilation must be sacrificed to assure dryness below.

FIGURE 6-2: COCKPIT AWNING & WINDSAIL

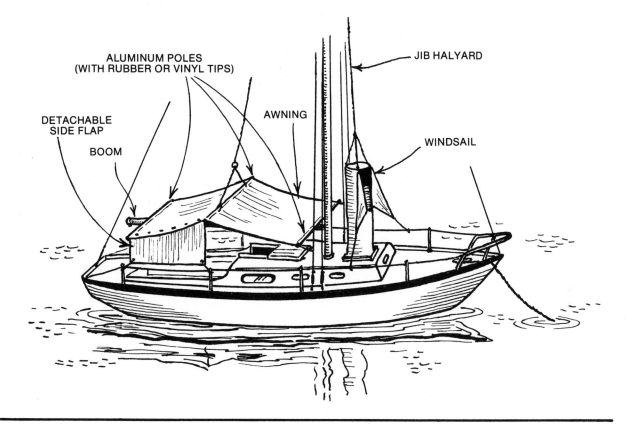

ALUMINUM POLES
(WITH RUBBER OR VINYL TIPS)

DETACHABLE
SIDE FLAP

BOOM

AWNING

JIB HALYARD

WINDSAIL

FIGURE 6-3: COMPANIONWAY DODGER

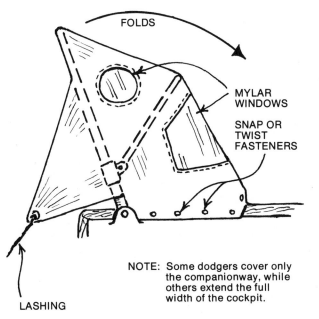

FOLDS

MYLAR
WINDOWS

SNAP OR
TWIST
FASTENERS

NOTE: Some dodgers cover only
the companionway, while
others extend the full
width of the cockpit.

LASHING

FIGURE 6-4: "ARTFUL" DODGER
(a cheap substitute intended
for a rainy day at anchor)

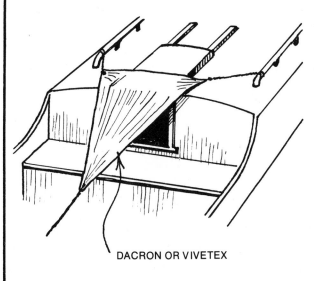

DACRON OR VIVETEX

FIGURE 6-5: REMOVABLE DORADE VENT

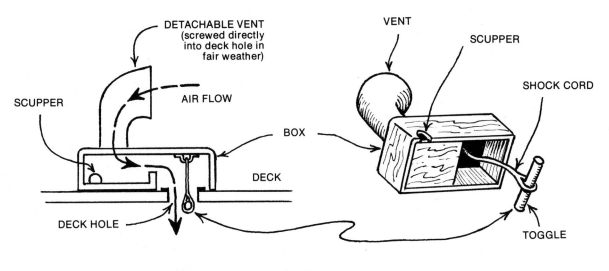

NOTE: In heavy weather at sea, vent and box are removed,
and metal cap is screwed into deck hole.

FIGURE 6-6: SIMPLE VENTILATION PLANS

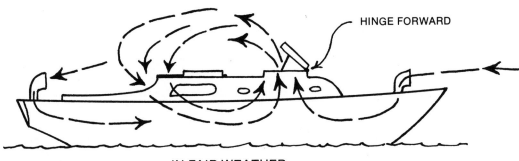

IN FAIR WEATHER

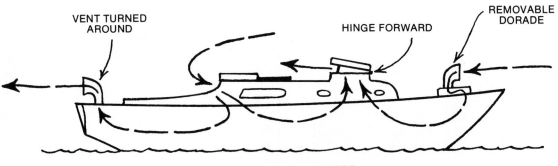

IN RAINY WEATHER

Figure 6-6 illustrates fair weather and rainy weather ventilation plans for a small cruiser at anchor. Contrary to typical stock boat hatch covers, which are usually hinged at their after ends, the forward cover shown in the illustration is hinged at its forward end. Forward hinging most often encourages better air circulation, prevents rain from being blown below, and provides a possible safety advantage in that there is less chance of the cover being swept or blown overboard if it has been left undogged in heavy weather. Actually, it is preferable that there be hinges forward *and* aft and that the hinging be made interchangeable with a removable rod or some other means in order that the hatch can be opened either way. Incidentally, a large *windsail* will funnel a tremendous amount of air through an open hatch. Most windsails are large-diameter cloth tubes secured directly over an open hatch; at the top of the tube are wind-catching cloth "wings" lashed to the rigging or life lines (see Figure 6-2). These ventilators can be bought from most large chandlers, or they can be constructed by sailmakers.

In cruising areas inhabited by mosquitoes or other insect pests, you may want screens. Screens block the flow of air into a cabin far more than many people realize, however, and so in hot weather I would avoid them unless the insects become quite unbearable. Very often mosquitoes will descend on a boat when the wind dies soon after dark; but not long afterward, a breeze will come up and dispel them. Then, too, mosquitoes often can be avoided by anchoring farther offshore or away from marshy areas. Nevertheless, in cool regions, where mosquitoes can be fierce (such as in certain parts of Maine), screens are a real blessing. When screens are used only occasionally, they can most conveniently be secured with Velcro strips. Velcro is a fastening material in tape form having two whiskery surfaces, one called "hook" and the other "pile." The tapes stick to each other when they are pressed together, yet they can be pulled apart quite easily. Pile tape is cemented around the edges of the opening to be screened and hook tape is sewn to the edges of soft nylon screening material that has been cut to the size of the opening. When screens are desired, the pile and hook tapes are pressed together, but when screens are not needed the tapes are peeled apart and the screens rolled up for easy stowage. Velcro screens can be bought in kit form with

An "Irwin 28" with a Bimini top set over the cockpit to provide shade while sailing. Notice the high boom, which allows standing headroom when the Bimini is down.

The sailors aboard this "Morgan 41," at anchor in a Maine harbor, appear to be using the companionway dodger and awning to keep the cockpit dry in wet weather.

complete instructions from prominent yacht chandlers. Incidentally, don't forget one or more fly swatters—the plastic kind that don't rust.

Another piece of gear that many sailors consider essential is a good swimming ladder. This article has been included here, in the section on comfort equipment, because swimming has primarily to do with comfort or entertainment, but the item could have been mentioned as safety equipment, since swimming without an easy means of reboarding the boat undoubtedly can be dangerous, especially when children or unskilled swimmers are overboard. A proper ladder should be sturdy yet not too heavy, be well padded to protect the topsides, and extend a foot or more below the surface of the water so that the bottom step can be reached easily. It is preferable that the ladder fold for easy stowage. Incidentally, to be extra cautious, hang some lines overboard and/or put the dinghy or rubber raft overboard when people are swimming from the boat; for there may be a stronger current than you expect, and there is always the possibility that a swimmer may get a cramp.

Many cruising boats carry cushions made to fit the cockpit seats exactly. If these are carried, they should be covered with a tough, waterproof cover such as naugahyde, and they should not be so long as to make stowage a problem. In my opinion, it is important that large, fitted cockpit cushions be provided with snaps or other fasteners to hold them in place; otherwise they may slide off their seats when the boat heels or when a person steps on them, and they could cause the person to lose his balance and fall.

Below decks, mattresses for the bunks should be covered on top with a waterproof material such as naugahyde, vinyl, or polyurethane-coated fabric, but a porous synthetic cloth should cover the bottoms in order that the mattresses can "breathe." Most boat mattresses are made of foam rubber or polyurethane foam. Having tried both materials, I prefer the latter, as it seems somewhat more comfortable, lighter, and more resistant to damage by overexposure to heat and sun. It has been said that polyurethane will break down in time and flatten slightly, but I have not found this to be true in eight years of using the material. Polyurethane mattresses should be at least four inches thick, however, for the best sitting comfort.

Sheets, blankets, and pillows will be needed, too, of course. The chore of making up bunks will be greatly simplified if the sheets are form-fitted to the mattresses like contour sheets. Blankets can be kept in zippered plastic bags to keep them dry and folded. In warm weather or during the daytime, the plastic bags containing blankets may be used for pillows.

Another important item for the cabin is window curtains. These not only afford privacy, but they keep out the sun, which can heat up the cabin, cause glare, and harm the finish on woodwork. Curtains may be secured with snaps or Velcro tapes, or they may swing or slide on rods. The latter method will require hoops or slides sewn to the curtains, and if there is a rake to the sides of the cabin house, rods may be required at the bottom as well as the top of the curtains.

In northern climes or temperate latitudes during the early spring or late fall, a small heater may be necessary for comfort. There are many different types, ranging from oil burners on large cruisers to compact alcohol or catalytic heaters suitable for small boats. Heating stoves or "fireplaces" that use solid fuel are made in small sizes, and they can burn briquettes of charcoal or coke, but they require proper venting with chimneys and *Charlie Nobles* (small smokestacks), so they are normally not very suitable for small craft. Kerosene heaters have reached a high degree of perfection in combustion efficiency and lack of odor, but for the very smallest cruisers, I prefer the tiny alcohol burners because of their compactness, cleanliness, and safety. The so-called catalytic heaters, which are flameless, have many good points, but they use white gasoline or LP-gas. These fuels are said to be safe when properly used in a well-designed catalytic heater that is leakproof and spillproof, but great care must be exercised in stowing the fuel and filling the heaters. In fact, filling should only be done on deck. As said earlier, gasoline and LP-gas are potentially explosive, and their fumes are heavier than air and thus difficult to dispel from a closed compartment. Any kind of heater should be well secured and insulated and located where it cannot come into contact with flammable materials. Also, adequate ventilation should be provided below deck. Electric heaters are relatively safe and efficient, but away from dockside or when shore power is inadequate, a 115-volt AC generator will be needed.

Cooking stoves and other equipment for the galley were discussed in Chapter 3. Stores, galley supplies, and consumable goods will be discussed in the next chapter under the section "Stocking Up." Most mechanical equipment, extra tanks, and instruments have already been discussed (in Chapter 3, 4, or 5), but a luxury item that has not been mentioned yet is hot water. One successful system for providing hot water uses a small water tank containing coils of copper tubing through which hot water from the engine's cooling system is passed, thereby heating the water stored in the tank. This method requires running the engine, of course, but small, well-insulated tanks will keep the water warm for up to twenty-four hours.

The Dinghy

One of the most important pieces of equipment for any well-found cruiser is a proper dinghy, or "dink." It serves not only as a supply carrier and transportation tender but also a lifeboat for certain emergencies and a work boat for such jobs as cleaning the topsides or carrying out an anchor after running aground. Furthermore, the dinghy is valuable for recreational purposes—rowing, sailing, crabbing or fishing, towing children, landing on remote shores, and exploring the heads of creeks, marshes, or other areas where the water is too shoal for the mother vessel. These activities are not only fun and interesting, but they allow temporary separation of crew members to relieve overcrowded conditions aboard a small boat on a long cruise in secluded regions.

Choosing a dinghy requires the consideration of many factors, including price, size, weight, capacity, stability, flotation, construction, ease of rowing and towing, ease of maintenance, capability of being stowed on board the mother vessel, and suitability for sailing. Size probably will be the primary consideration, because this affects the price, weight, capacity, and other factors. Ideally, the dinghy should be light enough for two people to lift and sufficiently small to stow handily, and yet large enough to carry at least three people safely in choppy waters. As said earlier, the dinghy normally will stow upside down on chocks mounted on the cabin house top, but on vessels with very small deck houses or flush decks, the boat will stow in a similar way on the deck. It should be securely lashed down, customarily with criss-crossed straps running over the boat's bottom and secured with slip knots or *pelican hooks* (hinged hooks with slip rings) to facilitate quick release of the straps.

There should be a *capacity plate* fastened to the inside of the dinghy's transom stating clearly how many people and how much weight the boat can carry in calm weather and the maximum horsepower of an outboard motor that can be carried safely if the boat is designed for outboard power. In addition, the capacity plate should carry flotation information. There ought to be sufficient flotation in the bow,

Sailing dinghies are available in many models. This one is an inexpensive plywood double-ender with bamboo spars. On a cruise, the dinghy can provide access to shallow areas that the mother vessel cannot navigate.

under the midships *thwart* (the plank seat extending across the boat), and under the stern thwart to float the boat level when she is swamped and to support her passengers and equipment. The Coast Guard is currently standardizing regulations on capacity, safe powering, and flotation, and so most small boats will have to conform to these standards. Incidentally, although they are not presently required, hand grips on the boat's bottom, perhaps cut into the skeg, are a good safety feature to facilitate holding on in the event of a capsize. Coast Guard statistics consistently show that most boating fatalities come from the capsizing or sinking of small boats, so don't overload the dinghy, and remember that federal law now requires a personal flotation device for each person in almost every kind of craft, even a dinghy.

An essential feature of a small cruiser's dink is its capability of being towed without yawing from side to side. Most dinghies will tow well, but a few, usually those with deep, sharp bows and little if any skeg, will yaw, especially when the *painter* (tow line) is secured at the stem head. The painter should

be spliced to an eye strap that is bolted quite low on the stem in order that the bow can be lifted slightly when the boat is being towed in difficult seas. The distance between the mother vessel and the dinghy being towed will depend on the sea conditions and the speed of the vessel. Usually it will take some experimentation to find the proper distance that will minimize yawing and resistance. In some cases, yawing can be eliminated by letting the dinghy ride on the back of a transverse wave created by the vessel's passage through the water, but at other times, when yawing is no problem, towing resistance can be minimized by adjusting the tow line so that the boat rides on the face of a transverse wave. At any rate, there should be an ample length of painter in order that the dinghy can be towed far astern when desirable. It is not a bad idea to attach some cork floats to the painter, by the way, to prevent it from getting caught in the mother vessel's propeller.

Before heading into rough waters, especially when steep following seas are anticipated, the dink should be brought aboard. In calm weather, this is not a difficult operation. The dinghy is brought alongside, and two people standing at the rail of the mother vessel can lift the boat aboard by simultaneously pulling up on the painter and a stern line made fast to the stern thwart or a metal transom ring. When the dinghy is lifted up to the rail it can be tilted over, lifted over the life lines, and then carried to its deck chocks. If the dinghy is very heavy, it can be brought aboard by rigging a bridle consisting of lines running from its stern and bow meeting at a ring or loop above the boat's center. The end of the main halyard is attached to the ring, and the boat can be lifted with the halyard winch. Of course, large cruisers may have a pair of boat *davits* (small lifting cranes), most often located at the vessel's stern.

Most modern dinghies are made of fiberglass, which is a very practical material, for it is relatively light and leakproof and requires little maintenance. About the only source of leaks on a fiberglass boat is at areas where screws or other fastenings penetrate the hull shell below the load waterline. Sometimes a wood skeg is screwed to the bottom, and it may work loose and permit leaks around the screw holes. It is usually better if the skeg is bolted on, because bolts can be kept tight more easily. Better still is a skeg of molded fiberglass unless the boat will be repeatedly hauled up on a sandy beach, which will abrade the fiberglass and wear it through in time.

Some dinks are made of clear, transparent plastic. In clear waters these boats provide a means of viewing the seabed and watching aquatic life, and they also can be secured on deck over an open hatchway and still allow light to enter the cabin. One word of warning, however: Plastic boats are not as strong as those made of fiberglass. In fact, it is possible for the former to split open if severely stressed. Aluminum dinks are very light, but they are noisy and perhaps subject to some corrosion in extremely salty water. Inflatable rubber boats are handy and often quite seaworthy, but rubber lacks the longevity of fiberglass.

Every dinghy should be fitted with a permanent fender of either rope, canvas-covered soft rubber, or preferably vinyl which runs entirely around the gunwales in order that the topsides of the mother vessel will not be marred when the boat is brought alongside. Bolts for the painter's eye strap or ring should have very large washers or perhaps a backing block so that the bolts cannot be pulled through the

stem. There should be two positions for oarlocks: one amidships so that the boat will be properly trimmed when it is being rowed with a single person aboard, and the other position forward so that proper trim can be maintained when there are passengers seated aft.

As a lifeboat, the typical dinghy is somewhat limited. It may be adequate to take a small crew off the vessel in fair weather when she must be abandoned because of an uncontrollable fire or some other emergency, but in heavy weather offshore, the dink may be almost useless. Every vessel going to sea should be equipped with a proper inflatable rubber life raft having at least two separate air compartments and large enough to hold the entire crew whether or not a dinghy is carried on deck.

Sailing dinghies are quite a bit more expensive than nonsailing models, but in my opinion the extra cost for sail is worth it when cruising will be done in protected waters. Not only is dinghy sailing fun and great entertainment for children, but it provides a means of exploring lengthy creeks, of seeing what is around the next bend in a shallow river. Sailing dinghy rigs are usually compact affairs with spars that will stow on deck or on the cabin top, lashed to the hand rails. Quite often the spars are folding or collapsible to assure compactness and ease of stowing. One such type, related to the ancient *sliding gunter* rig, is illustrated in Figure 6-7. Notice that a short vertical spar attaches with hooks to an unstayed, stumpy mast, which is stepped through a hole in the forward thwart. Running rigging consists merely of a simple boom downhaul, an outhaul, and a one-part main sheet, which attaches to a traveler and is led through two blocks to a cleat.

Of course, the boat also needs a rudder and tiller and some means of preventing leeway. Most dinghies of this type have dagger boards that slide in and out of small wells similar to the one illustrated in Figure 6-7. The well should be raked in the direction shown and be provided with a cap to prevent water from splashing in when the boat is being towed.

Stowing the Gear

After all the gear and equipment described has been acquired, a logical stowage plan must be devised, and once devised, the basic plan should be adhered to in order to minimize searches for needed equipment. The old expression "a place for everything and everything in its place" was probably originated

FIGURE 6-7: SAILING
            DINGHY

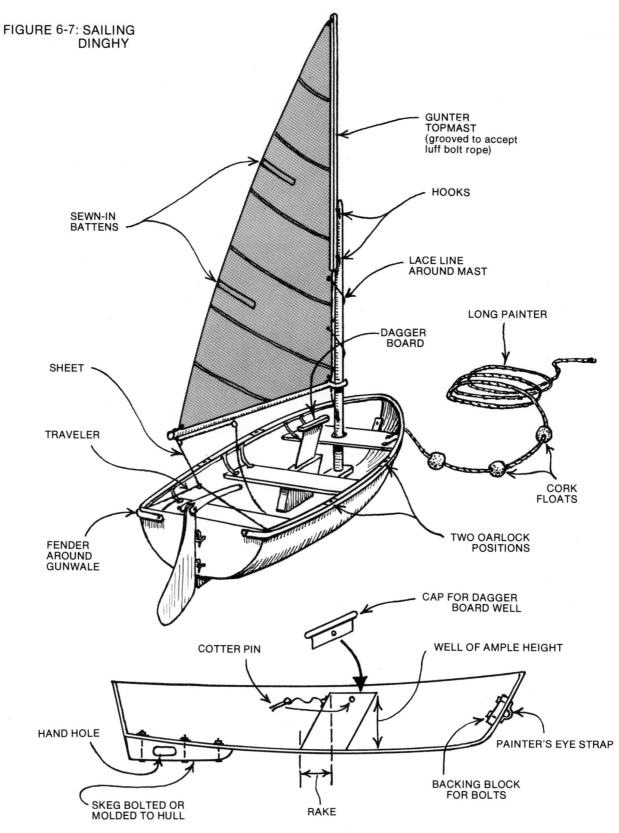

GUNTER
TOPMAST
(grooved to accept
luff bolt rope)

HOOKS

LACE LINE
AROUND MAST

LONG PAINTER

SEWN-IN
BATTENS

DAGGER
BOARD

SHEET

TRAVELER

CORK
FLOATS

FENDER
AROUND
GUNWALE

TWO OARLOCK
POSITIONS

CAP FOR DAGGER
BOARD WELL

COTTER PIN

WELL OF AMPLE HEIGHT

HAND HOLE

PAINTER'S EYE STRAP

SKEG BOLTED OR
MOLDED TO HULL

RAKE

BACKING BLOCK
FOR BOLTS

by a very wise boatman. As a matter of fact, it is not a bad idea to keep a ship's notebook, which lists—in addition to procedures for getting underway and securing and such information as tank capacities —the stowage locations of all important gear. With such a notebook any guest coming aboard or anyone who borrows or charters the boat can quickly learn where the equipment is kept without having to search for it.

Another means of designating stowage areas for particular equipment is with the use of a label gun. This instrument, which can be bought in most stationery stores or elsewhere, prints letters on durable plastic tapes, which can be stuck on almost any smooth surface. Such labels as "navigation gear," "snatch blocks," "sewing kit," "flares," and so forth assure, within reason, that the gear not only will be found, but that it will be returned to its proper place. At least, if the gear is not returned, there is no excuse, and the captain has a perfect right to break out his cat-o'-nine-tails. Be sure to stow the most needed items in the most accessible locations, and always keep safety gear where it can be reached in a hurry.

Although this chapter has covered most cruising equipment associated with the hull, a few important extras associated with the rig have not yet been covered. These items will be discussed in Chapter 9, which deals with cruising rigs and sailing short-handed.

7

Cruise Planning and Activities

After acquiring a new boat and equipping her, the proud owner undoubtedly will be anxious to start cruising. If he is a novice, however, he should use some restraint at first. He should not only know the basics of seamanship but be thoroughly familiar with his boat, know her handling characteristics, and see that she is properly fitted out or "well found" before the first cruise. Furthermore, the neophyte should familiarize himself as much as possible with the proposed cruising area. Even experienced sailors should be cautious about planning ambitious cruises in a brand new boat. It is wise to stay fairly close to home waters and familiar repair facilities until the boat is thoroughly shaken down and the inevitable "bugs" are worked out.

Preliminary Knowledge of the Cruising Area

The best single piece of advice to anyone contemplating a cruise in a particular area is to buy a cruising guide for that area. There are specific guides for almost all major cruising grounds in or near the United States (and in many other countries as well). Although the style and format of the guides vary tremendously, the information they cover is basically similar for every area—a brief history of the region; a list and brief description of marinas, yacht clubs, boat yards, sources of supplies, launching ramps, and other facilities; chart reproductions of specific anchorages; sometimes detailed sketches or photographs of harbors with advice on how to enter and moor; a description of local weather; major aids to navigation and ranges; radio information and sometimes tide tables; suggestions of things to do or see in the area; dangers (if any) or what to avoid; and so forth. Some cruising guides are spiral bound, contain advertisements, and are fairly cheaply produced, while others are quality hardback books that may be expensive. Whatever the form, however, the guide should be

sturdily constructed, should lie open with its pages flat, and should be reasonably waterproof. I have one vivid memory of an expensive cruising guide dripping dye from its cover and leaving stains all over the boat.

Some rather large, thin, privately printed volumes that are entitled cruising guides are actually *chart books*—collections of standardized charts covering the area, most often produced in one scale only and containing such information as printed courses and distances that are not found on government charts. Chart books can be very handy, but they are not the same, nor do they supply the same information, as true cruising guides. I also would recommend taking government charts of an appropriate scale as well as a chart book of the area being cruised (more will be said of charts in Chapter 8, which deals with navigation).

Obviously, cruising guides should be updated frequently, especially those containing changeable information. Guides containing tide tables, for instance, should be reprinted every year. When buying a guide, get the most current issue, and if there have been no recent revisions don't rely too heavily on advice that could be modified by physical change. For example, if the instructions for entering a certain harbor are to head northeast and line up the dead tree with the osprey's nest against a red house in the background, obviously the northeast course should be heeded, but don't be upset if there is no tree and the house is now white. In most U.S. cruising areas, frequently used harbors have buoys and channel markers to help people enter and leave, but secluded gunkholes may not be well marked. Cruising guides can be bought at most large boating chandleries or book stores or can be ordered from their publishers.

In addition to privately printed cruising guides, there are similar government publications that augment information shown on charts. These are the Coast Pilots published by the National Ocean Survey (formerly the U.S. Coast and Geodetic Survey). Coast Pilot books cover port facilities, information for navigating waterways and entering harbors, signal systems, aids to navigation, descriptions of U.S. coastlines, information on tides and currents, brief descriptions of anchorages, and so forth. As compared with most cruising guides, Coast Pilots are more formal and lack the history, anecdotes, suggested activities, and pen-and-ink sketches of harbor ranges found in some guides, but most Pilots are more scientific or technical, and, of course, are directly related to National Ocean Survey charts. Sailing Directions, published by the U.S. Naval Oceanographic Office (formerly known as the Hydrographic Office) are books (presently in seventy volumes but now being condensed into forty-three volumes) that cover foreign ports and coastlines. The newest Sailing Directions contain a wealth of condensed navigational information and even include some panoramic photographs with detailed drawings of prominent features. For extended cruises involving long passages, it is advisable to carry the Coast Pilot covering your cruising area (for cruises in U.S. waters, including those in Alaska, Hawaii, Puerto Rico, and the Virgin Islands), and Sailing Directions for foreign cruises. These books can be bought at or ordered through many navigational supply stores or they can be ordered directly from the publishers: The National Ocean Survey, National Oceanic and Atmospheric Administration, Rockville, Maryland 20852, or the U.S. Naval Oceanographic Office, Washington, D.C. 20390. Chart and publication catalogs are also available.

Tide and Current

Unless your cruising guide contains up-to-date tide and current tables (to do so, the guide would have to be reprinted in the same year as your cruise), it is a good idea to carry the government publications *Tidal Current Tables* and *Tide Tables*, produced by the National Ocean Survey. In many popular American cruising areas, tides and currents are not extreme, but knowledge of them is important. The tide, which is the vertical rise and fall of the water's surface (due primarily to the gravitational pull of the moon and, to a lesser degree, that of the sun), must be considered when navigating in shallow water and selecting an anchorage that will accommodate the boat's draft at low water. The current, which is the horizontal movement of the water, obviously affects the boat's headway and her lateral drift (depending on its strength and direction relative to the boat's heading).

Tide tables give the times and heights of high and low waters at specific important locations (primary reference stations). Tide heights are given in feet added to the depths of water shown on the chart (or subtracted, if the number is preceded by a minus sign). Secondary tables in the tide table books give tidal corrections for numerous subordinate locations near the primary reference stations. Foolproof instructions for figuring times and heights of the tide are given along with the tables. Remember, however, that weather conditions (the strength and direction of the wind and barometric pressure) can greatly affect the accuracy of the tables. Wind tends to pile water up along a shore against which the wind is blowing and lower the water's height along a shore away from which the wind is blowing; while very low pressure may cause a definite rise in the tide above its normal state shown in the tables (or vice versa for very high barometric pressure).

The tables also show tidal *ranges* (the difference between low water and high water heights). The difference in height between *mean high water* (the average of all high waters) and *mean low water* (the average of all low waters) is the *mean range*. The difference in height between *mean low water springs* (the average level of low waters during spring tides) and *mean high water springs* (the average level of high waters during spring tides) is the *spring range*. During spring tides, which occur when the earth, sun, and moon are in line (when the moon is new or full), tides are more extreme, with very high and low waters. The opposite of the springs are *neap tides*, occurring when the earth, sun, and moon are at right angles to each other (near the first and third quarters of the moon), which produce very moderate tidal ranges. A common misconception, especially among novice boatmen, is that the word *spring* (in *spring tides*) refers to the season, and that therefore those extreme tides occur only at that time of year. In truth, of course, spring (and neap) tides occur twice each month. The greatest tidal ranges occur when the new or full moon is in *perigee* (at the point on its orbit that is closest to the earth), while the smallest ranges occur when the quarter moon is in *apogee* (at the point on its orbit that is farthest from the earth).

In the majority of American cruising waters, there are two high waters and two low waters every lunar day (twenty-four hours and fifty minutes); thus the tide changes about every six hours and twelve minutes. It is often possible to estimate the state of the tide without consulting tables merely by remembering its height about twenty-five hours earlier, but it is seldom possible to estimate the tide even roughly by remembering its height twelve and a half hours earlier because of the inequality

FIGURE 7-1: TIDE

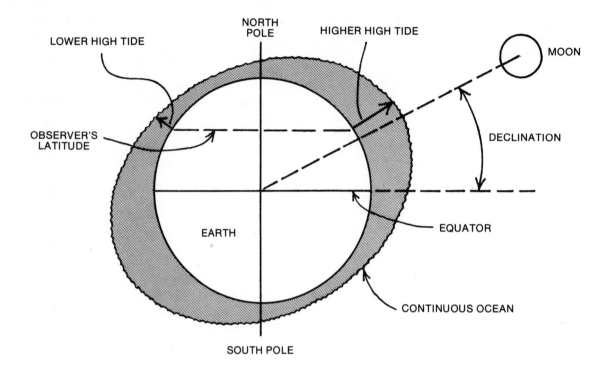

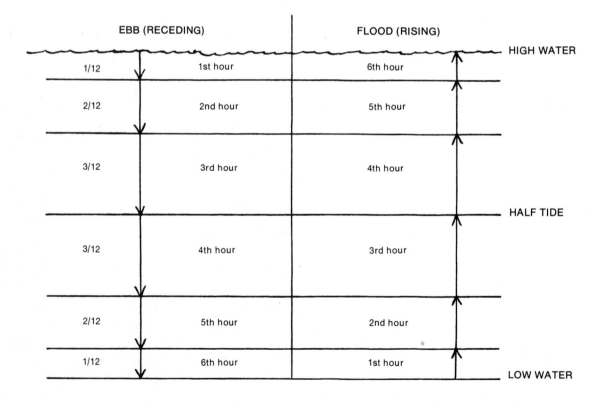

between high and low tides due to the moon's *declination* (its angular distance north or south of an extension of the equator as shown in Figure 7-1). Since the "humps" of water on both sides of the earth (caused by the moon's attraction) are directly under the moon, they become asymmetrical with respect to any parallel of latitude (except on the equator), and because the humps remain under the moon as the earth turns, there will be lower and higher low and high tides. This is explained in Figure 7-1.

Not only are there *semidiurnal* tides (those with high and low waters occurring twice a day), but there also are *diurnal tides* (those with high and low waters occurring only once a day). The former tides are found on the U.S. east coast and the west coast of Florida, while diurnal tides occur on the American Gulf coast, although their range is very slight. Tides on the Pacific coast usually have considerable inequality, and they are *mixed tides*—that is to say, they are partly diurnal and partly semidiurnal. The most extreme tides in the United States (excluding Alaska) occur along the northern sea coasts, especially in eastern Maine. These tides have a range of eighteen feet or more in some localities. Farther south the tides are much less extreme, but they are still considerable, ranging up to seven feet or more in such areas as the western end of Long Island Sound, the Savannah River, and Los Angeles during spring tides.

A very simple rule of thumb for determining the height of a semidiurnal tide at any given hour when the time of high or low water is known is the so-called *twelfths rule*, shown in Figure 7-1. The tide moves up or down one-twelfth of its range during the first or sixth hour of low or high water, two-twelfths during the second or fifth hour, and three-twelfths during the third or fourth hour. Of course, it should go without saying that water height should be observed whenever possible by looking at high water marks, such as discolored rocks, exposed barnacles, seaweed, lines of jetsam, and so on along the shore, in order to help judge the state of the tide and verify the accuracy of the table.

Although one might think that areas having considerable tides would also have strong currents, this is not necessarily so. In fact, the opposite may be true, for in some areas such as the Gulf of Maine, tides are large, but currents are weak; while in other areas, such as the Race off Long Island Sound or in Nantucket Sound, the tides are small but currents can be quite strong. In order to judge the strength of the current accurately, it is important not only to consult the tables but also to observe continually the effect of the current's flow on buoys, lobster pots, and stationary objects in the water. Unusual wind and weather conditions can have a great effect on the accuracy of current as well as tide tables.

Tidal current charts present the current graphically and show the direction and the velocity of flow in many cruising areas. These charts are usually correlated with the tide or current tables so that one can determine the strength and direction of the current each hour after high or low water or after maximum current or *slack water* (no current).

National Ocean Survey *Tidal Current Tables* use a similar system to the *Tide Tables*. Times of slack water and times and velocities of maximum currents are given for each day in primary tables (Table I) at principal reference stations, and secondary tables (Table II) give corrections in hours and minutes (to be added to or subtracted from the times given in Table I) for numerous subordinate locations near the main reference stations. Times and velocities of maximum currents (in Table I) are given when the current is *flooding* (flowing into an inlet) and *ebbing* (flowing out). Times given in tables are standard, and so an hour must be added for daylight-saving time.

When observing the current against a buoy or another object, it is safest to go close enough to the object to get a good look at its wake. Current can be "read" from a distance by observing the direction in which a buoy leans; however, this practice can cause confusion, since some buoys, usually those anchored with a bridle, may lean the "wrong way." In other words, the buoy will occasionally lean toward the direction from which the current is flowing instead of away, as one would normally expect. More will be said about current in Chapter 8, which deals with navigation, but the novice boatman should be warned here that if he is going into an area of strong currents, he should be sure his boat has sufficient power and a large enough propeller to drive the boat against a strong flow. In most U.S. cruising areas the current is not extremely fast, but in some rivers or in narrow straits the flow can be very strong indeed. For example, in the Race at the entrance to Long Island Sound, in the Cape Cod Canal, and at the entrance to San Francisco Bay the current can reach a velocity of about four knots. In certain parts of the Pacific Northwest the current can be considerably stronger, up to eight knots in some constricted waters. Of course, unusually strong tidal currents can be (and usually should be) avoided by passing through the area during slack water or at times when the current is favorable.

Regional Weather

One of the most important factors in the success of a cruise is the weather. Every effort should be made to learn about the general weather pattern of the cruising area from Coast Pilots, cruising guides, and other sources and to study weather maps and listen to reports immediately before casting off. If there is even a possibility of bad weather, the cruise should be planned so that protected harbors are readily available, and, whenever possible, courses should be oriented in such a way that expected heavy winds are favorable (not "dead on the nose" against you). Then, too, it is always advisable to allow sufficient cruising time for one or two layover days for "holing up" in a snug anchorage in the event of a hard blow. A pressing appointment or some other urgency that necessitates a return home in foul weather could be hazardous or, at the very least, disheartening to many cruising wives, children, or inexperienced guests.

Special caution is required when making coastal passages, because there are few situations with more potential danger than being caught in exposed waters on a lee shore in heavy weather. Make certain of the following: (1) that the boat is seaworthy (Chapters 1 and 2), (2) that she is properly fitted out and equipped for heavy weather (Chapters 2 and 6), (3) that weather reports are carefully checked just prior to getting underway and periodically during the passage, (4) that there are accessible inlets to duck into in the event of unexpected bad weather (otherwise you must be prepared to go far offshore for ample sea room), (5) that the boat has suitable heavy weather sails and can make good progress to windward under these sails in a hard blow, and (6) that you have ample crew and that they are able and not prone to violent seasickness.

Of course, it is important to select a good time of year for cruising. Generally speaking, midsummer is the most suitable time in northern parts of the country, but in the middle and southern parts of the east coast the weather can be unsuitably hot, humid, and calm in July and early August. On parts of the west coast, the hottest weather may come a little later, because the prevailing winds there are onshore,

blowing over water that may be considerably cooler than the land. This is particularly evident in northern California, where the hottest weather often doesn't come until September due to the northwesterly winds displacing the surface water which causes the upwelling of cold subsurface water, thereby keeping sea temperatures in that region low until late in the summer. This same condition is very conducive to fog when warm, moist maritime air passes over the cold ocean near the coast.

Many southern cruising grounds—Florida, the Gulf of California, and the West Indies—are popular in the winter, but some of these places should be considered for summer cruising as well. In fact, southern waters are sometimes subject to very strong winds in the winter when cold, high-pressure continental air masses drop down into the United States from Canada. These cause the unpleasant and sometimes dangerous northers that periodically hit Florida and the Bahamas on the east coast and can even cause fierce winds on the west coast of Mexico, especially where they are funneled through mountains into the Gulf of Tehuantepec. On the other hand, summer cruising in many southern areas can be done in milder weather when charter rates and other costs are considerably less and when waters are often less crowded. The weather may be hot and humid at times, but usually not unbearably so.

In late summer and early fall, the cruising yachtsman must be ever alert for hurricane warnings, especially on the east, Gulf, and southwest coasts of this country. Figure 7-2 shows the breeding grounds of hurricanes and some typical tracks of these intense tropical storms. Notice that they are born in hot, humid regions over the oceans, where they begin as counterclockwise-turning depressions (low pressure areas). From their points of origin, hurricanes in the northern hemisphere tend to move in a westerly to northwesterly direction, and then many of them curve northward until they reach the latitudes of prevailing westerly winds (between 30 and 60 degrees latitude), at which time they curve toward the northeast. Hurricanes born off the west coast of Mexico occasionally curve into southern California, and those born in the mid-Atlantic or the Caribbean may curve into the Gulf coast or strike the east coast of the United States. Although the tracks shown in Figure 7-2 are typical, many tropical storms are highly erratic and wander around a great deal; thus, sailors should follow weather reports closely and plan cruises so that protected

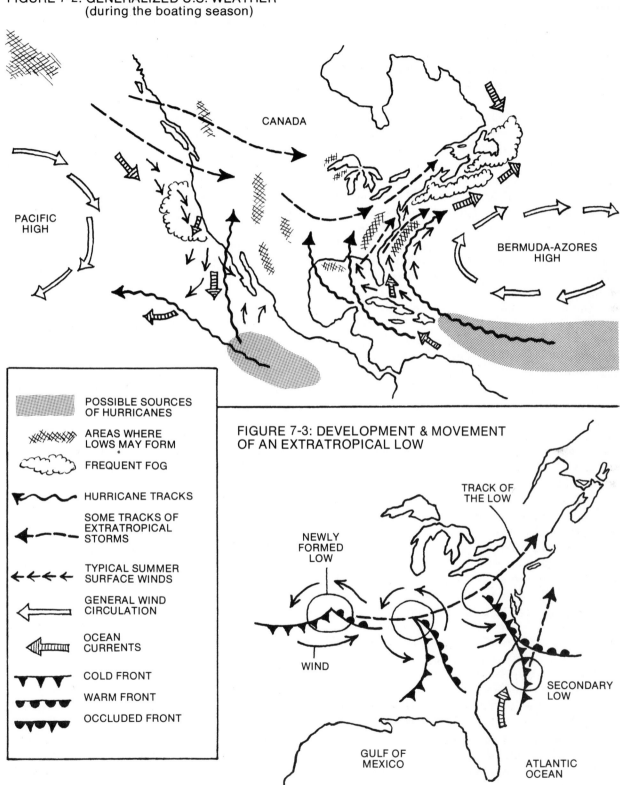

FIGURE 7-2: GENERALIZED U.S. WEATHER
(during the boating season)

CANADA

PACIFIC
HIGH

BERMUDA-AZORES
HIGH

POSSIBLE SOURCES
OF HURRICANES

AREAS WHERE
LOWS MAY FORM

FREQUENT FOG

HURRICANE TRACKS

SOME TRACKS OF
EXTRATROPICAL
STORMS

TYPICAL SUMMER
SURFACE WINDS

GENERAL WIND
CIRCULATION

OCEAN
CURRENTS

COLD FRONT

WARM FRONT

OCCLUDED FRONT

**FIGURE 7-3: DEVELOPMENT & MOVEMENT
OF AN EXTRATROPICAL LOW**

TRACK OF
THE LOW

NEWLY
FORMED
LOW

WIND

SECONDARY
LOW

GULF OF
MEXICO

ATLANTIC
OCEAN

harbors are never far away during the hurricane season.

Figure 7-2 also shows typical tracks of extratropical storms that travel from west to east across the United States. These storms, which are far more frequent and intense in the colder seasons than in the summer, often result from friction of opposing winds at the border between cold and warm air masses. A V-shaped wave is formed at some point along the border or "front," with an area of low pressure at the wave's crest, a cold front (the edge of an advancing cold air mass) to the left of the crest, and a warm front (the edge of an advancing warm air mass) to the right of the crest. As the winds swirl around the low in a counterclockwise direction, the cold front swings southeastward, pivoting on its end at the crest, and gradually overtakes the slower-moving warm front. The two fronts eventually meet and occlude below the crest, while the whole system moves across the country in an easterly or northeasterly direction. This sequence is illustrated in Figure 7-3.

Many extratropical lows that affect the United States originate in the north Pacific and, after striking the west coast, often travel entirely across the country. Some types of lows, however, form over the land, usually near mountains or hot desert regions. Quite often extratropical lows will traverse the northern part of the United States in summer, but regions farther south may well be affected by the fronts—especially the cold front, which is pushed to the south of the depression. Sometimes a secondary depression will form along the trailing cold front of an extratropical low. A region noted for the development of secondary lows is the area off Cape Hatteras, North Carolina, when a cold front strikes the warm, moist air carried north by the Gulf Stream. The secondary depression will usually move northeastward along the Atlantic coast. The tracks of extratropical storms can be quite erratic, but usually they run in curves from the northwest United States, dipping southward, and then swinging northeastward across the eastern part of the country. Occasionally lows that form over the Pacific may swing southward early and strike the west coast as far south as southern California. Vessels in the path of an extratropical low will very often be forewarned by a falling barometer and the thickening of high altitude clouds (cirrus, cirrostratus, or cirrocumulus) and then the filling in of middle altitude clouds (altostratus or perhaps altocumulus followed by darker, globular stratocumulus when the air is vertically unstable).

See Figure 7-4 for cloud types. The warm front usually will approach from the southwest, and its appearance will bring nimbostratus clouds with rain and sometimes thunderstorms in unstable air. After passage of the warm front, the wind will veer and a brief period of fair weather will follow before altocumulus clouds appear and then cumulonimbus (thunderheads), presaging the cold front approaching from a more northwesterly direction. This front will generally bring the more severe weather with stronger winds, but it should pass by quite rapidly, and fair weather with a fresh wind from the northwest will follow in most instances.

Figure 7-2 also shows the simplified pattern of summer surface winds on the coasts of the United States. Of course, most of this country lies in the zone of prevailing westerlies, and the upper winds usually come from the west or southwest and steer the general weather pattern in an easterly direction, but summer surface winds are very often controlled by large areas of high pressure in the Pacific and Atlantic Oceans. The west coast is affected by the clockwise rotation of winds around the Pacific high and the flow of air from this high to a frequent low pressure area over the southwestern part of the country and the Gulf of California; thus in midsummer the west coast winds are usually from northwesterly directions. The east coast is affected by the clockwise rotation of winds around the Bermuda-Azores high, which causes frequent southerlies, often with an easterly component along the southern part of the east coast and the Gulf coast but with a westerly component along the northern part of the eastern seaboard. These winds bring warm, moist air ashore and create conditions that are conducive to isolated, air mass thunderstorms, especially when the land is very hot. These storms can be quite violent, but usually they don't last long, and the sailor is forewarned by towering cumulus clouds (most often to the west of him) that may develop into thunderheads. The west coast has comparatively few thunderstorms.

Fog

In some parts of this country fog can be a persistent problem. Although there are many types of fog, the cruising sailor is probably most often seriously affected by *advection* fog, which forms when warm, moist air is cooled as it passes over colder water (or land). The most troublesome regions during the summer months are along the northeastern

FIGURE 7-4: CLOUDS

CIRROCUMULUS "mackerel sky"
(over 20,000 ft.) can predict approach
of warm front in unstable air

ALTOSTRATUS (about 19,000 ft.) gray sheet
often warns of approaching warm front

CUMULONIMBUS "thunderhead" (thunderstorm
cloud)—can reach height of cirrus

CIRRUS "mares' tails" (over 25,000 ft.)
if thick often advanced forerunners
(24 hours or more) ahead of a front

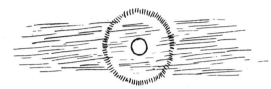

CIRROSTRATUS (over 20,000 ft.) whitish sheet
often causing halo around sun—can warn of
approaching warm front

ALTOCUMULUS (over 12,000 ft.) like sheep—
can warn of cold front in unstable air

STRATOCUMULUS (about 8,000 ft.) dark globular rolls

CUMULUS (over 4,000 ft.) fair
weather unless extreme towering up

NIMBOSTRATUS
(about 3,000 ft.)
dark rain cloud

STRATUS (about 1,500 ft.) gray sheet

seaboard, especially in Maine and points east when southerly winds blowing over the Gulf Stream meet cold water carried south by the Labrador Current, and also along the northern coast of California when warm maritime air moving eastward blows over the upwelling cold coastal water. The Gulf coast is subject to this type of fog in the winter when cold river water meets warmer moist air over the Gulf of Mexico, and the Great Lakes also have their share of fog, especially in the early summer when the water is still extremely cold, and warm, moisture-laden air moves up from the Mississippi River Valley.

Fog is formed when water vapor in the air condenses into suspended droplets. This can be brought about by increasing the air's moisture content to saturation or by lowering the air's temperature to its *dew point* (the temperature at which condensation takes place). When there is a considerable and continuing *spread* (difference) between the air temperature and the dew point, fog is not very likely, but when the spread decreases to little or no difference, fog is very probable. Many of the better weather broadcasts give the dew point, and so if the boatman carries a thermometer he may have some forewarning of fog. The *sling psychrometer* is a handy instrument for determining the relative humidity and dew point, but it requires the use of special tables. The instrument consists of a pair of thermometers mounted side by side and loosely attached to a handle so that they can be whirled around in the air. One of the thermometers merely gives the air temperature, but the other, which has its bulb covered with wet muslin, gives a lower temperature reading, depending on the amount of moisture in the air, when the bulb is cooled by evaporation as the psychrometer is whirled. Considerable difference between the two thermometer readings would indicate low humidity and dew point and thus little chance of fog unless the spread decreases through a drop in temperature and/or an increase in humidity.

Another type of fog that can annoy the boatman is radiation fog, but this kind forms at night over land, and it seldom drifts far out over the water. This fog results from the land cooling off in the evening and thus cooling humid air just above the ground until its dew point is reached. A few hours after sunrise, radiation fog will usually "burn off" or actually be lifted by the sun heating the ground. A fresh breeze will also dispel this fog or prevent its formation.

Fog tactics will depend to a large extent on what kind of fog the boatman encounters. In radiation fog, for instance, it may be best to head offshore to obtain better visibility, but in advection sea fog, it may pay to cautiously navigate coastal inland waterways where the water is warmer and will be less apt to cool the humid air to its dew point. In some cases it may pay to hug a lee shore when the onshore breeze and warm land cause the fog to lift over a low bank, but in other cases, quite often when there is a spread of only one or two degrees between the air temperature and the dew point, the lifting of the air over a high cliff will lower its temperature to the dew point and form fog. Be watchful for fog during warm, humid weather when onshore winds with southerly components blow across cold waters. To keep informed of fog possibilities and other weather conditions, the cruising boatman should study weather maps whenever he can and listen to weather broadcasts. Along the U.S. coasts a great many stations transmit continuous weather bureau forecasts over VHF-FM, 162.55, 162.40, or 163.275 MHz. Fog piloting will be discussed in Chapter 8.

Distant Cruising Areas

As mentioned earlier, the boat owner can transport his boat to areas away from his home waters in a variety of ways. He can sail his boat there, but this often takes more time than he can spare. Sometimes he can find friends who will take his boat part way, but such arrangements may be difficult to make, and the boat owner must be sure his friends are thoroughly capable seamen. There are reliable boat delivery services, but they are not cheap, nor is transportation by ship or truck. Probably the simplest and least expensive means of transportation is with a boat trailer towed behind the family car, but obviously this requires a small trailerable cruiser, one having shallow draft, beam less than eight feet, and normally a length under about twenty-six feet overall.

For cruising in remote areas, it is often better to forget about using one's own boat. I understand there is at least one boat swapping service, Yacht Swap, 18 Pond Street, Boston, Massachusetts, through which boat exchanges can be made. However, many owners might be reluctant to let strangers use their yachts, and I should think that swapping arrangements could be difficult to work out. Very probably the simplest and most reliable means of acquiring a cruiser away from home waters is by chartering through a reputable agency. Dependable boats usually can be acquired through the better-known yacht brokers, who will charter to you directly or refer you to a reputable company that specializes in yacht charters. Such companies generally offer *crewed boats* (with a professional captain and crew) or individual *bareboats* (without crew), and some of the larger chartering operations, such as Caribbean Sailing Yachts, Ltd., have fleets of identical, well-equipped bareboats continually available. These fleets usually include boats in two general size categories: those around thirty to thirty-five feet LOA, which will accommodate four people; and those in the neighborhood of forty feet LOA, having three cabins and usually a center cockpit, which will accommodate six people. In most cases, these bareboats are completely stocked, and they are not unreasonably expensive when the costs are shared by two or three couples. Obviously, the skipper must have had prior sailing and cruising experience before chartering a bareboat, and it is helpful if he can get a boat that is similar in size and type to his own or to one that he is used to handling.

If you are chartering for the first time, be sure you have a complete understanding with the chartering company as to rates, down payment, insurance, and so on. Find out what equipment and supplies will be provided by the company; learn what stores, clothing, bedding, and utensils you are expected to bring; and inquire about restrictions (if any) regarding your qualifications as a skipper, the distance you can take the boat, and whether pets or children can be taken. Most of the better charter operations provide nearly all the equipment that will be needed, complete charts and a cruising guide of the area, and a good instruction or operation manual for each bareboat. A few small companies that charter stock boats, however, unless owned by private individuals, provide very minimal equipment. In fact, I once chartered from such a company a stock cruiser that had almost no spares of anything. There was only one anchor, one anchor line, one battery, one can of freon for the horn, one flashlight, no spare winch handles, one jib, and so on. It certainly is safest to carry a reasonable number of spares,

Many inland waterways provide picturesque and protected routes to distant cruising grounds. They sometimes have strong currents, however, and in certain marshy areas mosquitos abound.

especially when cruising in unfamiliar waters, because sails can blow out, batteries can run down, freon cans might leak, and the boat might drag her anchor. And be sure the compass is accurately adjusted; ours was off 14 degrees on one heading.

If you own a small trailerable cruiser, you may want to take your own boat overland to a distant cruising ground. Although this is a relatively simple means of transporting a boat, a number of safety requirements and precautions are necessary. First of all, of course, you must learn the legal regulations for trailers from the Department of Motor Vehicles of the state in which the trailer will be used. Such regulations include controls and requirements relating to speeds, licenses, brakes, size of the boat, lights,

and so forth. Boat trailer construction and safety features should conform to standards set forth by the Society of Automotive Engineers and those of the American Boat and Yacht Council (published in the ABYC book, *Safety Standards for Small Craft*). Generally speaking, the automobile that does the towing will need a sturdy hitch that is bolted to the car's frame, not merely attached to the bumper. Ball hitches must be of adequate diameter for the load to be pulled (details are in the ABYC book), and there should be two safety chains secured to the frame of the car. Of course, many specific details about trailing your particular boat can be obtained from the manufacturer of your boat or the dealer from whom you buy the trailer.

The "Cal 21" is a fast, retractable-keel cruiser, shown on her trailer, *above,* and under sail, *below.* Note how low she sits on the trailer for easy towing, boarding, and launching. Also note the method of securing the mast.

FIGURE 7-5: RAISING AND LOWERING A SMALL CRUISER'S MAST

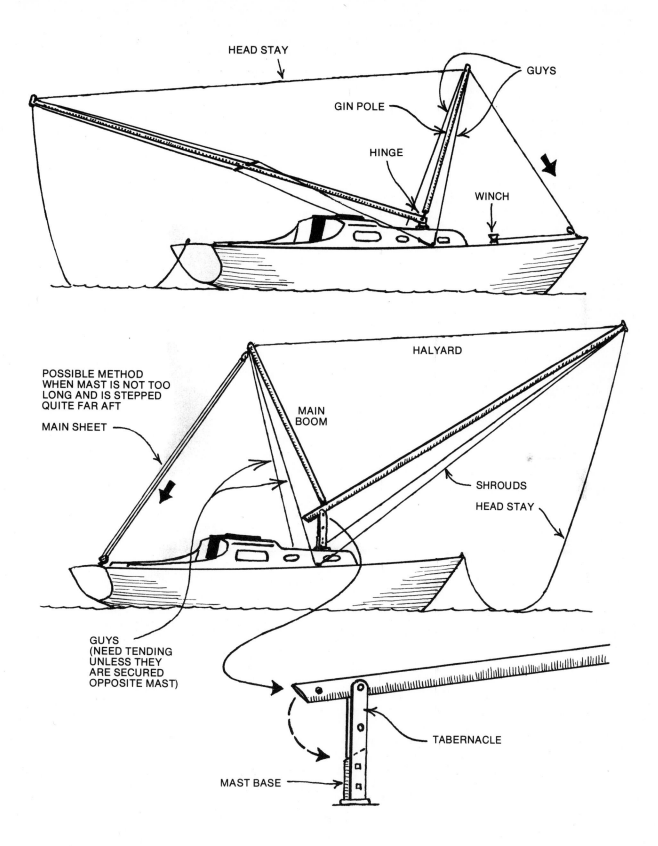

HEAD STAY

GUYS

GIN POLE

HINGE

WINCH

HALYARD

POSSIBLE METHOD
WHEN MAST IS NOT TOO
LONG AND IS STEPPED
QUITE FAR AFT

MAIN SHEET

MAIN
BOOM

SHROUDS

HEAD STAY

GUYS
(NEED TENDING
UNLESS THEY
ARE SECURED
OPPOSITE MAST)

TABERNACLE

MAST BASE

The boat being towed must be firmly seated on the trailer and securely tied down and the mast and rigging well secured. Heavy gear in the boat should be kept out of her stern while she is being towed, and hard gear should be padded so that its movement during sudden stops or on bumpy roads will not result in damage. Needless to say, you should exercise extra driving caution. Your speed should be moderate, and the distance you keep behind the car ahead must be ample.

When you reach the cruising ground, the boat should be taken to a suitable launching site that has a ramp or at least a gentle slope to the water with firm ground and a surface affording good traction. Cruising guides will usually give the locations of ramps. Since the trailer will be backed into the water so that the boat can be floated off, it is often necessary to submerge or wet the wheel bearings. Be sure they are allowed to cool before submersion and that they are kept well greased. Raising the mast of a small trailerable cruiser is usually not a great problem, because simple systems for the operation have been worked out. On most boats, the mast is hinged at the step on the cabin top or has a *tabernacle* (a short pedestal with a pin that supports the mast heel) in order that the mast can be folded up or down. Its raising or lowering is generally accomplished with a *gin pole* (a leverage pole) as illustrated in Figure 7-5. Some systems have a special winch operable from the mast step to simplify the procedure. On some small boats the mast can be raised or lowered forward so that the main boom can be used as the gin pole (see Figure 7-5).

Miscellaneous Activities on a Cruise

There is really very little excuse for anyone to become bored on a boat, especially a sailboat, but occasionally a lengthy cruise will prove somewhat monotonous or tedious to a child or a greenhorn guest. In such a case the skipper is usually to blame, either through his treatment of the crew or through lack of imagination in cruise planning.

The key to successful crew treatment is allowing everyone aboard, young or old, experienced or neophyte, the opportunity to participate. Of course, some guests who are new to cruising may be perfectly content to relax and "let George do it," and in this case, I don't think the skipper should insist on too much participation. At least he should try to keep a happy ship and avoid emulating Captain Bligh. Most crew, however, whether they initially realize it or not, will enjoy taking an active part in running the boat. Young people will usually find elementary piloting to be entertaining and will appreciate being given a certain amount of responsibility, and almost any guest or child will get a kick out of handling sails and taking an occasional short trick at the helm. In fact, most people will enjoy learning new and useful skills, provided the instruction is given in moderate doses, and, of course, the skipper will have fun teaching.

As for imagination in cruise planning, a key factor on a long cruise is variety. There should be ample opportunities to sail, swim, use the dinghy, relax in quiet anchorages, and perhaps fish, bird watch, or otherwise enjoy nature; but plans also should afford opportunities to go ashore in order to shop, sightsee, bathe, or merely stretch one's legs. The cook and most guests will enjoy an occasional meal in a good shoreside restaurant. Include in the cruising itinerary a variety of ports of call. Aside from quiet gunkholes, take in an occasional regatta, group rendezvous, or sightseeing area.

SIGHTS TO SEE. More than a few areas of historic interest, especially colonial buildings on the east coast, are located on or near navigable waterways. Some of the most interesting spots are marine museums, some of which have their own boat slips or moorings for guests. The most famous example of this kind of operation is the Mystic Seaport Museum in Mystic, Connecticut. This is a truly fascinating exhibit, but it is so popular during the summer that reservations for slips should be obtained well in advance of a visit. Mystic has inspired similar but perhaps less ambitious marine displays in many sections of the country. On the Chesapeake Bay at St. Michaels, Maryland, there is an excellent museum with a protected anchorage and mooring facilities. Of course, many picturesque ports may be visited by boat, allowing guests to take photographs, sketch, or paint. Be sure to consult your cruising guide for worthwhile sights to see in your cruising area.

REGATTAS AND RENDEZVOUS. Attending regattas and group rendezvous also can be great fun. These are social gatherings, and they usually involve *rafting*, lashing a number of boats together side by side. A group rendezvous is an informal get-together of friends or members of a particular yacht club. Sometimes several or many boats cruise in company

Above, among the interesting places to stop on a cruise is the Mystic Seaport, viewed here from New York Yacht Club Station 10 at the maritime museum. Visiting yachts are in the foreground. In the background are masts of the whaleship *Charles W. Morgan* at left and the mariner training ship *Joseph Conrad* at center. *Below*, many fishing ports along the way are picturesque subjects for sketching, watercolor painting, or photography.

on yacht club or group cruises, or boats cruise separately but meet at prearranged ports or anchorages. When cruising unfamiliar waters, traveling in company often provides security and mutual helpfulness.

Regattas are more formal, organized gatherings that feature boat races and usually a social function at a club house on shore. Large regattas include a variety of interesting and colorful sights. Races might include those for one-design sailboats, large cruising boats, motorboats, and/or character craft such as schooners, log canoes, or workboats. Despite Damon Runyon's celebrated remark that watching a sailboat race is like watching the grass grow, racing boats in action can be a beautiful and thrilling sight when the spectator understands the sport and stations himself in the right location. The most interesting spots from which to view a race are usually at the starting line and at turning marks. From those locations the spectator can station himself close enough to the action to get a good view without interfering with the racers, and he has the opportunity to observe tactics, boat maneuvering, and sail handling. Be sure, however, that you are far enough away from the racers that you do not disturb their wind.

Since rendezvous and regattas nearly always involve rafting, a few words should be said about this procedure of lashing boats together. In most cases only one boat in the raft is anchored (usually the first one to arrive or the one on which the subsequent party will be given). Obviously, her ground tackle must be of sufficient size, weight, and scope to hold all the boats made fast to her even if the wind happens to pipe up. The anchored vessel should receive others on each side of her. It is a good idea to use all the fenders available, of course, and each craft should be lashed to her neighbor with a pair of spring lines as well as a bow and stern line for each neighbor (see Figure 7-6). An important point to remember when going alongside another boat to raft is to look aloft and see that your spreaders are kept well clear of those on the other craft. Remember that when the boats roll from the wash of a passing motorboat, masts may tend to converge as a result of one boat being on the face of a wave while her neighbor is on the wave's back (see Figure 7-7).

This raft-up on a river in the Chesapeake Bay is remarkable in that all these Cruising Club of America boats are lashed together while underway. Motivation power is being supplied primarily by the single spinnaker.

Cruise Planning and Activities 101

FIGURE 7-6: LEAVING A RAFT

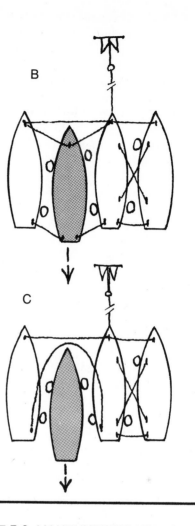

A

SPRING LINES

ANCHOR

FENDER

B

C

FIGURE 7-7: RAFTING PROBLEMS

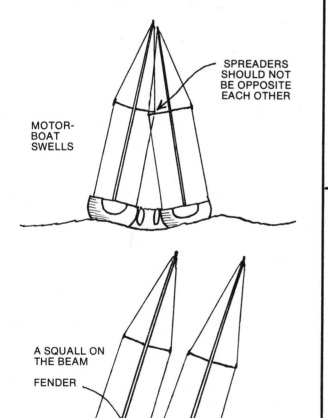

SPREADERS SHOULD NOT BE OPPOSITE EACH OTHER

MOTOR-BOAT SWELLS

A SQUALL ON THE BEAM

FENDER

FIGURE 7-8: MANEUVERING WHILE LASHED SIDE-BY-SIDE

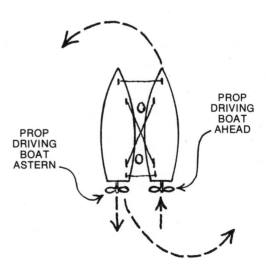

PROP DRIVING BOAT ASTERN

PROP DRIVING BOAT AHEAD

Quite often boats remain rafted all through the night, but this is really not very safe. There is always the possibility of a storm or sudden wind squall arriving while everyone is asleep. Even if the single anchor is able to hold all the boats, there may be an abrupt shift of wind when the squall strikes, and the boats will be struck broadside. This means they may heel considerably, and the lee rail of each boat might underride the fender of her neighbor to leeward. A windward boat will be lowering her lee rail at the same time the adjacent rail on the leeward boat will be rising; thus an underride is quite possible. This is shown in Figure 7-7.

An almost inevitable problem with rafting is that one or two of the inside boats will want to be among the first to depart. It is difficult to extricate an inside boat without breaking up the entire raft, and the operation usually results in confusion, countercommands, and lack of coordination in general. Figure 7-6 shows a standard departure procedure that minimizes the problem when the boats are *wind-rode* (lying to the wind rather than to the current). Notice that the springs on both sides of the boat to be extricated are removed, and then as she drifts astern slightly, a line is passed from the bow of one of her neighbors to the other neighbor's bow. Without this line, the bows of the two neighbors would be blown apart by the wind very quickly. Next, a stern line from one neighbor to the other is passed around the bow of the boat that is leaving, and finally, the original bow and stern lines on the boat being moved are cast off so that she can be backed out of her berth in the raft. Of course, crew should be stationed along the rails of all boats involved to fend off, and the boat leaving should have her rudder amidships until her bow is well clear of the raft before she is turned.

Incidentally, a handy means of maneuvering two boats in a very constricted area is to lash them together side by side in order that they can be handled like one twin-screw vessel. Turns can be made within a very small circle when one boat reverses her engine while the other goes ahead. Obviously, the latter would turn in the direction toward her neighbor whose engine is in reverse (see Figure 7-8).

VARIATIONS IN SAILING. The activity of sailing itself can be varied in ways that will break the routine of a long cruise. On short passages with fresh winds in fair weather, normal sailing under working canvas will be thoroughly enjoyable to most people whether they be veterans or novices; but during a lengthy passage on only one point of sailing in hot weather with little breeze, sailing can become tedious even to an old salt. In the latter case, it can be comfortable and convenient to rig up a self-steering system or to hoist light sails that will permit fast sailing with the awning set. These improvisations will be discussed in Chapter 9. Other ways to vary the sailing routine are to have occasional brushes (informal races) with boats nearby, to try out heavy weather rigs in fresh winds (see Chapter 9), and to sail the dinghy when your cruiser is at anchor in a protected harbor or river.

FISHING AND CRABBING. It is fun to try fishing from your boat. While underway when the boat is moving slowly, it is simple to drop over a trolling line. In many bays or rivers along the east coast, for instance, it is perfectly possible to catch a sizable striped bass or bluefish that will be delicious to eat. A sailboat generally does not make the best fishing boat, but if the fish are biting, they can be caught from almost any kind of vessel. By all means put over a trolling line when small fish such as alewives are breaking and there is a flock of screaming gulls whirling and hovering over them. This indicates that the small fish are being hotly pursued by larger ones that might greedily snatch a spoon, a feather, or some other inviting lure.

Crabs are found along most coasts of the United States. Some of these delectable crustaceans can be caught with a crab net by wading along the shore and prodding them from their hiding places under the mud or sand or in seaweed, or they can be lured from under rocks with bait. Swimming crabs such as the famous blue crab can be caught from the anchored boat by hanging a scrap of meat (or preferably an old fish head) on a piece of string several feet below the surface of the water. When a crab begins to feed, it is pulled up to the surface very slowly and stealthily so that it can be dipped up with a sudden lunge of the net. During the spawning season, it is even possible to dip up mating "doublers" without bait while the boat is underway, but this is usually frowned on by conservationists even when females are thrown back. Further suggestions for fishing and crabbing are given in Appendix B.

SWIMMING AND SNORKELING. In regions where the water is clear and warm enough for lengthy swimming, snorkeling can be fascinating. For the experienced swimmer, it requires little training and not much equipment. All that one really needs is a good, tight-fitting face mask and a breathing tube, preferably a J-shaped type without crude valves to keep the water out. Flippers are definitely helpful but not essential. The snorkeler simply floats on his stomach over a shoal area and stares down through the glass in his mask to the seabed, which may present an intriguing and perhaps colorful spectacle of aquatic life, especially in the West Indies or even in the southern parts of the United States. The beginning snorkeler should be cautioned against getting too much exposure to the sun, for the clear water will tend to magnify the sun's rays. It is sometimes a good idea to wear an old pair of pajamas or at least a T-shirt over one's bathing suit for sunburn protection.

There are few dangers for good swimmers in most U.S. cruising areas when common-sense safety rules are observed. These rules include avoiding swimming immediately after meals, in strong currents, in heavy surf or large breaking seas, by oneself in deep water, during thunderstorms, and in areas where there is heavy power boat traffic. Furthermore,

the swimmer should be very cautious in areas where there are potentially dangerous forms of marine life such as sharks, barracuda, moray eels, sting rays, sea urchins, or potent stinging nettles. In warm waters where sharks or barracuda have been seen, it is safest to have an out-of-water observer keep a lookout for these fish, which ordinarily do not attack swimmers, but which very often behave unpredictably. Rules for shark protection are: (1) avoid swimming at night and in deep water offshore; (2) don't wear bright trinkets such as bracelets when swimming; (3) come out of the water at once if you cut yourself; and (4) when spearfishing, immediately remove from the water any bleeding fish. Sea urchins and sting rays are dangerous only if you step on them while wading, and moray eels are no threat unless you reach into a crevice in the rocks or coral where they are hiding. Most stinging jellyfish in this country cannot seriously injure a person (provided he is not stung in the eyes), but the Portuguese man-of-war (*Physalia*), which is not often seen except in some warm coastal or offshore waters, has a very severe sting. This creature is easily identified

This handsome yawl appears to be returning from a cruise. Notice the tied-off halyards, the shroud rollers to prevent chafe, the well-taped cotter pins in the turnbuckles, the large *Dorade* vent forward, the large fenders, and the protective sail covers.

by its floating air bladder with a bluish vertical crest or "sail," which supports the stinging tentacles that hang down many feet below the water's surface.

BIRD WATCHING. Another cruising activity that can be very entertaining is bird watching. A great variety of bird life can be seen on nearly all waters of the United States. Aside from the ever-present gulls and frequently seen terns, there are birds found on or close to shore near the water's edge such as the so-called shore birds (plovers, oyster catchers, sandpipers, yellowlegs, turnstones); the waders (herons, egrets, ibises, bitterns, rails); the dabblers or shallow water feeders (swans and tipping or dabbling ducks including mallards, baldpates, pintails, black ducks, and teals); and miscellaneous birds such as geese, ospreys, marsh hawks, and so forth. In addition, there are the open water divers such as grebes, loons, cormorants, anhingas, and the diving ducks, which include canvasbacks, scoters, scaup, mergansers, ruddy ducks, and so on. It is most helpful to have a local "field list" of commonly seen birds in your area. Such lists, often obtainable from the National Audubon Society or from local bird clubs, tell not only in what locality a particular bird can be seen, but also about its habitat, time of occurrence, and abundance each month. Of course, bird identification books should be carried, too. Highly recommended are *A Field Guide to the Birds* by R. T. Peterson (Houghton Mifflin Company); *Birds of North America* by Robbins, Bruun, Zim, and Singer (Doubleday and Company); *Birds of the West Indies* by James Bond (Houghton Mifflin Company); and *Complete Field Guide to American Wildlife* by H. H. Collins, Jr. (Harper and Row). The last book is also a useful guide for collecting shells and identifying fish or other forms of marine life.

Perhaps the most spectacular times for bird watching from a boat are during the spring and especially the fall migrations. The majority of waterfowl migrate by way of four main flyways. Two of these are along the Atlantic and Pacific seaboards, while a third is through the Mississippi Valley and into or across the Great Lakes region. A major branch from the Atlantic flyway leaves the main artery along the east coast in the vicinity of the Chesapeake Bay and crosses the northern Great Lakes on the way to central and western Canada and Alaska. To me, there are few experiences more stirring than to be sailing on a crisp fall day when hundreds of gleaming white swans with outstretched necks are flying overhead in V-shaped flights, filling the air with their strange, shrill calls.

ECOLOGY STUDIES. In the present age, when we are becoming increasingly concerned with problems of overpopulation, pollution, and the ruination of our environment, it is important to learn all one can about the ecology of his cruising area in the interest of forestalling its gradual deterioration. Our concern should not be limited merely to the preservation of game. We should be vitally interested in the quality of water and shore and their capability of supporting all forms of natural life (including ours) in an ecological system that is properly balanced and self-sustaining. In the Chesapeake Bay area, an organization dedicated to conservation and preservation, the Chesapeake Bay Foundation, is currently sponsoring or at least encouraging "ecology cruises," whereby young people (especially high school students) or other interested landsmen are taken on short cruises to get a first-hand exposure to the local marine environment, learn how it is threatened, and recognize the value of saving it. Cruise boats are generally run by volunteer yachtsmen, and simple, easily workable ecological study equipment is carried. Details of the equipment, studies, and tests are shown in Appendix B, an "Ecology Cruise Guide" that was prepared by the Chesapeake Bay Foundation. This syllabus is appropriate for many bodies of water in the United States, and hopefully ecology cruises will catch on in other parts of the country.

STAR WATCHING. Still another fascinating if not vital activity for the cruising sailor is star watching. Anchored away from the shore, he usually will have an unobstructed view of the heavens, and there will be clear nights when one cannot help being impressed by the multitude of celestial bodies overhead. It is both entertaining and educational to try to identify the major stars, planets, and constellations.

The novice star watcher in the United States should begin his study of the heavens by orienting the prominent northern constellations with Polaris, the North Star. As most people know, the two end stars, known as the "pointers," on the bowl of the Big Dipper point toward Polaris. The distance from the pointer star nearest Polaris to Polaris is about four and a half times the distance between the two pointers. Polaris, which is actually the end of the handle of the Little Dipper (Ursa Minor), is located very close to the celestial north pole, and this star appears to rotate around the pole once every

FIGURE 7-9: ROUGH GUIDE TO LOCATING THE STARS

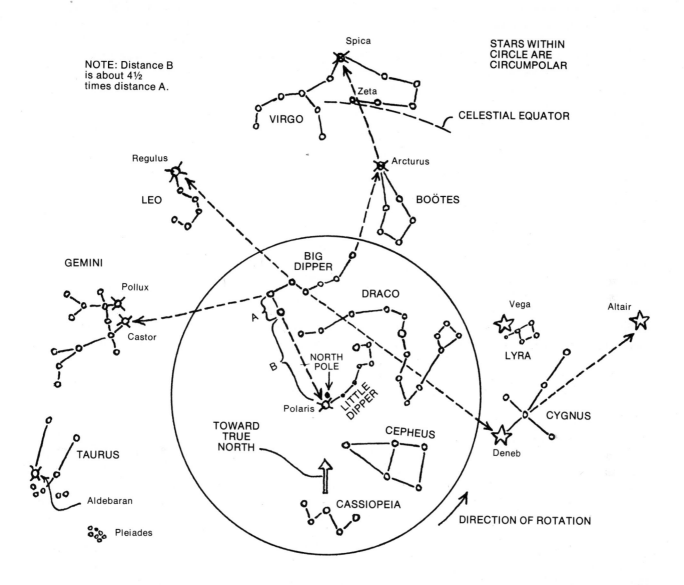

twenty-four hours as the earth turns on its axis. Likewise, all the northern constellations turn around the celestial north pole, and those near Polaris, which never sink below the horizon, are termed *circumpolar*. Of course, whether or not the stars rise or set will depend on the latitude of the observer. If he is far south near the equator, for instance, Polaris will be very close to the horizon, but if he is far north Polaris will be high in the sky. In fact, the altitude of Polaris will be very nearly equal to the latitude of the observer. The circumpolar star groups seen from the middle latitudes of the United States

(perhaps 40 degrees north latitude where the altitude of Polaris is about 40 degrees) include the Big Dipper, which is really a part of the constellation Ursa Major; the Little Dipper, of course; Draco, the serpentine constellation that seems to wrap itself around the Little Dipper; Cassiopeia, the M- or W-shaped constellation on the side of Polaris opposite the Big Dipper; and Cepheus, the five-star group looking like a square capped with a triangle, the point of which lies between the middle of Cassiopeia and the bowl of the Little Dipper.

The positions of the circumpolar constellations

relative to Polaris and the positions in the sky of the more southerly constellations, which rise and set, depend not only on the time of night, but also on the season of the year. Due to the earth's revolution around the sun, new constellations south of the circumpolar stars are seen as the seasons change and many stars seen during one season cannot be seen during the next. To tell what stars can be seen during each season and where and when to see them, carry star maps. Two good, non-technical books containing maps are *Stars* by Zim and Baker (Golden Press) or *The Stars, a New Way to See Them* by H. A. Rey (Houghton Mifflin Company). In addition, the National Geographic Society periodically publishes a fine large map of the heavens that includes planet positions and monthly star charts for both hemispheres.

Figure 7-9 is a simplified chart of the north circumpolar constellations with dashed-line directional arrows pointing toward prominent constellations that rise and set and are a considerable distance away from the celestial north pole. Those constellations inside the circle are circumpolar from middle U.S. latitudes (near 40 degrees north latitude), and the star positions are approximations of those seen in the early evening near the first of June. Notice that Cassiopeia is shown directly below Polaris. In this position and when the constellation is directly above the North Star, a line from the middle star of Cassiopeia through Polaris points to true north. The Big Dipper can be used not only to locate Polaris, but also to locate the star Regulus, for the two stars on the opposite side of the bowl from the "pointers" are aimed at Regulus, the dot at the end of the backward question mark in the constellation Leo, visible during the spring in the direction "beneath" the bottom of the Big Dipper's bowl. In the opposite direction the same two bowl stars point to Deneb in the crosslike constellation Cygnus (the swan) visible during the summer and fall. The Big Dipper's handle curves toward Arcturus in the constellation Boötes and then on to Spica in Virgo. Between Arcturus and Spica is the small star Zeta (in Virgo), which lies exactly on the celestial equator and therefore will rise and set due east or west. Both Boötes and Virgo are spring constellations, but they are also seen during a great part of the summer.

Predominating stars in midsummer are Deneb, Vega in the constellation Lyra, and Altair in Aquila (the eagle). These three stars are often referred to as the Great Summer Triangle. The two bird constellations, Cygnus and Aquila, are not very far apart, but the latter is closer to the celestial equator. Altair's *declination* (distance from the celestial equator) is only about 9 degrees north. Vega is the brightest and most western of the three stars forming the triangle, and it forms a near right angle between Deneb and Altair. By the way, the preferable pronunciation of *Vega* is "Veega," not "Vāga," as General Motors pronounces it.

On the opposite side of Polaris almost directly across from Vega is the constellation Gemini (the twins), with the bright stars Pollux and Castor as heads of the twins (see Figure 7-9). These are not summer stars, however. The two stars at the bottom of the Big Dipper's bowl point very close to Castor. Not far from the outside foot of the most northerly twin (which has Castor for a head) is the head of the constellation Taurus (the bull). This star group is readily identified on fall and winter evenings by the star cluster above and to the right of the bull's head, known as the Pleiades, and also by the prominent reddish star Aldebaran, near the bull's eye (almost in line with the two bottom stars in Castor's left foot, as shown in Figure 7-9). Another prominent star group seen in the fall is the Great Square of Pegasus, which is located almost directly south of Cassiopeia. But so much for an introduction to star watching.

RAINY WEATHER ACTIVITIES. Before finishing this section on miscellaneous cruising activities, the cruise planner should be reminded that there could be a day or so of stormy, rainy weather when the boat is anchored away from shore facilities that provide entertainment. When the crew is compelled or desires to stay aboard in bad weather, games such as cards, Scrabble (which comes in a magnetized form), crossword puzzles, and so forth will come in handy. At this time, furthermore, a good ship's library will be invaluable. Aside from cruising guides, pilot books, and books on birds and stars, there should be some light reading in the form of "pulp" novels or "who-dun-its." There should also be some good boating reference books and seamanship manuals, for this is a good time to review the basics of seamanship or to increase one's nautical knowledge, and even to learn certain manual skills such as new knots, splices, and so forth. Another suggestion is that a set of classic cruising or voyaging books be carried. One such set of small-size books that will fit into a compact bookshelf is the "Mariners Library" published by Rupert Hart-Davis Ltd. (London). These books, which include the voyages of Slocum, Voss, W. A. Robinson, and other famous small-boat sailors, are not only entertaining, but they are instructive as well. In fact, they are just about perfect for reading in a snug cabin while a storm rages above the deck.

Stocking Up

The amount and variety of stores carried on a cruise will depend primarily on the size of the crew, the intended length of the cruise, the number of ports to be visited, the intended frequency of stops, and the availability of supplies at the ports of call. In addition to groceries, of course, supplies must include many other items, such as drugstore supplies, galley equipment, and suitable clothing. A basic list of stores and supplies (not including safety, deck, or comfort gear, which have been discussed) is as follows:

1. Fuels. Gasoline or diesel oil (keep tanks full whenever possible to minimize condensation); alcohol, LP-gas, or kerosene for stove or perhaps lights.

2. Ice. Block ice for icebox, plastic bags of cubes, a sturdy, well-insulated cooler filled with ice cubes, and perhaps dry ice (frozen carbon dioxide) when available, with ice tongs or carrying bag.

3. Water. Two tanks or one tank and plastic jugs of water, one fill hose, bottled drinking water (if tank water has bad taste).

4. Plastic and paper supplies. Garbage bags, plastic or rubber garbage can, plastic forks and spoons, paper plates, paper cups, paper towels, toilet paper, napkins, and writing or notebook paper and pens or pencils.

5. Cleaning supplies. Hand soap (possibly salt water soap also), liquid detergent with screw-on top, mildly abrasive soap powder, wax for fiberglass, metal polish, scouring pads, talcum powder (for removing grease from raw teak), dish mop, brush with stiff nylon bristles (for skidproof fiberglass surfaces).

6. Galley supplies. Heavy can opener (and spare), beer can opener (and spare), bottle opener with corkscrew, ice pick, small wooden bucket for chopping ice, matches, spark gun for lighting stove (with spare flints), asbestos glove, asbestos pad or wood grate for hot pots (if there is no wood section of the counter), pot holders, *flame tamer* (a hollow metal plate that can be put on the stove's burner to produce very low heat), stainless steel eating utensils, large serving spoons, carving knife, paring knife, perforated spoon, cooking fork, vegetable peeler, measuring cup, funnel, deep frying pan with lid,

deep pots with lids, double boiler, pressure cooker, folding stove-top toaster of stainless steel, perhaps a portable stove-top oven (if there is no permanent oven), a set of large stacking plastic bowls, plastic plates, soup or cereal bowls, cups and saucers or mugs, glasses, a set of plastic food containers with tight-fitting lids (Tupperware is outstanding for variety of sizes and shapes and the tightness of lids), and a large plastic container for liquids with a screw-on top.

7. Condiments and dried goods. Salt, pepper, assorted spices, sugar, powdered cream or milk, powdered coffee, ice tea mix or tea bags, bouillon cubes, dried onions, gravy mixes, dried soups, tomato catsup, Worcestershire sauce, vinegar, vegetable oil, mayonnaise, salad dressing mix, quick rice, quick oatmeal, chipped beef, and pancake mix.

8. Canned foods. Stews, ham, chicken, corned beef hash, franks, baked beans, potatoes, seafood, soups (clam chowder, consommé, vichyssoise, black bean, cream of mushroom), vegetables (asparagus, tomatoes, artichokes), fruit (Mandarin oranges, pineapples, grapefruit segments), jars of cheese, pickles, and marmalade, jam, or jellies.

9. Fresh foods. Fruit (oranges or tangerines, peaches, plums, grapes), bacon, meat (ham or beef steaks), fried chicken (but beware of grease on raw teak), precooked stew or roast, eggs (in plastic egg box), lunch meats, cheese, butter or margarine (in a plastic tub), milk in a leakproof container (there is a Tupperware container into which a milk carton will fit), bread, crackers, sea biscuits, pretzels, cookies, frozen baked goods, potatoes, onions, carrot and celery strips (prewashed and precut, stowed in a plastic bag), lettuce, cucumbers, and tomatoes.

10. Drinks. Canned beer, liquor, wine, soft drinks (cola, ginger ale, tonic), and canned fruit juices.

11. Linens and bedding. Towels, dish towels, wash cloths, sheets (preferably fitted), blankets or sleeping bags, pillows, and pillowcases.

12. Clothes. Foul weather gear (preferably of PVC or polyurethane-covered nylon, colored yellow, with a front-opening jacket closed with snaps), hats (to keep the sun off your face and to keep your head warm in cold weather), shirts with long sleeves (for protection from the sun), slacks or long trousers (when legs become overexposed), shorts, bathing suits, lightweight shore clothes (suitable for wearing in a restaurant when eating ashore), a heavy sweater, lightweight jacket (when cruising in cold waters), suitable deck shoes (with skidproof rubber soles), lightweight flexible rubber boots (that may be rolled

up into a compact package), gloves and scarf (in cold weather), plenty of socks, sunglasses, and a carrying bag of a soft material (never a suitcase). Always wear deck shoes to prevent skidding and stubbing toes, and carry a knife.

13. Medical supplies, toilet articles, etc. Standard first aid kit with complete instruction book (including adequate bandages, gauze, burn ointment, antiseptic, adhesive tape, etc.) an antibiotic, a pain killer such as Darvon, Demerol, or codeine (consult your doctor), aspirin, seasickness remedy such as Dramamine or Marezine (if Dramamine causes drowsiness), sunburn cream ("Afil" and "Sun Dare" are recommended), diarrhea medicine (perhaps paregoric or Parepectolin), laxative (milk of magnesia tablets, prune juice, or cascara), vaseline, sanitary napkins (which make excellent bandages for serious cuts), insect spray and repellent, personal toilet articles (comb, toothbrush, dental floss, razor, shaving cream), and smoking gear (cigarettes, pipes, tobacco, and skidproof ashtrays).

These supply lists may seem rather formidable, but many items, with the exception of fresh foods, of course, are semipermanent, being taken on board at the beginning of the sailing season and not taken ashore until the boat is decommissioned for winter storage. Some items, not damaged by freezing, can be left aboard indefinitely. In putting aboard stores and supplies, pay very careful attention to stowage. Items must be stowed securely where they will not fall or spill during knockdowns or when the boat pitches and rolls. Also, all supplies and equipment should be returned to their stowage locations immediately after use. It is very important not only for convenience but for safety as well that equipment can be found quickly, without a search. Of course, gear and supplies that are used frequently should be kept in the most available and convenient locations. Supplementary stores can be stowed in hard-to-reach lockers, but oft-needed items should be handy. For example, don't stow condiments needed for cooking directly behind the stove when reaching them will require removing a pot from the stove or reaching over a hot flame.

Water, ice, and fuel are usually among the last supplies taken aboard before leaving on a cruise, but if possible some ice should be put aboard on the day before leaving so that the box will be cool when it receives the full load of ice and fresh foods just before getting underway. Also, fuel tanks should be kept reasonably full all the time, if possible, in the interest of minimizing condensation in the tanks and consequently water in the fuel. I don't believe, however, in topping up or overfilling the tanks, especially on a sailboat, because fuel may flow out the air vent on a rough day when the boat heels. Furthermore, it may be possible for a small amount of fuel to leak out of a fill pipe at the flexible hose connection when the tank is filled up to its filler cap, and also some room is needed for fuel expansion. As for keeping the water tanks filled, an important consideration is how the boat's trim is affected. She should be trimmed in such a way that one deck scupper on each side of the boat is at the low point of the sheer line in order that no puddles of water, which in time could cause staining or rot, will be allowed to remain on deck when the boat is moored. Water tanks located some distance from a vessel's center of gravity will obviously affect her trim. As said before, it is advisable to carry your own hose for filling the water tanks, because marina hoses are sometimes stolen, and in some remote areas hoses are never provided.

With the conclusion of this section on stocking up, most aspects of cruise planning have been covered except for those having to do with navigation, which will be covered in more detail in the next chapter.

8

Thoughts on Small Boat Navigation

It is far beyond the scope of this book to attempt a thorough discussion of navigation. There are many helpful, comprehensive books on the subject, a few of which will be mentioned later. This chapter will merely introduce the neophyte to the basic, everyday problems of *piloting* and *dead reckoning* as done from the deck of a small- to medium-sized cruising sailboat. Piloting might be defined as close-to-shore navigation when the boat's position is obtained from visible, stationary objects (such as landmarks and buoys), sound signals, and soundings. In the simplest terms, dead reckoning is the practice of finding the boat's position by keeping track of the distance she travels over a known course.

Basic Tools

The most essential or useful tools for piloting and dead reckoning are charts, a compass, binoculars, an instrument for taking a *bearing* (the horizontal direction of an object with respect to the boat or with respect to north) such as a *pelorus* (a gimbaled compass card with a sighting vane), a *hand bearing compass* (a small compass with a hand grip and sights) or a *sextant* (an instrument using a sight, arc, and mirrors for measuring angles, most often the altitude of celestial bodies), *parallel rules* (movable parallel straightedges used to shift on a chart the position of courses or bearings) or a *course protractor-plotter* (an instrument that has a semicircular arc, usually of clear plastic, marked in degrees and used in conjunction with a straight ruler for plotting courses or bearings on a chart), dividers (for measuring distances on the chart), a radio direction finder (RDF), a depth sounder and/or lead line, a log or speedometer, and a clock and stopwatch or wristwatch with a sweep second hand.

Four navigation book suggestions are: *Piloting and Dead Reckoning* by H. H. Shufeldt and G. D. Dunlap (Naval Institute Press), *Navigation and Finding Fish with Electronics* by G. D. Dunlap (International Marine Publishing Company), *Electronic Navigation Made Easy* by John D. Lenk (John F. Rider Publisher, Inc.), and the standard tome, *American Practical Navigator* by Nathaniel Bowditch (U.S. Navy Hydrographic Office), commonly known as *Bowditch*. The Bowditch book is quite thick and some of it will be of little use to the average boatman, but it is a positive treasury of information. Then, too, there are the navigation-related publications described in the last chapter—cruising guides, tide tables, tidal current tables, chart books, Coast Pilots, and Sailing Directions. The U.S. Coast Guard publishes the *List of Lights and Other Marine Aids,* commonly called *Light Lists* (obtainable from the Government Printing Office) describing visual (lighted and unlighted), sound, and radio beacon aids to navigation. *Notice to Mariners* is published weekly by the U.S. Naval Oceanographic Office to keep mariners abreast of worldwide changes in charts, navigation aids, and so forth. *Local Notice to Mariners* gives similar information within the limits of the various U.S. Coast Guard districts, and the publication is obtainable from the Coast Guard.

Charts

Aside from the compass, charts undoubtedly are the most essential navigational aid on a cruising boat. They give the navigator a wealth of information—water depth; bottom characteristics; channels; navigation aids such as buoys, markers, and lighthouses; obstructions such as rocks, wrecks, and fish traps; the delineation of shoals with *fathom lines* (curved lines joining all positions having the same depth of water); landmarks; heights of certain prominent navigation aids; sound signals; radio beacons; and so forth. Furthermore, charts have very important *compass roses* (see Figure 8-1)—graduated compass circles printed in convenient locations in order to help the navigator find his position on the chart from directional bearings or find his correct compass heading from a course line drawn on the chart (to be explained later). As can be seen in Figure 8-1, the compass rose has two 360-degree scales, one inside the other. The 0-degree mark of the outer scale points to *true north* (located at the geographic north pole, the northern end of the earth's axis), while the 0-degree mark of the inner scale points toward the *magnetic north pole*, located somewhat north of Hudson Bay, the spot toward

FIGURE 8-1: COMPASS ROSE

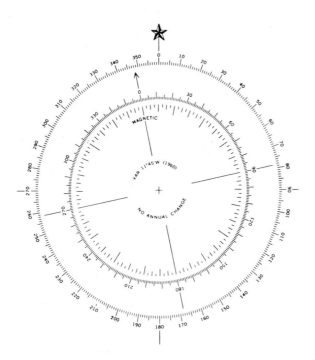

which the needle (or north mark) on a magnetic compass points. The angular difference between the true north meridian and the magnetic north meridian at any location is called *variation*. Annual change of variation (if any) is printed near the center of the compass rose.

The scale of a chart is often a source of confusion to beginning navigators. A "small-scale" chart is often thought of as one that shows a lot of detail covering a small section of the earth, when in actuality it shows little detail but covers a large area. It should be remembered that *small scale is large area*, and *large scale is small area*. Charts used by the coastal navigator and gunkholer are *general charts* with scales of from 1:100,000 to 1:600,000 for coastwise navigation offshore from coastal shoals; *coast charts* with scales of 1:50,000 to 1:100,000 for close-to-shore coastal and sound or bay navigation; and *harbor charts* with scales larger than 1:50,000 for entering and leaving anchorages, harbors, fairly small rivers, and so on. The scale ratio means that one unit of measurement on the chart is equal to the large number in the ratio of the same unit on earth. For example, a scale of 1:50,000 would mean that one inch on the chart equals 50,000 inches on earth.

On charts of the Gulf and east coasts of the United States, water depths are measured from a *datum* or plane of reference at mean low water, the average of all low waters, as explained in the previous chapter. On the west coast, however, water depths are measured from a datum at *mean lower low water*—the average of the lower low waters. Be sure to check the chart's legend to see whether depths are shown in feet or fathoms (one fathom equals six feet), and check the chart's date to assure that the information shown is current. For coastal navigation in the United States most charts are *Mercator projections*—that is, meridians of longitude and parallels of latitude are shown as straight parallel lines intersecting each other at right angles. This

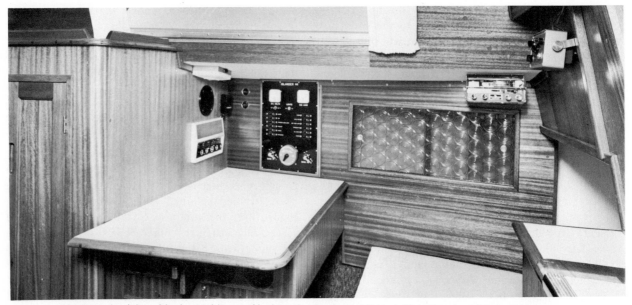

Navigator's niche with chart table on a Yachtcraft 44, a large kit boat. Note the size of the working area.

system of transferring a spherical map (as shown on a globe) to a flat map (as shown on a chart) causes considerable distortion through expansion of area in the high latitudes. There are charts of the Great Lakes, however, that use the *polyconic projection*, showing the central meridian as being straight but other meridians curving slightly on either side of center and converging toward the top of the chart. Actually, on a large-scale chart of this projection, all meridians will look like converging straight lines. The parallels of latitude, however, are shown as curved arcs of large nonconcentric circles equally spaced at the central meridian.

The Compass

When installing a compass, the major considerations will be that its location should afford protection for the instrument, provide good visibility for the helmsman, and be where *deviation* is minimal. Deviation is the magnetic compass error caused by local shipboard attraction of ferrous metals or electrical equipment. In addition, the compass must be gimbaled adequately so that it stays level when the boat pitches, rolls, or heels. Sailboat compasses, unlike many of those made for power boats, are constructed so that they can remain level at high angles of heel. The usual compass location on a boat with wheel steering is in a *binnacle* (a case or stand for housing the compass) directly ahead of the wheel. On boats with tiller steering the compass may be mounted in the bridge deck or behind a window or dome in the after end of the cabin trunk. Sometimes there are twin installations on either side of the companionway to allow good compass visibility for the helmsman on either tack. The drawback of twin compasses, however, is that their deviation errors seldom agree exactly, and, of course, they cost twice as much. A compass should be installed with the *lubber line* (the reference mark or post on the compass bowl that indicates the boat's heading) exactly parallel with the boat's centerline.

The most serious deviation on boats built of materials other than iron or steel are from such objects as the engine, iron or steel tanks, iron keel ballast, electrical components of the engine and electronic instruments, radios, and iron or non-stainless-steel fittings. The compass must be installed as far as possible from ferrous metal objects and electrical gear. Electric wiring anywhere near the compass should be twisted with each conductor wound around the other to help cancel out their magnetic fields. Regardless of how well the compass is installed, however, there almost always will be some deviation, and so the compass should be *adjusted* by having its deviation errors reduced to a minimum with corrective magnets, and what errors remain after adjustment should be noted on all headings and recorded on a *deviation card* posted near the compass.

Before going on extended cruises in strange waters, especially where fog is prevalent, it is safest to have the compass corrected by a professional adjuster, but in many cases reasonably accurate adjustments can be made by the boat owner himself. Most compasses are fitted with corrector magnets—athwartships north-south (NS) correctors controlled with a slotted head screw adjuster, and fore-and-aft east-west (EW) correctors similarly controlled. The screw adjusters must be turned with a nonmagnetic screwdriver. One means of adjusting the compass is to line up from your boat two objects marked on the chart while heading first in a northerly direction, then in an easterly, southerly, and westerly direction and to compare the magnetic bearing of a line drawn through the objects on the chart with compass bearings of the objects in order to find the deviation errors on all the *cardinal* (N, E, S, and W) headings (a brief discussion of taking bearings will come later).

Figure 8-2 gives an example of how deviation errors can be found from two such objects shown on the chart that can be lined up to form a *range*. The angle between the range shown on the chart (a straight line drawn between the two objects) and magnetic north (obtained from the inner compass rose on the chart) is compared with the compass bearing angle that lies between the range (seen when the two objects are in line) and north shown on the boat's compass. The difference between the two angles is deviation. If the compass bearing is less than the magnetic bearing, the deviation is east, and, of course, if the compass bearing is greater than the magnetic bearing, the deviation is west. An easy way to remember this is to think of the phrase "compass least, error east" or "compass best, error west."

When adjusting the compass, deviation is found on a northerly heading (as shown in Figure 8-2), and one-half the error is removed by turning the NS corrector screw on the compass. Then, while headed east, half the error is removed by adjusting the EW corrector. Next, half the error is removed by adjusting the NS corrector while headed south,

FIGURE 8-2:
DEVIATION &
COMPASS
ADJUSTING

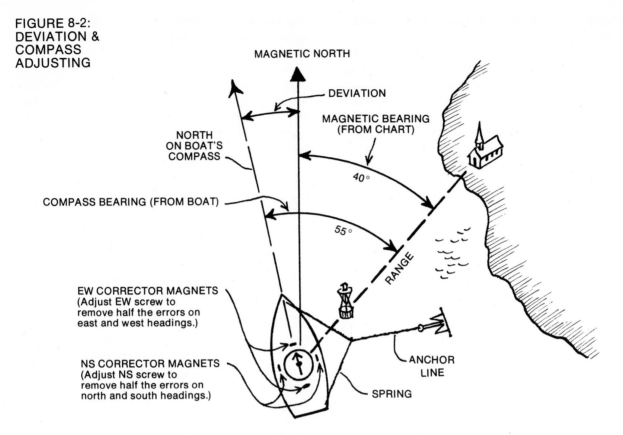

MAGNETIC NORTH

DEVIATION

MAGNETIC BEARING
(FROM CHART)

NORTH
ON BOAT'S
COMPASS

COMPASS BEARING (FROM BOAT)

40°

55°

RANGE

EW CORRECTOR MAGNETS
(Adjust EW screw to
remove half the errors on
east and west headings.)

NS CORRECTOR MAGNETS
(Adjust NS screw to
remove half the errors on
north and south headings.)

ANCHOR
LINE

SPRING

NOTE: After finding the deviation on the northerly heading, find it in a
similar way for easterly, southerly and then westerly headings.

FIGURE 8-3:
A SIMPLE
DEVIATION
CARD
(to be
mounted
near the
compass)

	FOR MAGNETIC COURSE		STEER	DEV.
N	000°		355°	(5E)
	045		042	(3E)
E	090		091	(1W)
	135		137	(2W)
S	180		184	(4W)
	225		228	(3W)
W	270		268	(2E)
	315		311	(4E)

and finally half the error is removed by adjusting the EW corrector while the boat is headed west. This entire process should be repeated to ensure accuracy. On all the cardinal headings, the boat should be in the same location with the range objects in line or very nearly so if the objects are far apart.

The compass can also be adjusted in a very simple way with the use of a *shadow pelorus*. This is an inexpensive instrument consisting of a gimbaled compass card or *azimuth scale* (a circular scale marked in degrees) with a vertical pin at the center for the purpose of casting a thin shadow on the scale. When using the shadow pelorus, a helmsman first steers the boat due east, and the pelorus is rotated so that the shadow falls exactly on the east or 90-degree mark on the azimuth scale. The helmsman then steers due west by the boat's compass, and if the shadow of the pin does not fall on the 270-degree mark of the scale, *half* the compass error is removed with its corrector magnets. Next, the process is repeated on north and south headings, and again half the error is removed.

After the compass has been adjusted, any remaining deviation should be noted by *swinging* (turning) the boat in all directions and recording (on a deviation card) the errors on cardinal and also *intercardinal* (NE, SE, SW, and NW) headings. The boat can be swung while underway, moving very slowly, or at anchor. With the latter method, she can be anchored from the bow and stern, or, under ideal wind and tide conditions, one anchor might be used with a spring line made fast to the anchor line and led aft in the manner suggested in Figure 8-2.

Still another method of checking deviation is to lash the boat snugly to the side and end of a dock, the heading of which is shown on a large-scale chart. Be sure, however, that there are no large masses of ferrous metal or electrical equipment that could attract the compass. For greatest accuracy, update the variation by applying the annual change shown in the center of the compass rose (see Figure 8-1).

A simple kind of deviation card that should not be confusing to an inexperienced helmsman is illustrated in Figure 8-3. The left-hand column, labeled "For Magnetic Course," lists the cardinal and intercardinal courses in degrees, while directly opposite them, in the right-hand column under the label "Steer," are the corresponding compass courses. A course in the right-hand list must be steered in order to make good its adjacent course in the

left-hand list. Deviation is seldom consistent. It varies on different headings and is subject to change from restowage or replacement of gear on board a boat; thus errors should be checked with bearings fairly frequently. Be especially careful about stowing supplies that might have been magnetized during their manufacture such as steel beer cans, and beware of placing portable radios or light meters near the compass. If it is necessary that the compass be near the engine, deviation should be checked with the engine running and then with it not running. On boats under sail some error may be caused by heeling.

Aside from deviation, the other compass error is variation, as explained in the previous section on charts. It is usually simplest to avoid the variation error by working directly from the magnetic compass rose on the chart, but on occasion the navigator might want to work from the true north rose or from a north-south meridian on a Mercator chart. Applying the deviation and variation errors can be confusing, especially when it comes to determining whether the errors should be added or subtracted. A recommended procedure is as follows: Write across a sheet of paper the letters C D M V T, which stand for Compass, Deviation, Magnetic, Variation, and True. You can remember the sequence of letters by thinking of the expression "Can Dead Men Vote Twice?" (or, reading from right to left, "Timid Virgins Make Dull Companions"). Next think of the letters AEC (as in Atomic Energy Commission), which stand for Add East Correcting. This means that when *correcting*, going from Compass to True (that is, taking the Compass heading, applying the Deviation to obtain the Magnetic heading, and then applying the Variation to obtain the True heading), you add easterly errors. Since you add east correcting, obviously you subtract west. When you are *uncorrecting*, going from True to Compass (taking the True heading, applying the Variation to obtain the Magnetic heading, and then applying the Deviation to obtain the Compass heading), you do the opposite of AEC; you subtract easterly errors and, of course, add westerly errors. If you have trouble remembering the letter sequence for correcting, remember that you read from C to T in the word "correct" and also in the expression C D M V T; thus reading from C to T is correcting.

An example of correcting the compass errors is as follows: You are steering due south (180 degrees) by the compass. The deviation is 8 degrees east, the variation is 4 degrees west, and you want the true heading. Jot down C D M V T; put *180* under C, *8 east* under D, and *4 west* under V. Since we are correcting (moving from C to T), we add easterly errors (remember AEC); thus we add 8 to 180 to get 188 Magnetic and subtract the 4 degrees westerly variation to get the True heading of 184 degrees.

Taking Bearings

As said before, bearings can be taken with a pelorus, a hand bearing compass, or a sextant, but the simplest method is to sight directly over the top of the boat's compass if possible. To use the compass this way, obviously it must be mounted in a location that permits sighting in all directions. If it is sufficiently elevated—being mounted atop a stand binnacle or pedestal just forward of the helm, for instance—the points or degree marks on the card might be aimed at the object whose bearing is being taken. In fact, some flat-top compasses are fitted with sighting vanes that may be turned in all directions. If the compass is mounted low, however, the person taking the bearing will have to sight in a rather crude way some distance above the compass card; consequently, the bearing will not be very accurate.

A more accurate but perhaps more troublesome means of taking a bearing is with a pelorus. The instrument has a lubber line, which must be set parallel to the boat's centerline; a nonmagnetic compass card, which can be rotated; and sighting vanes that can be turned independently of the card in any direction. The pelorus can be used to take *relative bearings* (those relative to the boat or her heading) by locking the card in position when its 0-degree mark is exactly on the lubber line; or bearings can be taken with reference to north by setting the pelorus card to agree with the compass, in which case the degree or point on the pelorus card corresponding to the boat's heading is set on the lubber line. Then, of course, the object whose bearing is sought is sighted through the vanes and its bearing is read from the card. Although a simple, small-craft pelorus need not be expensive, it is possible to save the cost of one by using a portable RDF set as a pelorus, since most modern sets have rotatable antennae fitted with sights that swing over a bearing circle marked in degrees or points.

A hand bearing compass is a very useful instrument for taking bearings, but a good one will not be cheap, and it may be difficult to hold steady in a seaway. Furthermore, its deviation will seldom agree exactly with that of the boat's compass. One advantage to carrying a hand bearer is that it will serve well as a spare compass, a recommended item for every boat that cruises extensively in strange waters.

Speaking from personal experience, I have found that a cheap plastic sextant (costing around fifteen dollars) is quite handy for taking bearings. Such a sextant is shown in Figure 8-4. Very precise angles can be measured between two objects, and fairly accurate magnetic bearings can be figured by measuring the angle between a distant object and the boat's bow or stern (a relative bearing) and then adding or subtracting this angle (depending on the object's location) to the boat's compass heading. This is explained in Figure 8-5. Notice that the boat is headed 75 degrees magnetic and the object (buoy) on the starboard bow is 40 degrees from dead ahead. It is plain to see that this angle must be added to the boat's heading to obtain the object's magnetic bearing, but the object on the port bow bearing 30 degrees from the bow must have its relative bearing (30 degrees) subtracted from the heading to obtain its magnetic bearing. This may sound complicated, but it should be evident after a brief study of the diagram.

The bow or stern reference points on the boat normally can be the sail track on the mainmast while sighting forward or a centerline permanent backstay when sighting aft, and the observer must be stationed exactly on the boat's centerline. Of course, the sextant must be held in a horizontal position when the angle between terrestrial objects is measured, and the object that is reflected in the sextant's mirror lies to the right of the object that is directly viewed through the sighting tube (see Figure 8-4). I find it most convenient to set the sextant's arm at 0 degrees on the index scale (so that the angle is 0) and sight through the tube at the distant object so that it is lined up with its reflected image in the mirror. Then the arm is moved (without moving the sextant itself, keeping the direct [unreflected] image of the object in view) until the reference point on the boat or other object to be reflected in the mirror is brought into view. The mirror image must be lined up exactly under the direct image, and then, of course, the angle is read from the scale. Operating instructions are nearly always provided with the sextant.

FIGURE 8-4: PLASTIC SEXTANT

FIGURE 8-6: A FIX FROM THREE LINES OF POSITION

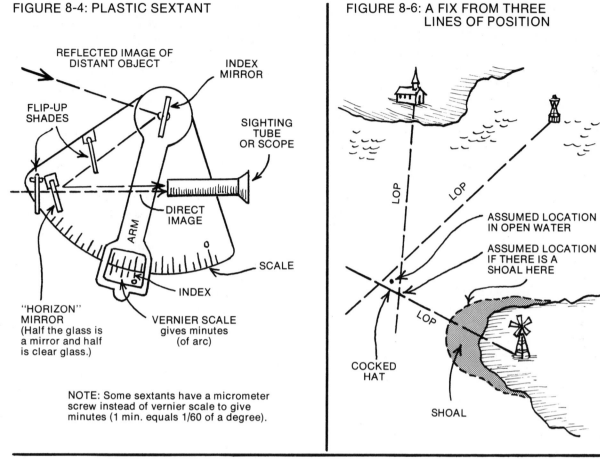

REFLECTED IMAGE OF DISTANT OBJECT

INDEX MIRROR

FLIP-UP SHADES

SIGHTING TUBE OR SCOPE

DIRECT IMAGE

ARM

SCALE

INDEX

"HORIZON" MIRROR
(Half the glass is a mirror and half is clear glass.)

VERNIER SCALE gives minutes (of arc)

NOTE: Some sextants have a micrometer screw instead of vernier scale to give minutes (1 min. equals 1/60 of a degree).

LOP

LOP

ASSUMED LOCATION IN OPEN WATER

ASSUMED LOCATION IF THERE IS A SHOAL HERE

LOP

COCKED HAT

SHOAL

FIGURE 8-5: MAGNETIC BEARINGS (USING THE SEXTANT)

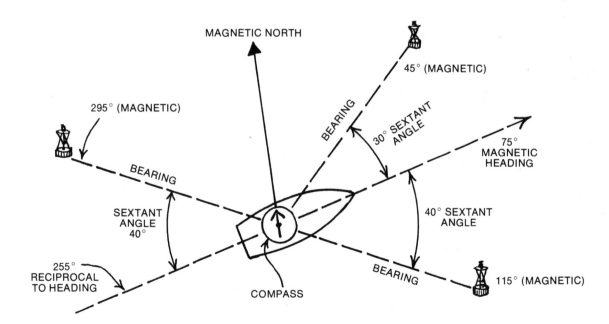

MAGNETIC NORTH

45° (MAGNETIC)

295° (MAGNETIC)

BEARING

BEARING

30° SEXTANT ANGLE

75° MAGNETIC HEADING

SEXTANT ANGLE 40°

40° SEXTANT ANGLE

255° RECIPROCAL TO HEADING

BEARING

115° (MAGNETIC)

COMPASS

Lines of Position and Fixes

A *line of position* (LOP) is a line on which a vessel is presumed to be located, and in piloting it usually is derived from the bearing of a distant charted object or from a range. With one LOP, the vessel's position can be anywhere on the line or its extension, but with a *fix* the position is more or less accurately pinpointed, normally with the crossing of two or more LOPs. Actually, three (or more) LOPs are rarely if ever sufficiently accurate to cross exactly at one point; thus there is usually a small triangle, often referred to as a *cocked hat*, at the center of the intersecting lines (see Figure 8-6). In this case, we should assume that the vessel is located at the center of the cocked hat, or, if there is a shoal nearby, at the corner of the triangle nearest the shoal.

When the distance to an object or the horizontal angle between two objects is known, the vessel lies on a *circle of position*, a circular LOP. Figure 8-7 shows a circle of position obtained by measuring the angle between two objects (a church steeple and a water tank). A simple method of drawing this circle on the chart is to draw a straight line between the two objects and subtract the horizontal angle (labeled Hor. A) from 90 degrees. Then draw toward the circle's approximate center radius lines

(RL 1 and RL 2) from the two objects so that the two radius lines make angles of 90 minus Hor. A with the line connecting the objects. The two radius lines will intersect at the circle's exact center so that an accurate circle of position can be drawn with a drawing compass. If the horizontal angle is greater than 90 degrees, the radius lines will be drawn so that they intersect on the far side of the line connecting the objects (so that this line is between the boat and the circle's center). To draw the angles on the chart a protractor or course plotter will be needed. Incidentally, there are instruments, such as the Webster *Reflectograph* and Weems *Position Finder*, that combine the function of a horizontal sextant with that of a three-arm plotter. The angles are measured with the instrument, and then it is laid directly on the chart to show the boat's position.

The dashed lines in Figure 8-7 demonstrate the constancy of the horizontal angle at any point on the circle of position. It is plain to see that to determine just where the boat is located on the circle, a fix must be obtained, normally by crossing the circle with a line of position or another circle of position. If another circle is used, it must cross the original circle at a fairly wide angle for greatest accuracy.

Distance away from a high object of known height

FIGURE 8-7: CIRCLE OF POSITION

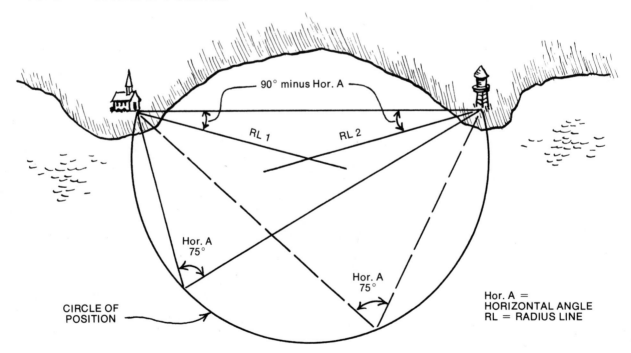

can be determined with the sextant by measuring the vertical angle between a line from the observer's eye to the top of the object and a line from the observer's eye to the sea horizon. A correction for *dip* (height of the observer's eye) should be applied, but this will normally be minor on a small boat. Distance can be read from "Distance by Vertical Angle" tables found in most books of nautical tables or in Bowditch (Table 9); or the following formula can be used with reasonable accuracy: distance off in miles equals height of the object in feet multiplied by .565 divided by the vertical angle in minutes. If the sea horizon cannot be seen, the angle can be measured from the top of the object to its bottom, and Table 22 in Bowditch is used for the dip correction. Heights of navigational aids sufficiently high to permit use of vertical angles for determining distance off can be obtained from your chart or light list. Sometimes a fix can be obtained by crossing one circle of position, which is derived from a horizontal angle between two objects, with another circle of position, which is derived from distance off, *i.e.* using the distance away from the object as the radius of the circle.

In areas where there are many buoys or other navigational aids or charted landmarks, fixes are usually obtained by crossing two or more bearings of different objects taken at approximately the same time. It is perfectly possible, however, to get a fairly accurate fix from just one object when bearings are used in conjunction with dead reckoning to obtain what is called a *running fix*. In this case, a bearing of an object is taken, and, at a later time, another bearing of the same object is taken. The earlier LOP is advanced along the course line the distance the boat has traveled between bearings, and the first LOP is crossed with the second LOP to make a fix as shown in Figure 8-8. The navigator knows only that the boat is somewhere on the first LOP when the original bearing is taken, but he does not know exactly where she is on the line. In the example illustrated, he heads due east for three miles (by the log) and then takes another bearing of the same object and obtains the second LOP. The first LOP is then moved due east for three miles and drawn on the chart so that it is exactly parallel to its original direction. It will cross the second LOP, and, since the boat must be somewhere on both LOPs, she must be where they cross; thus a fix is established. Of course, some inaccuracy is likely to result from unsteadiness in the boat's course or in the method of recording distance the boat travels between bearings. When drawing the LOPs on the chart, it is sound practice to label them with the bearing degrees and times the bearings were taken.

FIGURE 8-8: RUNNING FIX USING ONE OBJECT

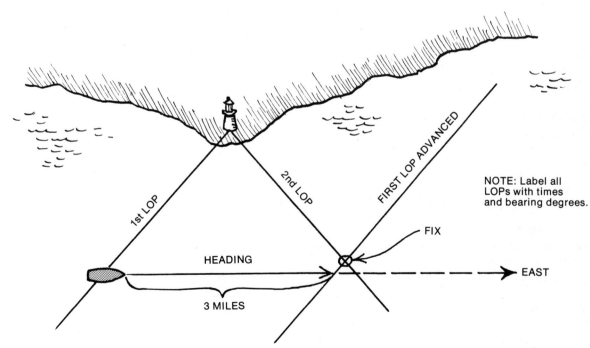

For a vessel passing by a landmark, there are two simple methods of determining distance off that do not require plotting on the chart. These methods, also utilizing nonsimultaneous bearings of one object, are commonly referred to as *bow-beam bearings* and *doubling the angle on the bow*. In the first case, a bearing is taken when the object is broad on the bow (bears 45 degrees from dead ahead), and a second bearing is taken when the object is exactly abeam (90 degrees from dead ahead). The *run* or distance the boat travels between bearings, normally read from the log, is equal to the distance from the boat to the object. An example is shown in Figure 8-9.

Basically, the same principle is involved with doubling the angle on the bow in that we are dealing with an isosceles triangle (a triangle having two equal sides). Let us suppose that the first bearing of the landmark is 25 degrees from dead ahead. We hold a straight course to pass by the landmark and then take another bearing when the object is 50 degrees from dead ahead. The first and second bearing lines and the boat's run form the sides of a triangle as shown in Figure 8-10. The angle between the second bearing line and the run is equal to 180 degrees (the number of degrees in a straight line) minus 50 degrees (the second bearing) or 130 degrees. Since the sum of the three angles in a plane triangle is 180 degrees, and we know two of the angles, 130 degrees and 25 degrees (the first bearing), the remaining angle is the sum of 25 and 130 subtracted from 180, or 25 degrees. Thus, with two equal angles, we have an isosceles triangle, and the boat's run is equal to her distance away from the object (see Figure 8-10). If the first bearing is 30 degrees and the second bearing 60 degrees, we also know that the distance to the object when it is abeam will be seven-eighths of the distance run between bearings. This is a special case of doubling the angle known as *the seven-eighths rule*.

Dead Reckoning

As said earlier, dead reckoning (DR) navigation is establishing a boat's position by keeping track of her course and the distance she travels. Distance may be determined with a log (described in Chapter 6) or with a speedometer. If a speedometer is used, of course, the boat's run must be timed in order to calculate the distance. The navigator may use a speed-time-distance calculator (obtainable from most chandlers or navigation supply stores), a logarithmic speed scale, or tables found in most navigation books, or he may use the simple formula: speed × time = distance. For example, if a boat travels at 5 knots (5 nautical miles per hour) for 2 hours, she travels 10 nautical miles. A nautical mile, incidentally, is equal to about 1.15 statute (land) miles or the length of one minute of latitude. When parts of hours are needed, speed × time (in minutes) in the above formula is divided by 60. A very handy DR rule is the *6 minutes rule:* the distance a boat goes in 6 minutes equals her speed divided by 10.

If the boat has no speedometer, her speed under power might be assessed from her tachometer, which shows the engine's revolutions per minute (rpm). Of course, trial runs at various rpm's will have to be made over a *measured mile* (markers or ranges that are exactly one mile apart) or a known distance between buoys or markers. In the latter case, the distance should be one that is easy to work with, perhaps a distance that is to the exact tenth of a mile and no longer than one mile nor less than four-tenths of a mile. Current, waves, and wind will very much affect the accuracy of this method of determining speed; therefore it is usually desirable to make each run (at each rpm for which speed is to be calculated) both ways (first in one direction between the markers and then in the other direction). Then the speed each way is calculated and the two speeds are averaged. With a sufficient number of speed determinations over a wide range of engine revolutions, a speed curve can be drawn on graph paper to show speed at all rpm's. When the boat has no tachometer, it may be possible to estimate her speed in a very approximate way by listening for certain vibrations that occur at particular speeds or by studying the wake or by noticing how the dinghy behaves when it is being towed. Speed also may be determined by throwing a floating object such as a chip of wood off the bow and timing with a stopwatch how long it takes the object to reach the stern.

Many authorities say that the term *dead reckoning* is derived from "ded" (short for *deduced*) reckoning, but Bowditch tells us that the expression is probably derived from the word *dead*, meaning stationary, and that it is reckoning relative to an object stationary in the water and therefore pertains to speed and courses through the water (not over the ground). For all practical purposes, however, we are concerned with distance and direction over the ground,

FIGURE 8-9: BOW-BEAM BEARING

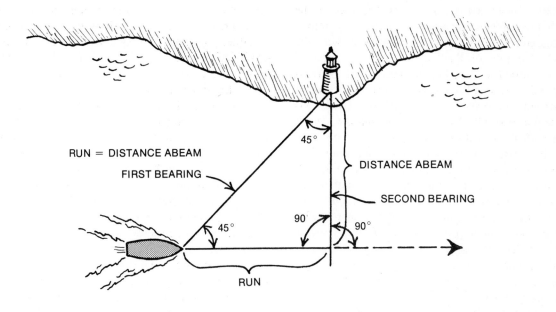

RUN = DISTANCE ABEAM

FIRST BEARING

DISTANCE ABEAM

SECOND BEARING

45°

45°

90°

90°

RUN

FIGURE 8-10: DOUBLING THE ANGLE ON THE BOW

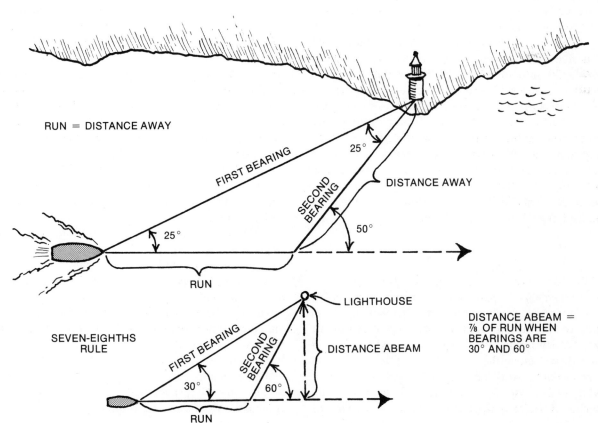

RUN = DISTANCE AWAY

FIRST BEARING

SECOND BEARING

25°

DISTANCE AWAY

25°

50°

RUN

SEVEN-EIGHTHS RULE

FIRST BEARING

SECOND BEARING

LIGHTHOUSE

DISTANCE ABEAM

30°

60°

RUN

DISTANCE ABEAM = ⅞ OF RUN WHEN BEARINGS ARE 30° AND 60°

and therefore allowance must be made for the effects of leeway and current.

Speed and direction of tidal currents can be obtained from the current tables as described in the last chapter. When the boat heads directly into a foul current or heads directly downstream with the current, the rate of flow, obviously, is subtracted from or added to the boat's speed, and there is no lateral movement involved. If the boat crosses the current, however, she will be pushed sideways to an extent that will depend on the angle her course makes with the direction of flow. A 90-degree angle (with the current abeam) obviously will cause the greatest lateral movement, while a small angle will cause little movement to the side. The usual means of figuring this is to draw a vector on the chart showing the distance and direction the current will push the boat away from her course, but there is a table called "Ratio of Boat Speed to Current Speed" (found in *Eldridge Tide and Pilot Book* or elsewhere) that permits almost instant figuring of the lateral movement.

A very simple rule of thumb for figuring the number of degrees a boat is deflected when crossing a current is the so-called *60 formula*. Divide the length of the course into 60, multiply this by the distance a beam current sets you, and the result gives the degrees needed to compensate. For example, if you plan to travel due south for 20 miles, and you figure the current will set you east 4 miles, divide 20 into 60, multiply the resulting 3 by 4, and the resulting 12 gives you the number of degrees you must steer west of your heading to make good a southerly course. Of course, this formula only holds true if the current is on the beam, but an approximation of lateral movement can be obtained for a current set that is 45 degrees from the course by multiplying the 60 formula result by two-thirds, or a set that is 30 degrees from the course by multiplying the result by one-half.

Fog Piloting

Fog was discussed in the last chapter, and it was mentioned that in advection fog it may be advisable to hug the shore where the water is relatively warm and is less apt to cool moisture-laden warm air to its dew point. In some areas where fog is prevalent—along the coast of Maine, for instance—lobster pot buoys can be very helpful to the navigator who sticks close to shore. Although some pots are anchored quite far offshore, most are near the

land in about ten feet of water. Be sure to keep the pot buoys between you and the shore, and observe the flow of water around the buoys to determine the direction and strength of the current.

In areas subject to fog, it is essential to have a reliable, adjusted compass with any uncorrected deviation errors posted near the helmsman. If chartering a boat in such areas, be sure to inquire about the deviation from the boat's owner or agent.

When there is fog in the early morning before you have departed from your anchorage or marina, it is often wise to delay getting underway in order to see if the visibility will clear during the heat of the day or until a fresh, fog-dispelling breeze arrives. If it does not clear and you must depart, plan a careful course from one buoy or channel marker to another. Of course, you should try to pass (to leeward if possible) near those that produce sound, such as bells, whistles, or gong buoys. Lighthouses, too, are usually equipped with horns that can be heard from a considerable distance. With the use of dead reckoning, estimate your time of arrival at the sound buoy, and if you do not hear or see it at the estimated time, stop the engine or heave to or perhaps anchor. Listen carefully and then try to determine if there is a current that could have set you off course. Anchoring should enable you to determine the current accurately by watching the flow of water past the boat. Bear in mind that some buoys depend on movement from wave action to produce sound; therefore, they may be difficult to hear in calm weather. Also, sound will not carry well against the wind. In addition, listen for foghorns, engines or bells on vessels, the sound of breakers, and sounds from shore such as automobiles, sirens, or church bells. In timing your DR runs you will find an ordinary cooking timer to be a handy instrument. Simply set the alarm for the time when you expect to spot a buoy, and if nothing is seen or heard at that time, heed the old railroad crossing advice, "stop, look, and listen."

When approaching land, try to pick a bold shore that will be relatively easy to see but one without dangerous outlying ledges or shoals. Near land, smells can be helpful. The odor of factory smoke or automobiles or the smell of pine trees and hayfields can be detected a considerable distance from a windward shore.

There should be *at least* two lookouts on deck, because the helmsman will have his eyes on the compass most of the time. If the fog is low, a lookout stationed up the mast may have better visibility, but when the fog is high, the lookout should be stationed as low as possible. A crew member who is not steering should be responsible for manning the horn and giving the proper fog signals. Under sail the horn is sounded at intervals of not more than one minute: when on the starboard tack, one blast; when on the port tack, two blasts in succession; and when with the wind abaft the beam, three blasts in succession. Under power the horn should be sounded at intervals of not more than one minute: a prolonged blast (U.S. Inland Rules). At anchor a bell is rung rapidly for about five seconds at intervals of not more than one minute.

Two commonly used means of finding a boat's position in conditions of poor visibility are with a *chain of soundings* or with a radio direction finder. The former involves soundings at a fixed speed with a lead line or depth sounder taken at regular intervals, perhaps every quarter of a mile on a fairly slow-moving cruiser. A straight line representing the course can be drawn on a piece of tracing paper, and the quarter-mile distances with the recorded water depths are marked along the line. Then lay the tracing paper on the chart in the general area where you think you are, orient the line with your compass course, and shift the paper around until your observed soundings coincide with those on the chart. This method will often work well if the seabed is somewhat irregular. Also, it is sometimes helpful, when the characteristics of the bottom are changeable and you have a flashing light depth sounder, to compare the type of seabed shown on the indicator (as mentioned in Chapter 5) with the type marked on the chart. For example, a soft mud bottom will make a broad echo flash, while a rocky bottom may produce multiple echo flashes. When comparing the water depths on the chart with those shown on the depth sounder, allow for the depth of the transducer below the waterline, and also, of course, allow for the state of the tide.

A generally more reliable means of finding your position is with the use of an RDF when there are sufficient radio beacons in your area. In fact, even one beacon can be helpful to obtain a running fix or a bow-beam bearing or to *home on* (head directly toward slowly). A small cruiser normally will carry a portable receiver that has a rotatable antenna, usually a horizontal bar on top of the set, which is usually called a *loop antenna* (because it was almost always circular on early models). When the antenna is rotated, the radio signal varies in strength so that there is a position where the volume is maximal and another where it is minimal. The latter position, called the *null*, is used to obtain a bearing on the transmitting beacon. An antenna pointer that reads against a 360-degree azimuth scale gives the direction from which the radio signal is coming. The location of the sending beacon can be found on a radio beacon chart included in the *Light Lists*, and its signal is identified by a simple code of dots and dashes. The system of transmission is fully explained in the *Light Lists*.

The 0- and 180-degree marks on the RDF's 360-degree scale are aligned parallel to the boat's keel, and the bearings will be relative to the vessel's bow. Magnetic bearings can be figured by obtaining from the helmsman the boat's compass heading at the exact moment the bearing is taken and adding the heading to the relative bearing. When the addition exceeds 360 degrees, 360 is subtracted, and the result is the bearing from magnetic north. Most of the better RDF sets have a null meter, a visual means of determining the null, which affords greater accuracy than determining the null audibly. Unless the RDF has a special *sensing antenna*, the loop antenna has *180-degree ambiguity*. In other words, there will be a null on the bearing line toward the transmitting station and also in the opposite direction; thus it is sometimes difficult to tell from which side the signal is coming. When in doubt, it may be advisable to head temporarily on a new course that puts the station almost on the beam until a significant change is noted in its bearing. It should then become apparent on which side of you the station is located.

In addition to marine radio beacons, some aeronautical beacons (obtainable from Department of Commerce aeronautical charts) and standard broadcast stations that are not too far inland can be used for radio direction finding. Locations of the latter stations can be obtained from *Coastal Warning Facilities* charts published by the U.S. Department of Commerce (National Ocean and Atmospheric Administration). A few major radio beacons are distance-finding stations that use a sound signal in conjunction with the radio signal in order that a navigator can time the difference between the two signals and thereby calculate how far he is away from the beacon. The time difference in seconds divided by 5.5 will give a close approximation of the distance to the beacon in nautical miles.

Accuracy of RDF navigation will depend on a number of factors—operator skill, the quality of the set, distance away from the beacon, refraction of the radio waves, and deviation. As a general rule, the closer you are to a beacon, the more accurate its bearing will be. Refraction or bending of the waves can be caused by their passing over land or prominent structures or from the atmosphere. In regard to the latter cause, daytime bearings taken well after sunrise and well before sunset are the most accurate. Deviation for an RDF is similar to compass deviation. It is caused by metal objects on board, especially metallic loops formed by rigging, life lines, stanchions, and so on, that interconnect to form a closed continuity of metal. A portable RDF set should always be used in the same location on the boat and in a position, usually fairly elevated, where deviation is minimal. To check for deviation, you should be within sight of a radio beacon and compare its radio bearing with its visual bearing. In some cases it may be advisable to make up a deviation card similar to that used with the compass.

Eyeball Navigation

In clear weather in some parts of the southern United States or in other areas easily accessible from this country, such as the Bahama Islands, it is possible to use what is commonly referred to as *eyeball navigation*. This is a form of pilotage that has to do with judging the water's depth by its appearance, especially its color. Eyeball pilotage is most dependable when the sun is high and when it is behind you. When it is not directly overhead, however, and when the shadow of the boat can be seen on the seabed, the depth of the water can be judged by the distance of the shadow from the boat. This is illustrated in Figure 8-11. In deep water the shadow is farther away from the boat than in shoal water.

Although it takes experience to become a skillful eyeball pilot, the following tips should be helpful to

FIGURE 8-11: JUDGING WATER DEPTH BY BOAT'S SHADOW

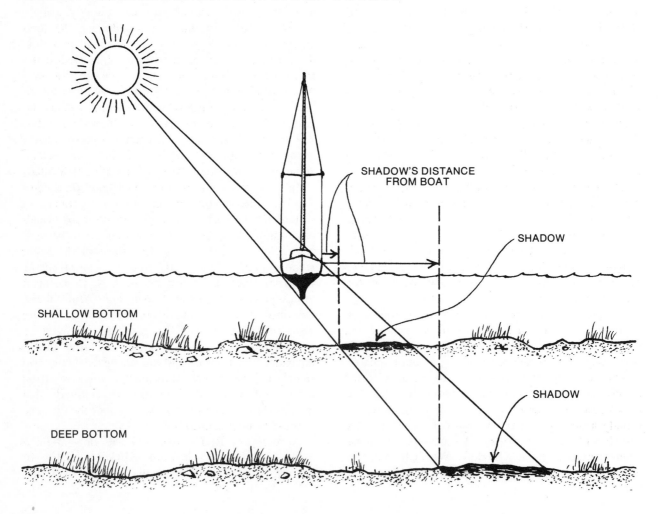

the beginner: Dark colors are generally safe waters, with dark blue being deeper than dark blue green. Dark browns usually indicate rocks or coral heads or possibly certain types of seaweed, but if the color is dark and the dark shape is somewhat indistinct there is probably sufficient water to allow passing over the shape slowly and cautiously. Distinct yellow brown or pale russet brown indicates shallow water over coral or rocks. Whitish green indicates very shallow water over a white sand bottom. Be very cautious when clouds pass in front of the sun, as their shadows completely change the color of the water.

Breakers or steep, choppy waves will usually occur over a submerged rock or shoal, but tide rips will also cause choppy seas. Seaweed often gives a greenish or olive brown cast to the water, and it will usually have a calming effect on the waves. If the weed tops break the surface, the water may appear smooth as a mirror in calm weather. When navigating through very shoal regions, it is advisable to carry a short lead line with markings every foot or a sounding pole similarly marked whether or not there is a depth sounder on board.

U.S. Buoyage Systems

Details of aids to navigation and buoyage systems can be found in Bowditch, the *Light Lists*, Coast Pilots, in the Coast Guard publication *Aids to Marine Navigation of the United States*, or elsewhere. United States buoys and channel markers follow the so-called lateral system recommended by the International Marine Conference of 1889. This is the system often associated with the simple remembrance aid "red right returning." The expression actually means that you leave red markers to starboard and black markers to port when entering a channel or harbor "from seaward." Since all channels do not lead directly from seaward, however, certain arbitrary assumptions are made as follows: From seaward is in a southerly direction along the Atlantic coast, in a northerly and westerly direction along the Gulf coast, in a northerly direction along the Pacific coast, and in a westerly and northerly direction on the Great Lakes (except for Lake Michigan, where the direction is southerly).

The basic U.S. buoy types are shown in Figure 8-12. Notice that the red buoys are marked with even numbers, and black buoys are marked with odd numbers. The numbers increase from seaward with the lowest numbers beginning at the entrance of a

river, bay, or channel. To facilitate recognition, certain unlighted buoys are given distinctive shapes in the form of cylinders or inverted cones. The former are called *cans*, and when they are painted a solid color (without bands or stripes), they are black. The conical buoys are called *nuns*, and when they are a solid color, they are red. Buoys having horizontal bands of red and black are *junction* or *obstruction* markers (or *middle ground markers*) and, as their name implies, they mark obstructions or junctions in channels. These buoys can be passed on either side, but they should be given a fairly wide berth. The color of the topmost band indicates the side on which the preferred channel lies. If a junction buoy has a top band of red, the preferred channel lies to port when returning, and the buoy might be a nun; but a black top band would indicate the preferred channel is to starboard, and the buoy might be a can. Mid-channel buoys are those having black and white vertical stripes. They mark the fairway or middle of a channel, and they can be passed moderately close aboard on either side. (The Code of Federal Regulations recently has been revised to delete from the regulation concerning mid-channel buoys the words "and should be passed close to on either side.") A buoy is marked on the chart with an elongated diamond shape above a dot that pinpoints the buoy's exact location. It should be kept in mind, however, that the location is subject to very slight changes because an anchor chain cannot hold a buoy completely stationary in a strong wind or current. Also, buoys have been known to drag their anchors on rare occasions. During the boating season they are most apt to be out of position after severe storms.

Some typical sound and lighted buoys are shown in Figure 8-13. Red lights are on red buoys or junction buoys having a red top band, while green lights are on black buoys or junction buoys having a black top band. White lights are used on buoys of any color. Unless lights are fixed (steady) on red and black buoys, they will regularly flash or *occult* (show a steady light totally eclipsed at intervals). A quick flash warns navigators to be especially cautious. An interrupted quick flashing light is used on a junction or obstruction buoy, while a short-long flashing white light is used on a mid-channel buoy.

Some variations on the U.S. buoyage system occur on western rivers, in intracoastal waterways, and in areas where uniform state markers are used. When these areas are cruised, details of their markers should

FIGURE 8-12: U.S. BUOY SYSTEM

FIGURE 8-13: EXAMPLES OF SOUND & LIGHTED BUOYS

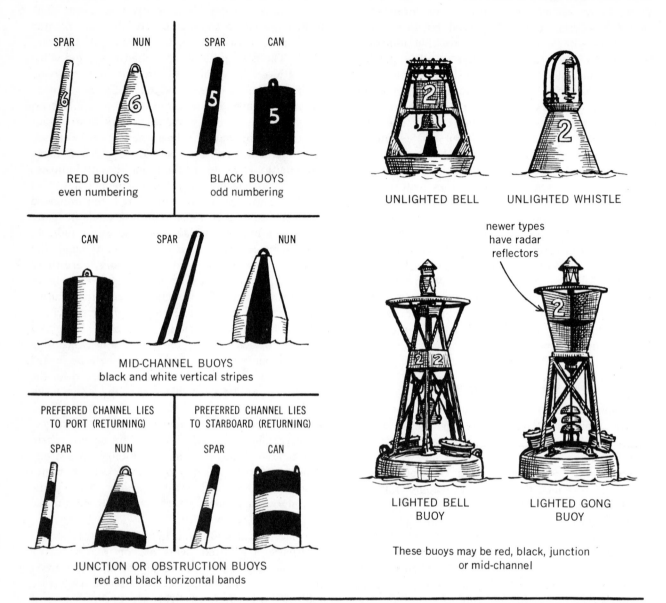

SPAR   NUN

SPAR   CAN

RED BUOYS
even numbering

BLACK BUOYS
odd numbering

CAN   SPAR   NUN

MID-CHANNEL BUOYS
black and white vertical stripes

PREFERRED CHANNEL LIES
TO PORT (RETURNING)

PREFERRED CHANNEL LIES
TO STARBOARD (RETURNING)

SPAR   NUN

SPAR   CAN

JUNCTION OR OBSTRUCTION BUOYS
red and black horizontal bands

UNLIGHTED BELL   UNLIGHTED WHISTLE

newer types
have radar
reflectors

LIGHTED BELL
BUOY

LIGHTED GONG
BUOY

These buoys may be red, black, junction
or mid-channel

NOTE: In addition to the above federal markers there are Intracoastal Waterway markers (along the Atlantic and Gulf coasts) and state markers within certain state areas (such as crowded inlets and lakes). However these marker systems are generally compatible. **Refer to text.**

Intracoastal Waterway aids to navigation are distinguished by a special yellow border or other yellow mark. On this waterway, black markers are on the port and red markers on the starboard side of the channel entering from north and east and traversed to south and west respectively.

State "Regulatory Markers" use international orange geometric shapes with a white background on a sign or buoy. They are as follows:

UNIFORM STATE REGULATORY MARKERS

COLOR OF SHAPE—INTERNATIONAL ORANGE. BACKGROUND—WHITE. Diamond with cross means BOATS KEEP OUT! Diamond shape warns of DANGER! Specific danger (such as rock) is usually lettered inside the diamond. Circle marks CONTROLLED AREA such as a speed limit (6 knots for example). Square or rectangle gives INFORMATION such as the availability of gas.

be studied in local chart books, *Light Lists*, or in the previously mentioned *Aids to Marine Navigation of the United States*. Intracoastal waterway markers and buoys have yellow borders or other yellow marks. On these waterways you leave black markers to port and red markers to starboard when entering from north and east, proceeding to south and west. Occasionally, there is a conflict between the intracoastal waterway system and conventional U.S. buoyage when the intracoastal coincides with a river or other body of water leading from the open sea. In this case, the markers or buoys are marked with yellow triangles or squares. A yellow square means that you must leave the marker to port and a yellow triangle means that you should leave it to starboard when following the intracoastal waterway from north to south on the Atlantic coast and from east to west on the Gulf coast. If you are not following the intracoastal waterway, however, disregard the yellow triangles and squares and be governed by the color and shape of the buoy in accordance with the conventional U.S. lateral system.

Uniform state aids to navigation are used on inland waterways such as lakes that are not under federal control. Black- or red-topped buoys signify that a cardinal system is used: A boat should pass to the north or east of a white buoy with a black top, and to the south or west of a white buoy with a red top. A white buoy with red stripes indicates that the boat should not pass between the buoy and the nearest shore. A boat leaves a solid black buoy to port and a solid red buoy to starboard when headed upstream. Uniform state regulatory markers, giving warnings or information, use orange colored geometric symbols on white buoys or markers. These are shown at the bottom of Figures 8-12 and 8-13.

It should be mentioned that many foreign waters are marked with an entirely different buoyage system. For instance, many European countries use the Uniform System of 1936 (recommended by a League of Nations subcommittee). Under this system, the navigator should think "black right returning." Also, can-shaped buoys are red, while nun-shaped buoys are black.

The best general advice that can be given in regard to understanding a particular marker or group of markers is to study your chart constantly. Sometimes channels can be followed by steering direct courses from one marker or buoy to the next, while at other times the same kind of markers should be given a fairly wide berth, and the course

from one marker to the next must be a slightly S-curved course. When any ambiguity of this kind exists, however, a quick glance at the chart will nearly always clear up the matter.

Grounding

Faulty navigation sometimes leads to running aground. In protected waters where the seabed is soft, grounding is seldom dangerous, but extra care with piloting must be taken when the bottom is hard and when there are rough seas or groundswells. Be especially cautious when the tide is high, because a grounding might leave the boat stranded for half a day or perhaps longer when the tides are diurnal. Obviously, it makes sense to proceed very slowly in conditions of poor visibility and when there is any uncertainty about the navigation.

A few simple hints for extricating a boat after she has grounded are as follows:

● When the keel touches the bottom, turn the helm immediately so that the boat heads for the nearest accessible deep water.

● If under sail, closehauled or reaching, try to come about at once and back the jib to help bring the boat around on the other tack.

● Should the tack fail due to the boat's stopping abruptly, lower sails immediately to avoid being driven further aground.

● If the tack is successful and you know you are headed for deeper water, trim sheets to encourage heeling, start the engine, and drive the boat forward under power if you have grounded on a soft bottom. Be sure, however, that the engine's water intake is submerged and that no large amounts of sediment from the bottom are being stirred up which could be sucked into the cooling system.

● In some instances, when the boat has not been turned after grounding, she might be backed off under power (with sails lowered) while the crew stands on the bow if the deepest part of the keel is aft. Be sure the rudder and propeller are free.

● It is sometimes possible to break the suction of a keel embedded in a soft bottom by rolling the boat from side to side.

● After grounding on a hard bottom, inspect the bilge to be sure the boat has not been holed. Should she be leaking badly, leave her where she is until all holes can be plugged, because if she is extricated, she could sink in deep water.

● When initial efforts to free the boat have failed, study the charts carefully and sound from the dinghy to determine exactly where the deep water is located.

● The boat might be pivoted and/or pulled toward deep water by kedging (putting out an anchor and hauling on its line).

● The kedge anchor can be carried out in the dinghy, or in some cases a small, lightweight anchor can be thrown far enough to allow kedging.

● A tackle, windlass, or large winch can be utilized to increase power on the kedge line.

● Heeling the boat to reduce her draft might be accomplished (1) with sails, (2) by putting weight on the end of the main boom, which is swung broad off, or (3) by careening (heeling) the boat with a halyard. Be sure the halyard block is on a swivel that can accept a lateral strain.

● When the boat is a centerboarder, her board should be fully retracted.

● If the boat still cannot be freed, wait for a rise in tide or hail a tow boat.

● When being pulled off by a tow boat, stand well clear of the tow line under strain, see that it is secured to a heavy bitt or through-bolted cleat, or perhaps secure the line around the base of the forward mast. If the line will be under very considerable strain and the strength of the towing cleat or the boat herself is questionable, attach the tow line to a bridle that runs entirely around the hull.

● Should you be in an area where there is a considerable range in tide, take care that the boat does not fall over on her side when she is left high and dry. She should either be shored up with wood props or be fitted with numerous fenders and padding on her low side and be allowed to heel gradually as the tide falls until she rests on her padded side.

An attempt to free a grounded sloop by inducing a heel. Notice that the dinghy has been brought up short to prevent her painter from fouling the propeller.

9

Cruising Rigs and
Sailing Short-Handed

Although not all sailors agree precisely on the best rig for cruising, most will concur on the basic premise that the ideal rig should supply the greatest power for the least amount of effort. In fact, a cruiser's sail plan should be almost as powerful as a racer's but much easier to handle. The average cruising skipper wants speed for the most sailing pleasure and for maximum efficiency in reaching his destination, yet he must be able to manage his boat easily when short-handed, because very often he may be off with his wife alone, with young children and wife, or with inexperienced guests.

Popular Cruising Rigs

To achieve reasonable speed, of course, the cruiser needs a large sail plan, especially if the boat is heavy, because a smart sailer requires a high ratio of sail area to displacement. For ease of handling, however, a large boat's rig should be divided into several sails of a manageable size. The most popular divided sail plans are the sloop, cutter, yawl, and ketch rigs. The schooner, so common in former times, has lost much popularity, partly because of its inefficiency over the modern racecourse and partly because it is a complicated rig requiring a relatively large crew.

The sloop has its working sails divided into only two components, mainsail and jib, as opposed to the other popular rigs, which are divided into three sails; therefore, it is generally appropriate to rig smaller size cruisers as sloops. The two-sail combination provides great efficiency when beating or close reaching, which is highly desirable, of course, as long as neither sail is too large to handle with ease.

The ketch rig may be most appropriate for a large cruiser, because this plan divides the sail area into three working sails of somewhat equivalent size so

that the largest, the mainsail, will not need to be excessively large, ensuring easy management without sacrifice to the total sail area. Then, too, a well-designed ketch is easily balanced—that is to say, weather or lee helm can be alleviated by altering the trim of the jib and mizzen. Good balance also can be maintained with a minimum of difficulty in heavy weather (more will be said of this a bit later). A major drawback of the ketch rig, however, is that aerodynamic efficiency is sacrificed when closehauled, because on this point of sailing, the large mizzen is severely backwinded by the mainsail.

For a medium-sized cruiser, a yawl rig may be very appropriate, for this rig is a sort of compromise between the sloop and the ketch. The faults and advantages of both the latter rigs are shared by the yawl but to a lesser degree. A cruising yawl's mainsail, being moderate in size, is generally handier than a sloop's but not so handy as a ketch's, while the mainsail's backwind against the mizzen hampers a yawl's speed to windward only slightly, because her mizzen is relatively small, and its function when beating is primarily to balance rather than to supply forward thrust.

For a medium- to large-sized cruiser, the cutter rig has quite a few advantages, because the rig is divided into three sails without the need for more than one mast. Of course, extra masts mean extra sails, spars, and rigging to buy and maintain. Also, the cutter's mast is nearly amidships, where it concentrates weight near the boat's center to minimize hobbyhorsing and where there is maximum beam for efficient staying of the mast and a wide, relatively stable platform for crew safety when they are forward handling sails. If the cutter's main boom is not extremely long, she should balance quite well in moderate winds under mainsail and a large fore staysail, an easily manageable rig, and in a sudden squall she should balance well enough under the fore staysail alone (see Figure 9-1). In light airs, of course, she can carry a large masthead reaching jib or Genoa or a large jib topsail and the fore staysail. For ease of carrying large overlapping jibs, however, the cutter's forestay should be quite far abaft the headstay, and it may be advisable to have the forestay detachable so that it can be brought back to the mast or shrouds to facilitate coming about with the Genoa or reacher set.

With any of the popular cruising rigs, it is highly desirable that the mainsail be small enough for one person to handle with reasonable ease, but, in my

127

FIGURE 9-1: BALANCE WITH REDUCED SAIL

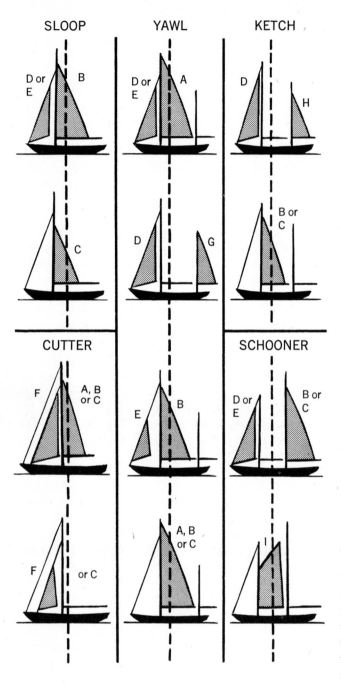

BROKEN LINES ARE TOTAL CENTER OF EFFORT UNDER FULL SAIL

A. full mainsail B. reefed main C. deeply reefed main D. jib
E. storm jib F. staysail G. mizzen H. reefed mizzen I. foresail

NOTE: Refer to the text for preferable reduced sail combinations.

opinion, it should not be so small that the boat cannot be sailed under mainsail alone. There are many times when you might want sail power and maneuverability with only the mainsail hoisted. Suppose, for example, that you are sailing up to your mooring in a crowded harbor. A flapping jib might interfere with picking up the float, and you may get slime or mud from the mooring line on your headsail when it is lowered. In most cases I think it is easier to enter a harbor or get underway with a minimum of effort and confusion and a maximum of visibility with the headsail lowered, provided, of course, the boat is maneuverable under mainsail alone.

Sail Selection

A boat used only for cruising in protected waters will not need as many sails as a completely equipped racer. In fact, carrying more sails than needed will waste valuable stowage space. However, if long coastal or offshore passages are planned, extra sails, especially those intended for heavy weather, should be aboard every well-found cruiser.

The minimum number of sails needed for a sloop used only for gunkhole cruising would be a mainsail, a working jib, and a large overlapping headsail to supply power in light to medium winds. The latter might be a reaching jib with a high clew that can be trimmed at certain times from the end of the main boom, or it can be what might be called a cruising Genoa. As opposed to a racing Genoa, the cruising version should have a *tack pendant* (a short wire strap at the tack) to raise the foot fairly high off the deck to prevent the sail from scooping up water and to provide good visibility. I would suggest that its cloth (Dacron) be of fairly heavy weight and that it have a slightly *hollow leech* (a reverse roach, having a concave curve) to minimize leech flutter in a fresh breeze. If the sail will never be used for racing, it might be helpful to have two or three short plastic battens sewn into the leech (Genoa battens are not allowed by racing rules). Many racing sails are treated with a plastic filler to minimize stretch, but this makes the sails stiff and difficult to handle. For a nonracing cruiser I would order sails of unfilled, soft Dacron; for if they are properly made, stretch will not be a serious problem, and the sails will not only be easier to manage, but they will take up less stowage space.

Working jibs vary in concept, but my own idea is a fairly large jib with a long luff, perhaps about

A 24-foot Sparkman & Stephens-designed ''Dolphin'' that seems to have her sail well matched for the breeze as evidenced by her speed, angle of heel, and good balance (note the helmsman's casual manner of steering).

four-fifths to five-sixths of the length of the head-stay. When the jib is boomless there usually should be a little overlap, because this helps control the leech and creates an effective slot between the jib and mainsail. I would suggest sewn-in plastic battens and very definitely a *head pendant* (a length of wire shackled to the head of the jib) for the purpose of keeping at least three turns of wire on the halyard winch when the halyard is composed of part wire and part rope. Without the pendant, the halyard's wire part usually will not reach the winch, and thus strength and stretch resistance will be sacrificed. Of course, the foot of the working jib also should be cut high for protection from the bow wave and to afford good visibility.

Special purpose sails that can be very useful at certain times are the spinnaker, drifter, mizzen staysail, storm trysail, and spitfire (storm jib). If you can afford it, I would certainly recommend a parachute spinnaker. It is fun to handle, and it supplies tremendous power when reaching and running in light to moderate winds. The sail itself is not unreasonably expensive, but it does require a lot of extra gear. For cruising only, I would suggest a spinnaker of medium-weight nylon, perhaps 1.2 ounces, without excessively wide *shoulders* (broad girth aloft). The drifter is a large, lightweight, full-cut jib used for close reaching or sailing closehauled in very light airs. It is usually made of the lightest weight Dacron and is *set flying*—that is to say, it has a wire luff and only one hank at the head. The mizzen staysail, which is set forward of the mizzen-mast on a yawl or ketch, can be a handy means of setting a considerable amount of extra sail when broad reaching on a ketch, but, in my opinion, the sail is little more than a frill on the typical modern yawl with its very short mizzenmast.

Storm sails may not be essential for a gunkhole cruiser that will never venture from protected waters, provided the boat has an effective means of reefing, but for offshore work or any extended passage-making the boat should have a spitfire and storm trysail or small storm mainsail. The spitfire is a small, flat, high-cut jib of fairly heavy weight and strong construction. It, too, should have a tack pendant to keep the foot high and a long head pendant to keep the wire portion of a wire and rope halyard on the winch. The head pendant should have one or two hanks to keep it close to the jib stay, especially at the top of the pendant. The storm trysail replaces the mainsail in very heavy weather. A typical modern trysail is bent to the mast with slides on a track (in most cases on the main-sail's track), and its head goes about as high as or slightly higher than midmast spreaders, where normally there is secured a set of lower shrouds leading slightly forward of the mast, counteracting the aftward pull of the trysail's head. The sail is cut very flat, and it can be sheeted to the end of the main boom or to either side deck opposite the cockpit. When the sail is sheeted to the boom, there should be a topping lift to help support the boom.

When ordering cruising sails, be sure to insist that they be given the same care in manufacture as racing sails. They should not only be strong and well constructed, but they should have proper draft curves, be free of wrinkles and *hard spots* (unwanted flat areas), and set as perfectly as sails intended for the keenest competition. All the sails discussed are illustrated in Figure 9-2.

Trouble-Free Rigging

Some important safety features of the rig frequently lacking on stock boats include:

• Adequate support under a deck-stepped mast. There should be a pipe or a sturdy post under such a step.

• Double lower shrouds widely spaced in the fore and aft direction to adequately support the mast and hold it steady in a seaway.

• Rigging toggles on all shrouds and stays. A toggle supplies a universal joint between the chain-plate and turnbuckle and prevents the latter from becoming fatigued.

• The main boom sufficiently short to be well clear of the permanent backstay and high enough to clear the heads of crew standing in the cockpit (except, perhaps, on very small cruisers).

• Upper shroud angles (those between the mast and the upper shrouds where they attach to the mast) of at least 12 degrees to minimize compression on the mast.

• Spreader sockets (where the spreaders join the mast) of ample strength. There have been a number of failures of aluminum sockets; therefore, those made of stainless steel are generally preferable. When the mast is aluminum, however, it is safest to have a barrier material such as plastic tape between the socket and mast to prevent the possibility of galvanic corrosion.

• A proper topping lift to support the main boom (instead of the usual strop attached to the permanent backstay). A topping lift from the end of the boom

FIGURE 9-2:
CRUISING
SAILS

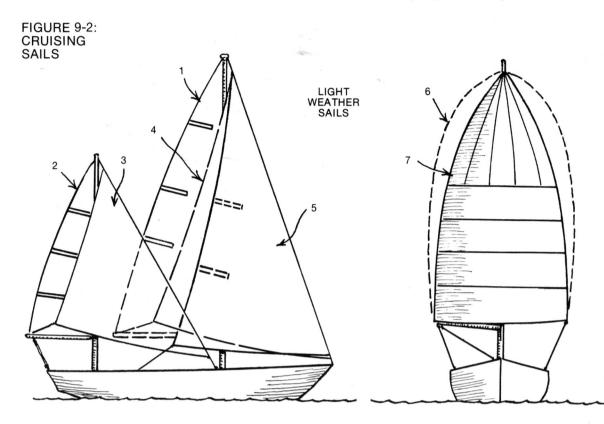

LIGHT
WEATHER
SAILS

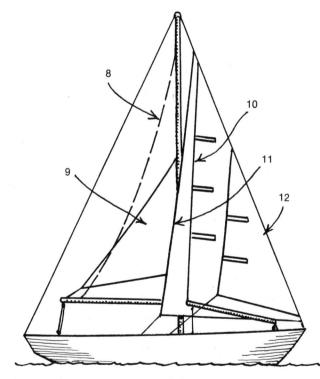

HEAVY WEATHER SAILS

1 MAINSAIL

2 MIZZEN (preferably with
full-length battens to
minimize mainsail's backwind)

3 MIZZEN STAYSAIL

4 DRIFTER OR REACHING JIB

5 CRUISING GENOA (short plastic
battens may be used if there is
no problem from their striking the
mast when tacking)

6 LIGHT AIR RACING SPINNAKER

7 CRUISING SPINNAKER

8 STORM MAINSAIL (sometimes
called a SWEDISH MAINSAIL)

9 STORM TRYSAIL

10 WORKING JIB (with boom)

11 WORKING JIB (loose-footed,
sometimes called a LAPPER)

12 SPITFIRE (STORM JIB)

to the masthead, preferably controllable at the mast so that the boom can be raised or lowered when it is broad off, permits the sail to be hoisted or lowered without need for the boat to be headed directly into the wind. The masthead lift also alleviates backstay stress, allows topping up of the boom, gives support to a reefed sail or storm trysail secured to the boom, and serves as an emergency halyard (when the lift is controllable at the mast).

• Masthead flotation on capsizable cruisers such as multihulls to prevent the possibility of turning turtle. The flotation tank should be streamlined to minimize windage.

• Cotter pins in lieu of lock nuts on turnbuckles. On racing boats, lock nuts are sometimes used (to prevent turnbuckles from coming unscrewed) in order to facilitate changing shroud or stay tension, but on a cruising boat, tension is seldom changed during the sailing season, and so the more reliable cotter pins are preferable, but they should be covered with tape (or otherwise covered) to prevent them from snagging and tearing sails.

• Fairleads on the mast for wire halyards to prevent them from jumping out of their sheaves and jamming.

• Shroud rollers to prevent chafe on jib sheets, and rollers or pads on the spreader tips to prevent chafe on large overlapping jibs.

• Stops at the end of all traveler tracks to prevent their slides from coming off.

• Cleats placed so that their axes make a slight angle with the direction of a line's pull to prevent jamming.

• All fittings through-bolted and with backing blocks whenever possible.

• Blocks of a proper size for their rope or wire and fitted with swivels when the direction of their lines' pull causes a twisting force.

• Ample size and strength to fittings and rigging, especially on nonracing cruisers, which need not be overly concerned about weight and windage aloft.

On cruising boats that are raced, the rigging is usually set up quite taut, especially the stays for optimal performance to windward, but I believe nonracing cruisers should carry their rigging less taut to avoid stressing the hull and to minimize high compression loads on the mast. The rigging should not be slack, however. It should be sufficiently snug to firmly support the mast and prevent its getting out of column or whipping excessively in rough seas. With modern, lightweight, thin-walled aluminum masts found on most stock boats, I think it is important to set up the shrouds and stays so that the mast is held as steady and straight as possible under all sailing conditions but without excessive rigging tension.

Labor-Saving Gear and Sail Reduction

The handling of a cruising rig is facilitated not only by having sails of a manageable size and proportion but also by the use of labor-saving systems. Some of these systems are not used on racing boats, because they often result in a slight loss in speed, but it is surprising to see the number of boats that never will be sailed in competition that lack the labor-savers. A prime example is the self-attending jib shown in Figure 9-3. This kind of jib is fitted with a boom and traveler so that the jib sheet need not be touched when the boat is tacked. The particular rig illustrated permits removal of the jib boom in order to keep the foredeck clear when a larger, overlapping jib with double sheets is used. The traveler might be a track and slide secured to the deck, or it might be a removable wire cable instead of the old-fashioned *horse* (bar traveler) illustrated.

Although a boomed jib usually does not allow the precision and versatility of trim possible with a loose-footed jib having double sheets, there is a trimming advantage with the type of boom that has its forward end located slightly abaft the jib tack. As the sheet is eased, the jib is given an increasing amount of draft or camber, because the distance from tack to clew is considerably greater when the sail is closehauled than when broad off. This point is illustrated in Figure 9-4. If the clew of the boomed jib is very high, the boom may ride up and twist the sail when the sheet is eased; thus a high-cut jib may need to have the forward end of its boom mounted on a *pedestal* (a stand, often with a pipe base, for raising the height of a fitting). Most probably the pedestal will have to be permanently through-bolted to the deck or otherwise permanently secured, which means it will clutter up the deck to some extent, but at least it affords a good point of attachment for the forward sheet block.

A real boon to the inland and coastal cruising sailor is *roller furling*. This is a means of reducing the area of a sail (usually a headsail) or furling it entirely by winding it up on its luff. The sail is sewn on a luff wire or rod that is rotated by pulling on a furling line wound around a drum just below the tack (see Figure 9-5). The rolled-up sail is unfurled simply by hauling on its sheet and slacking

FIGURE 9-3: SELF-ATTENDING JIB

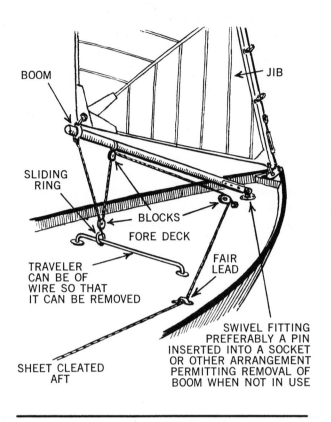

BOOM

JIB

SLIDING RING

BLOCKS

FORE DECK

TRAVELER CAN BE OF WIRE SO THAT IT CAN BE REMOVED

FAIR LEAD

SHEET CLEATED AFT

SWIVEL FITTING PREFERABLY A PIN INSERTED INTO A SOCKET OR OTHER ARRANGEMENT PERMITTING REMOVAL OF BOOM WHEN NOT IN USE

FIGURE 9-4: SHORT JIB BOOM

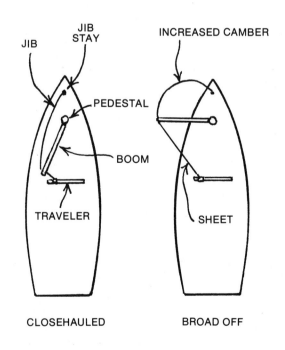

JIB

JIB STAY

INCREASED CAMBER

PEDESTAL

BOOM

TRAVELER

SHEET

CLOSEHAULED

BROAD OFF

the furling line until the desired area is unwound. Both lines can be led back to the cockpit so that the roller sail can be reduced to any area or be completely furled without anyone leaving the cockpit.

This system works very easily and is excellent for cruising in protected waters, but, in my opinion, most standard roller furling gears for jibs have disadvantages for offshore work and racing. For the latter purpose, a rod luff with no headstay is most efficient, but it is risky to depend entirely on the luff's rod as the only means of forward mast support, because rods or their attachment fittings have been known to break. Furthermore, the jib and rod might have to be lowered if the sail should happen to be damaged or blow out. A safer practice is to have a wire luff that is set just behind a permanent headstay as shown in the illustration; for racing, however, there will be considerable sag in the jib's luff in a fresh breeze that will hurt the boat's windward ability. This will not matter on a cruising boat, provided the luff can be made reasonably taut with a large halyard winch; but for lengthy passages offshore with ample crew, specialized individual headsails with sail size, shape, cloth weight, and draft matched to the weather condition for which each sail was designed is better than trying to make one roller furling sail do for all conditions.

Since a roller sail is usually left hoisted (but furled), a small part of it is always exposed to the sun and weather; thus it should be protected with a sail cover, for even Dacron (the synthetic cloth from which most modern sails are made) is subject to sun rot and staining from mildew. A handy means of accomplishing this is to sew a narrow strip of protective cover cloth such as Acrylon to the leech and also to the foot of the sail if it is high cut (see Figure 9-5). If the jib has a luff wire, I would recommend a *twist stopper* or "keeper" (as shown in the illustration) at the head of the sail to prevent the halyard from twisting if the upper swivel should bind when the luff is being rotated. Twisting may also occur when the jib is being hoisted, and this could cause the halyard to foul if it is comprised of a tackle (for extra power) such as the two-part arrangement shown in Figure 9-5.

Roller furling gears are also used on twin headsails for easy downwind sailing. The system was first devised by Otway Waller in 1930, and later improved by Paul Hammond, but it has been further modified, perfected, and standardized by Wright Britton, a well-known offshore sailor and president of Britton Yacht Systems, Inc., who calls the sails

"Roller Jeni Wings." Two identical headsails are sewn on one roller furling luff wire that is tacked down just forward of the mast as shown in Figure 9-6. The sails are held out by poles that have their inboard ends secured to a slide on a mast track. The poles are stowed by sliding their inboard ends up to the top of the track. When sailing downwind, of course, the inboard ends of poles are slid down to the bottom of the track and the twin sails are boomed out on each side of the boat. The sails can be reduced in area for various strengths of wind

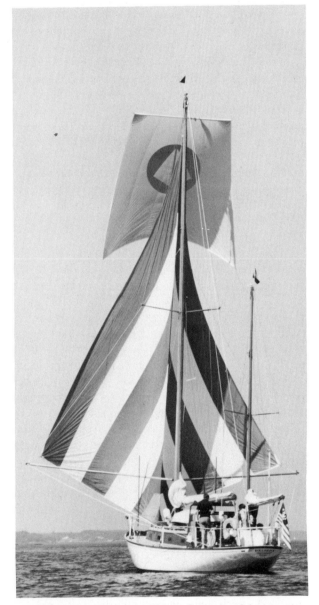

Roller Jeni Wings on Wright Britton's 40-foot yawl, *Delight.* The squaresail, for extra power in light airs, is placed high.

with the roller furling gear. Details of this gear's operation can be obtained from either Britton Yacht Systems (108 East 30th Street, New York, New York 10016) or the well-known firm Ratsey and Lapthorn, which makes the sails.

Roller furling even can be used on mainsails, but this requires a specially cut, loose-footed, high-clewed sail with a luff wire, and the rig lacks the sailing efficiency of a standard mainsail. Nevertheless, such an arrangement is handy and sometimes very suitable for mainsails on motor sailers.

Of course, sails attached to booms also can be reduced with roller reefing—rolling a sail up on its boom rather than on a luff wire. With this arrangement the boom is rotated with a geared mechanism at the gooseneck. Of course, the halyard must be slacked and the sail slides must be slid off their track (or unlaced) as the boom is turned. A few suggestions concerning this system are as follows: The roller mechanism should be the strongest available and the gears housed to protect the sail. There should be a large flange and/or hollow waist around the boom to accept the rolled-up luff and keep it from sliding forward, where it might become jammed in the mechanism. It is preferable that the boom be tapered, having a larger diameter aft than forward to prevent the after end of the boom from drooping excessively when a deep reef is rolled in. Don't rely on a wire-to-rope tail splice in the halyard to support the reefed sail. Use an all-wire halyard on a reel winch, or, if a rope tail is used, see that it is joined to the wire part of the halyard with eye splices.

A labor-saving method of changing sails is with *slide magazines* and *track switches.* Both of these devices are illustrated in Figure 9-7. The magazine is a short channel bar of bronze or stainless steel on which the luff (or foot) slides of an unbent sail are stored. When sail is bent on, the magazine is simply snapped onto the mast just below the sail track, and when sail is hoisted, the slides run out of the magazine onto the track. There is at least one company that makes a magazine for jib hanks. This device is essentially a rod that holds the piston hanks open so that they can run onto the jib's stay when the sail is hoisted. The hank magazine is a handy and fast method of changing to a light- or heavy-weather jib when there is a change in the wind velocity or sea condition. The track switch is used in conjunction with a short section of track secured to the mast alongside the lower part of the mainsail track as shown in the illustration. With this system, a small, heavy-weather mainsail or storm

FIGURE 9-5: ROLLER FURLING

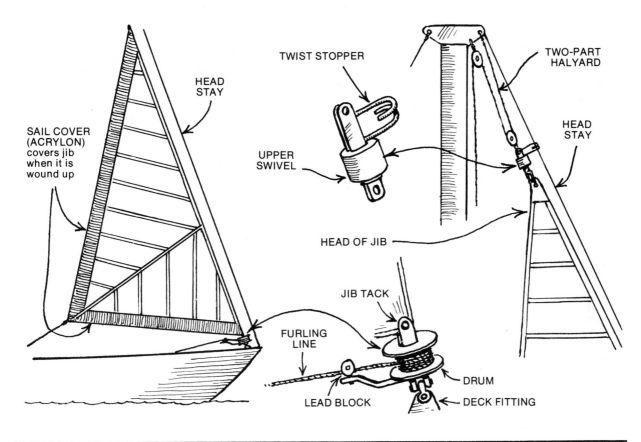

HEAD STAY

TWIST STOPPER

TWO-PART HALYARD

SAIL COVER (ACRYLON) covers jib when it is wound up

UPPER SWIVEL

HEAD STAY

HEAD OF JIB

JIB TACK

FURLING LINE

DRUM

LEAD BLOCK

DECK FITTING

FIGURE 9-6: ROLLER TWINS (THE BRITTON SYSTEM)

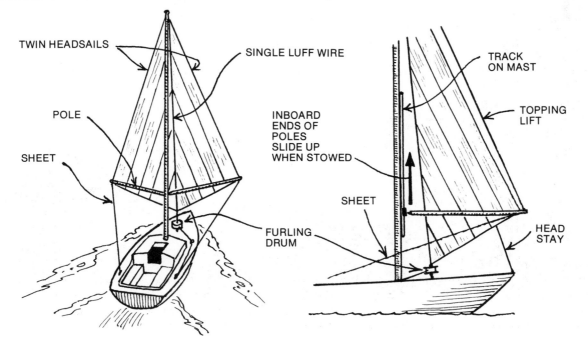

TWIN HEADSAILS

SINGLE LUFF WIRE

TRACK ON MAST

POLE

INBOARD ENDS OF POLES SLIDE UP WHEN STOWED

TOPPING LIFT

SHEET

SHEET

FURLING DRUM

HEAD STAY

trysail can be left bent on the side track. In a blow when there is too much wind for the full mainsail, that sail is lowered, the switch is pushed over to the side track, the halyard is changed, and the smaller sail is hoisted. Of course, this saves the trouble of turning in a deep reef in the full-size mainsail.

While discussing sail reduction, it should be pointed out that reefing or provisions for conveniently changing sails will probably be needed on every cruiser regardless of her rig. Although sail can be reduced with a minimum of effort on a yawl, ketch, or cutter by simply lowering her mainsail in a sudden squall, it is better to carry some sail bent to the after side of the mainmast when beating or close reaching for prolonged periods in a blow with

rough seas. A reefed mainsail, a small storm mainsail, or a storm trysail used with a small, high-cut jib will provide an effective aerodynamic slot for better drive, will centralize the rig while moving the center of effort slightly farther forward of the designed total center of effort (see Figure 9-1) to improve balance when the boat is heeled, and will provide some support for the mast to help prevent it from whipping back and forth when the boat pitches in rough seas. Be sure, however, that the head of the smaller or reduced sail set on the mainmast comes reasonably close to the point of attachment of a forward leading stay or shroud, so that the pull of the head will be counteracted by the forward pull of the stay.

The short jib boom on this Morgan "Out Island 41" not only permits self-tacking but automatically adjusts the sail's camber as the sheet is eased. This boat is a popular tri-cabin, center-cockpit cruiser with a long, shallow keel.

FIGURE 9-7: TRACK SWITCH AND SLIDE MAGAZINE

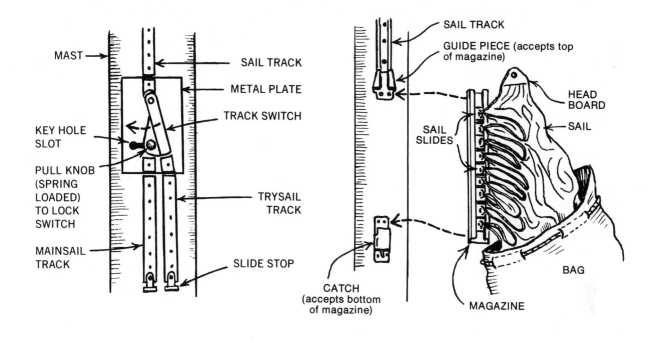

FIGURE 9-8: OLD-FASHIONED LABOR-SAVING DEVICES

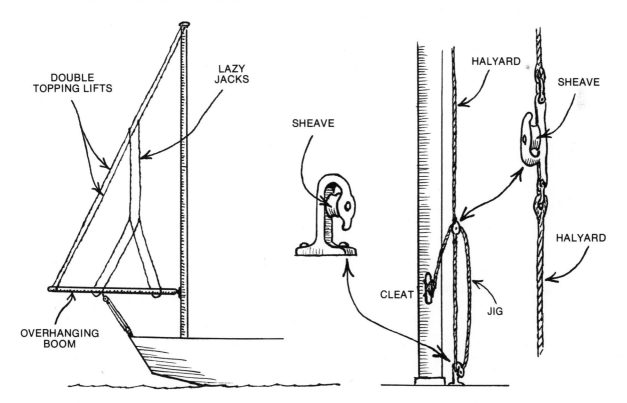

Ancient labor-savers seldom seen on modern boats are *lazy jacks*. Their absence is not really surprising, since they complicate the rig somewhat and cause some chafe and windage. Lazy jacks are lines or parts of lines leading from double topping lifts (see Figure 9-8) or from the mast down to the boom. Their purpose is to hold the sail securely after it has been lowered but prior to furling to prevent the sail from flapping excessively and blowing overboard. This gear can be of great value on old-fashioned boats that have long bowsprits or long booms that overhang at the stern.

Another piece of gear rarely seen on modern boats is a halyard *jig*, an open block spliced onto the halyard in a location slightly above the cleat when the sail is hoisted and another open block mounted on deck at the base of the mast as shown in Figure 9-8. The purpose of this rig is to obviate the need for a halyard winch to tighten the luff. When the sail is almost hoisted (by pulling it up hand-over-hand) and extra power is needed to stretch the luff taut, the bottom part of the halyard is slipped under the deck block, then passed over the block spliced on the halyard, and presto, a purchase or simple tackle is formed. The device normally is used with a rope halyard, and at least the part below the spliced-on block should be rope. Since rope stretches more than wire, jigs are not considered very suitable for racing boats. For cruisers, however, rope halyards of prestretched Dacron, which has relatively little stretch, can be quite satisfactory for mainsails and mizzens.

Sailing in Comfort

Sailing is seldom uncomfortable except in extremely hot weather and in cold and wet heavy weather. In the latter case, the companionway dodger and the weather cloths discussed in Chapter 6 can be invaluable. Of course, the proper clothing mentioned in Chapter 7 can make a big difference in your comfort, too.

In hot weather a Bimini top, described earlier, will provide shade without blocking off the breeze, but a good top may be expensive and somewhat cumbersome. A hot-weather rig I have found very comfortable and fun to handle when the wind is fair is the spinnaker and awning. With this rig, the mainsail is simply lowered, and the regular boat's awning (described in Chapter 6) is set over the main boom so that a large shady area with full standing headroom is provided (see Figure 6-2) and the parachute spinnaker is carried in the customary way. The spinnaker alone drives the boat nearly as fast with the mainsail down. Furthermore, the 'chute is considerably more manageable when there is no mainsail to blanket it. In fact, it is possible to sail by the lee on a broad reach without the 'chute collapsing. Once the sail is properly set and trimmed there is very little to do but steer a straight course or a slightly weaving one in shifty winds.

About the only difficulty you might have with this rig is lowering the sail when short-handed in a freshening breeze. Actually, a medium-weight spinnaker (perhaps 1.2 ounces) can be carried dead downwind in quite a fresh wind, because there is no side force on the sail, and the boat's forward speed is subtracted from the true wind velocity to lessen the apparent wind. But problems can develop when you try to hand the 'chute if there is no other sail set. The solution, of course, is to hoist another sail, the mainsail perhaps, or a large headsail, which will blanket the spinnaker. The boat should be headed off before the wind so that the 'chute will stay well blanketed to make it easier to lower. Details on spinnaker handling can be found in two of the author's earlier books, *Hand, Reef and Steer* and *The Racing-Cruiser*.

Sailing Short-Handed and Simple Self-Steering

As mentioned earlier, most cruising in protected waters is done short-handed. Thus it is important for the skipper to think in terms of self-reliance and to rig his boat so that he can manage her alone or with one other person.

To rig the boat for the simplest management when sailing short-handed, most running rigging should be led to the cockpit, preferably within easy reach of the helmsman. Those lines handled from the cockpit would probably include all sheets, spinnaker gear, and most halyards. Some seamen, however, might prefer that jib halyards be cleated on the mast in order that the man handing the jib can control the halyard as he is lowering and muzzling the sail. This leaves the helmsman free to slack the jib sheet and keep one hand on the helm as the sail is lowered. If the boat is being single-handed without a self-steering rig, steering lines usually can be rigged quite easily by running two light lines from the helm through snatch blocks on each side deck and then leading forward. Of course, this enables the single-hander to steer while he is forward. When he makes a brief trip forward for some purpose other than handing or hoisting a sail, his boat might be balanced well enough by altering sail trim and/or lashing or otherwise securing the helm so that she will sail herself temporarily, thus obviating the need for steering lines. These lines will probably be required, however, if sail is raised or lowered, because this will change the vessel's balance.

The key ingredients for successful short-handed cruising are forethought and preparedness. The skipper must plan far ahead, anticipate problems and requirements, and lay out his gear well in advance of when it will be needed. For instance, the anchor and rode should be in position and ready for use at all times; properly coiled docking lines and fenders ought to be placed where needed well ahead of docking; blocks for steering lines and other purposes should be in position before they are needed; the horn, sail stops, winch handles, and all gear that might be required must be readily available, and the engine should be ready for quick use.

A great boon for those who sail short-handed, especially single-handers, are self-steering systems. Although self-steerers are most useful on long voyages away from crowded waters, they can be useful even on relatively short passages when course changes are infrequent and boat traffic is minimal. It is often convenient for the helmsman to leave the helm unattended so that he can study his chart, attend to some chore on deck, or simply go forward to sit in the shade.

There are all kinds of self-steering methods. Some involve the use of special sails such as the twin wings already mentioned; other systems, commonly called *autopilots*, use helm-controlling electric motors, which are activated by a magnetic compass or a very small metal or plastic wind vane, while still other methods employ large plywood or cloth wind vanes that move the helm mechanically through direct leverage or gears without the help of electric motors. Autopilots can be very expensive, but simple types designed to control the tiller on small- to medium-sized cruisers sell for less than $350. The major drawback of autopilots is their drain on the batteries. The drain may not be great on a well-balanced, easy-steering boat in fair weather and smooth water, but on a lengthy passage, especially if the vessel is poorly balanced or the seas cause her to yaw, the batteries may need charging quite often.

Nonelectronic wind vane steerers save the batteries, but they require at least a gentle breeze, and they will not hold the boat on a compass course unless the wind is unusually steady, because they steer a course that is more or less a constant angle to the apparent wind. These vane steerers come in several different forms. Some have no underwater parts and steer by direct action of the vane acting on the helm, while others have underwater appendages, either in the form of a *servo trim tab* (a small auxiliary rudder hinged to the trailing edge of the main rudder), an extra separate rudder, or an athwartships swinging pendulum that controls the helm.

For large cruisers, especially those making lengthy offshore passages, I would recommend those vane steerers with underwater parts, as they are more powerful and generally more reliable. However, they also are more cumbersome and more difficult to remove entirely when not in use, and they can be quite expensive. A small, well-balanced cruiser can carry a relatively inexpensive and easily removable vane having no underwater parts, but the vane usually must be quite large for sufficient power when its turning axis is vertical. On the other hand,

This gaily decorated wind vane turns on a vertical axis and operates its own rudder blade, which is hoisted as shown to minimize drag when not in use.

if the axis is horizontal the vane can be much smaller, because it gains power through greater leverage. This point is illustrated in Figure 9-9, which shows a vane similar to the British-made QME (Quantock Marine Enterprises) self-steerer. The beauty of this kind of gear is that it is completely removable, and there is no need to leave mounting frames, brackets, or gudgeons that may deface the stern or transom; but, as said before, I don't think a wind vane alone is as reliable for most boats as a well-designed vane with underwater parts.

Our thirty-foot fin-keel cruiser has a QME vane, which came in kit form directly from England and cost a mere $68. The kit can be assembled in a couple of hours by a nonmechanical person such as myself, but the supporting strut will have to be bolted to the afterdeck, lead weights (not included in the kit) must be added, and the vane should be varnished (or painted) soon to inhibit warping. The vane can be removed simply by lifting it out of the supporting strut, and the strut is taken in with very little difficulty by removing two bolts. The strut can be mounted off-center so that the vane will clear the permanent backstay when it tips on its horizontal axis.

To operate the self-steerer, the boat is put on course, and her sails are trimmed so that the helm is well balanced (without weather or lee helm). Then, with a control line, the vane is turned so that its edge is headed into the apparent wind. At this point, the vane will be parallel to the shroud telltales and it will be standing up straight (not tipped over). Next, steering lines, leading from the vane's vertical drum through lead blocks on each

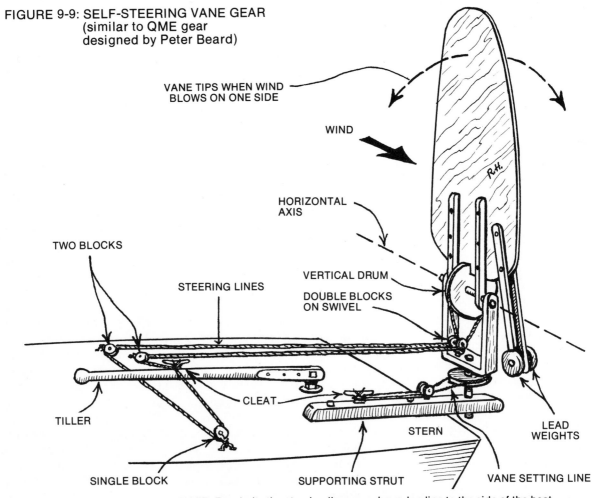

FIGURE 9-9: SELF-STEERING VANE GEAR
(similar to QME gear
designed by Peter Beard)

VANE TIPS WHEN WIND BLOWS ON ONE SIDE

WIND

HORIZONTAL AXIS

TWO BLOCKS

STEERING LINES

VERTICAL DRUM

DOUBLE BLOCKS ON SWIVEL

CLEAT

TILLER

STERN

LEAD WEIGHTS

SINGLE BLOCK

SUPPORTING STRUT

VANE SETTING LINE

NOTE: For clarity the steering lines are shown leading to the side of the boat opposite the supporting strut, but in actual practice the steering lines would probably be led to the side on which the strut is mounted as illustrated in Figure 9-10.

FIGURE 9-10: RIGGING THE VANE GEAR

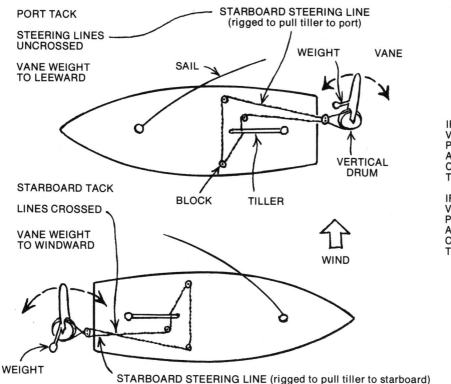

PORT TACK

STEERING LINES UNCROSSED

VANE WEIGHT TO LEEWARD

STARBOARD STEERING LINE (rigged to pull tiller to port)

SAIL

WEIGHT   VANE

VERTICAL DRUM

STARBOARD TACK

LINES CROSSED

VANE WEIGHT TO WINDWARD

BLOCK   TILLER

WIND

WEIGHT

STARBOARD STEERING LINE (rigged to pull tiller to starboard)

IF BOAT LUFFS UP, VANE TIPS AFT, PULLS STBD. LINE AND TILLER UP, CAUSING THE BOAT TO HEAD OFF.

IF BOAT BEARS OFF, VANE TIPS FORWARD, PULLS PORT LINE AND TILLER DOWN, CAUSING THE BOAT TO HEAD UP.

side of the cockpit (as shown in Figure 9-10), are cleated or otherwise secured to the helm while it is positioned to hold the boat on a straight course. At this point, the vane will take over steering. Should the boat begin to luff or bear off, the wind will strike the vane on its side, causing it to tip over. This will cause a pull on the appropriate tiller line, thereby correcting the course.

The vane works quite well on our boat when beating or reaching except in light or extremely variable winds, but I have found that sometimes it takes considerable fiddling with the gear to make it work satisfactorily. Operating instructions are clear in general, but one important point was not clear in my particular set of instructions, which perhaps was intended for a slightly different vane model. The point I had to learn through trial and error was that the steering lines often had to be crossed. On the port tack with the counterbalancing weight to leeward, the steering lines are uncrossed, but on the starboard tack with the weight to windward, the lines must be crossed. This is explained in Figure 9-10. Crossing the lines is accomplished quite

easily with plastic clips that are located near the base of the vane unit. My instructions also failed to specify the weight of the counterbalance, but I found it should be about fourteen pounds, just enough to hold the vane upright when there is no breeze.

Most vane systems will not work well when the wind is dead astern, because in fresh winds, following seas may tend to slew the boat off course, and in moderate to light airs, the boat's speed is subtracted from the true wind's velocity to reduce the strength of the apparent wind. Thus systems using self-steering sails are often most appropriate when the wind is aft. Most methods using two headsails boomed out on opposite sides of the boat work best if the headsail sheets are secured to the tiller as shown in Figure 9-11. The sails steer most effectively if they are angled slightly forward of athwartships—that is to say, when their leeches are slightly forward of their luffs, as illustrated. Then, when the boat yaws off her downwind course, there is greater pressure on the windward sail, and its sheet pulls the helm to windward, thereby causing

FIGURE 9-11: SELF-STEERING SAILS

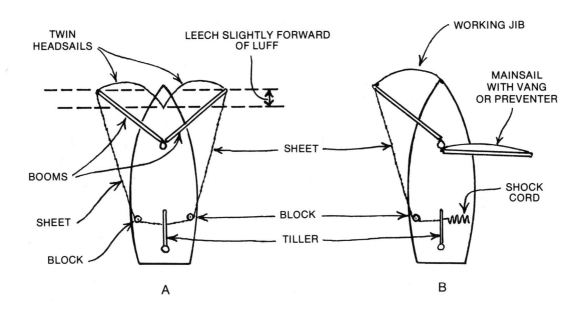

the boat to bear off to her proper course. Wright Britton told me, however, that with his twin wings there is no need to secure the sheets to the helm for self-steering. The sails alone will usually hold the boat on course.

There are some rather complicated ways of rigging self-steering sails and connecting them to the helm, but one simple rig I have used occasionally is illustrated in Figure 9-11, B. This method may not be as effective as twin headsail arrangements, but it requires no extra specialized sails or equipment. The mainsail is carried in the normal way but held forward with a vang or preventer to prevent an all-standing jibe, and a large working jib is boomed out with the spinnaker pole. The jib sheet is led aft to a block on the cockpit coaming and thence to the tiller, where it is secured, as shown in the sketch. On the opposite side of the tiller, a short length of elastic shock cord is used to counteract the sheet's pull.

The system works in the following way: When the boat bears away from her course and sails by the lee, the jib becomes partially blanketed by the mainsail. At this point there is less pull on the sheet and the

shock cord pulls the helm down, which, of course, causes the boat to head up and return to her proper course. When the boat luffs up, however, heading higher than her proper course, the jib fills, and the sheet exerts a greater pull than the shock cord, thereby causing the helm to move to windward, turning the boat back to her original course. Some experimentation will be needed to obtain the correct tension on the shock cord. Tension can be regulated not only by tightening or slacking the cord, but also by changing its position on the tiller. When the cord is fastened near the tiller's forward end, there is greater leverage on the rudder and less tension is required; but if the cord is secured to the tiller's after end, there is less leverage and more tension is required.

The final and most important advice on self-steering and sailing short-handed is: *Don't fail to keep a lookout when the boat is steering herself.* Many collisions and near misses have occurred when helms were unmanned. In crowded waters there should always be someone on deck, and he should look around frequently, because speeding motorboats can converge on his vessel in minutes.

10

Marinas, Yacht Clubs, and Anchorages

In her home port, a cruising boat is usually berthed at a wharf or *slip* (a narrow waterway between wharfs), or she is anchored in a harbor with a permanent-type anchor, commonly called a *mooring*. There are advantages and disadvantages to each system. An offshore mooring affords greater peace and privacy, generally better ventilation, fewer insects, and less danger of marring the topsides; but getting aboard the boat and getting ashore take time, and the convenience of shore electricity must be sacrificed. Ease of boarding and disembarking will depend primarily on the availability and efficiency of *tender service* (ferry service in launches between shore and anchored boats provided by many marinas or yacht clubs). In some places tender service is very good, but there are bound to be times when it is not operating or when crowds cause unavoidable delays; thus it is highly advisable that the owner of a boat moored offshore keep a dinghy ashore so that he will not have to rely on the tender at all times for transportation.

In some popular harbors, conditions are becoming so crowded that boats must be moored from their sterns as well as their bows in order to restrict their swinging to the wind or current. While less desirable than a single bow mooring, it is better than nothing in crowded areas, where the boat owner is lucky to get any kind of berth at all.

Marinas

In this book, a *marina* will be considered a commercial operation open to the public, as opposed to a yacht club, which is a private organization. Some marinas are humble affairs with only simple

A perfect, nearly land-locked harbor with cruising sailboats on permanent moorings.

143

docking facilities, drinking water, and a gas pump or two, but others are quite elaborate, having such facilities as 115-volt shore power, ice machines, toilets, showers, a laundromat, sewage disposal facilities for holding tanks, a small shop selling groceries and boat fittings, and perhaps even a boat repair service, restaurant, cocktail lounge, and swimming pool. Charges for dockage in a typical marina are based on the overall length of the boat, but rates vary according to the location, quality, and extent of the facilities. An average charge for a Long Island Sound marina having ample but modest facilities, for example, might be about twenty-five cents per foot per night at the time of this writing. Most marinas offer special weekly, monthly, or perhaps semiannual rates as well.

When you are off cruising and you wish to enter a strange marina, approach that part of the installation where the *dockmaster* is stationed. The dockmaster, often called *harbormaster* when he is in charge of the whole harbor, is there for the purpose of berthing and servicing boats, enforcing rules, collecting fees, and so forth, and he is generally stationed in a small control shack or office at the end of a pier near the marina's entrance or near the gasoline pumps. He will give you docking directions after he knows the length of your boat, her draft, and how long you want to stay. Sailboats should not stay in front of gas pumps for any longer than necessary, because a great source of profit for most marinas comes from fueling large power boats. During summer holidays or weekends many marinas, especially those near large cities, will be very crowded, making it advisable to make berthing reservations in advance of your cruise, especially if you plan to stay for any length of time.

Before making fast at a strange marina slip or dock, find out the state of the tide and its range in order to determine the amount of slack that should be given to the docking lines and to make sure you will not become grounded when the tide falls. Figure 10-1 shows the dock lines used when lying alongside a pier. The breast lines (shown as dashes) running out abeam of the boat are seldom needed. In fact, they should not be used if they cannot be tended (periodically slacked or tightened) when there is an extreme range in the tide, because a change in tide could cause the lines to break, hang or heel the boat, or pull off the cleats. Breast lines do serve the function of holding the boat close to the dock, but in many cases, if the stern has a tendency to swing out, the stern line may be led through a centerline chock as shown in Figure 10-1, or it may be secured to the outboard corner of the transom, helping hold the stern in. When there is a considerable range in the tide, the dock lines should be led far forward and aft from their point of attachment on the boat to the place where they are secured on the dock in order that the lines will need little if any slacking as the tide falls. This point is illustrated in Figure 10-2. Notice that an extremely low tide will stretch a bow line secured to the dock far ahead of the bow no more than a moderately low tide will stretch a bow line when it is secured only slightly forward of the bow. In other words, the slack needed for the bow line for boat A is the same as for boat B, despite the greater drop in tide in the case of A. Spring lines (shown in Figure 10-1), which prevent forward and backward drift, may not be needed when the bow and stern lines are led far forward and aft if the boat is secured for only a brief period of time and there will be someone on board at all times.

While she is secured alongside a dock or pier, the boat must be well protected with fenders. Most marinas have some form of chafe protection fastened to their docks or slip pilings, but the protection may be inadequate or worn or may leave marks on the topsides. When mooring alongside a dock with pilings, the boat's fenders will usually roll off the pilings, or the boat will drift forward or backward slightly so that the fenders will not make contact with the pilings. One solution is to use a fender board, a plank hung horizontally over the topsides, resting against two fenders hung from the boat. An even simpler solution is to make the fenders fast around the offending pilings, but you must be careful not to leave your fenders behind when you depart. Also beware of getting tar or creosote on your fenders and lines.

Slips present quite a different docking problem. The boat is made fast by four lines—bow and stern lines on both the port and starboard sides. Thus she can be held away from dock walls and pilings, and there is no need for fenders. The difficulty with this type of berth, however, is maneuvering an auxiliary sailboat in and out of the slip. The average sailboat is most easily berthed by going into the slip bow first and then leaving stern first, but if there are no side docks, the crew must leave the boat and reboard her over the bow. This is not as easy as leaving and boarding over the stern; therefore, many skippers prefer to back their boats into their slips. When there is little wind and current, backing in is no problem.

FIGURE 10-1: DOCK LINES

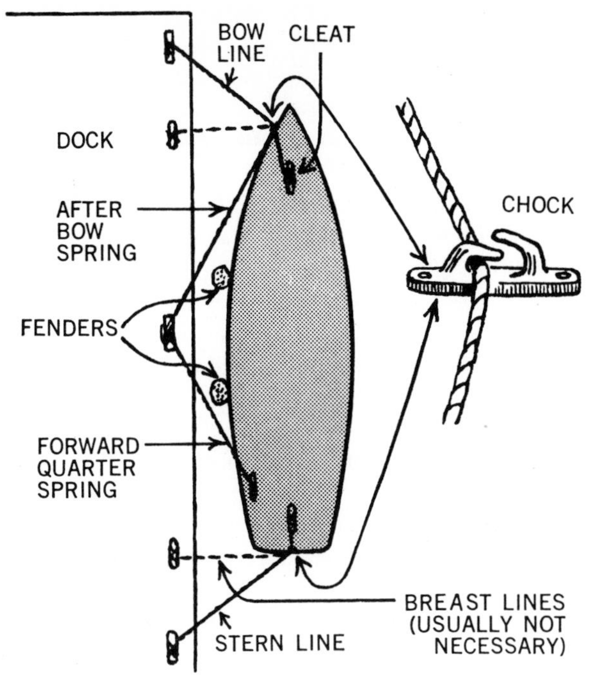

BOW LINE

CLEAT

DOCK

AFTER BOW SPRING

FENDERS

FORWARD QUARTER SPRING

CHOCK

STERN LINE

BREAST LINES (USUALLY NOT NECESSARY)

FIGURE 10-3: MANEUVERING AN AUXILIARY INTO A SLIP WITH A CROSSWIND

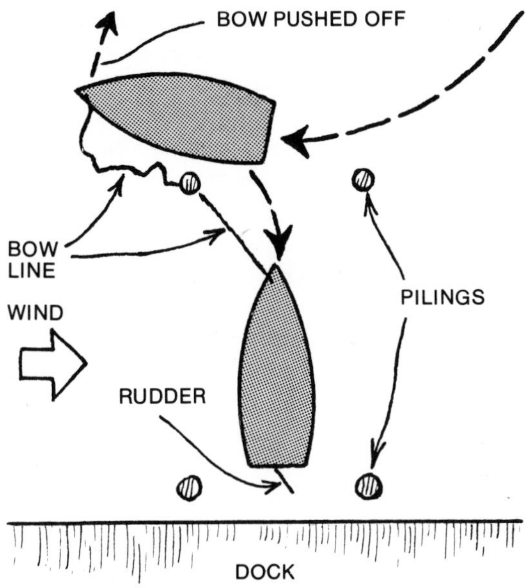

BOW PUSHED OFF

BOW LINE

WIND

RUDDER

PILINGS

DOCK

FIGURE 10-2: TIDE & DOCK LINE ADJUSTMENT

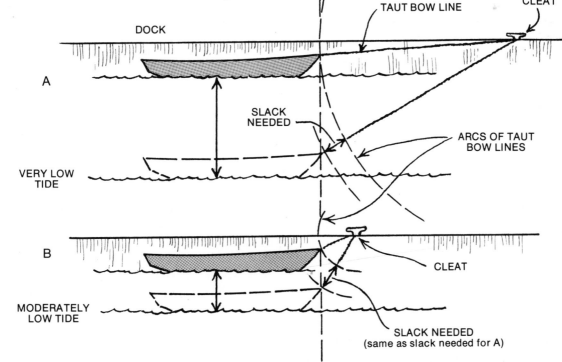

TAUT BOW LINE

CLEAT

DOCK

A

SLACK NEEDED

ARCS OF TAUT BOW LINES

VERY LOW TIDE

B

CLEAT

MODERATELY LOW TIDE

SLACK NEEDED
(same as slack needed for A)

But the normal auxiliary sailboat, with her propeller forward of the rudder, a cutaway forefoot, and great windage forward, may be difficult to back. In a fresh breeze her bow will blow off, and no matter which way the helm is turned, she will back her stern into the wind. One means of coping with this difficulty is illustrated in Figure 10-3. With the wind blowing from one side of the slip, as shown, the approaching boat heads into the wind and comes alongside the outermost windward piling. A crew member on the bow puts a looped line on the piling or grabs a line that is left coiled on the piling. Then, as the boat is backed into the slip and her bow begins to blow off, the bow man keeps a tension on the line to control the backward heading. Notice that the rudder is turned away from the wind in order to help prevent the stern from turning to windward.

Proper conduct and good manners in a marina are largely a matter of common sense. People aboard boats berthed in extremely close proximity should make every effort to be considerate of their neighbors, especially with respect to noise. Radios and televisions should have their volume controls turned as low as possible, and there should be no late parties on deck with raucous laughter and loud singing. Skippers of sailboats with aluminum masts should be sure that the halyards are tied off to prevent them from flapping in the wind and beating an annoying tattoo against the mast. Keep the dock area near your boat clear, and *never* throw garbage overboard. Whenever possible use the marina bathrooms instead of the boat's head if it discharges directly overboard. Also, while tied up in a marina, refrain from pumping oily bilge water overboard except in a real emergency. Have respect for your neighbors' privacy, and draw the curtains over your own windows or ports at night.

Yacht Clubs

There are many different kinds of yacht clubs, ranging from very informal organizations to highly social clubs that often are steeped in tradition and ceremony, and there are even a few clubs that require a certain amount of nautical experience of a candidate before he is eligible for membership. Some clubs have no physical facilities, but most own a clubhouse and have a harbor with docks, slips, or moorings. Although a few clubs are quite expensive and sometimes have formidable waiting lists of membership candidates, the vast majority of yacht clubs are not difficult to join, nor are their dues

and initiation fees unreasonable. Yacht club costs vary tremendously, but initiation fees generally are between $10 and $2,000, with an average of about $200, while annual dues may vary between $10 and $400, with an average of about $100. In any event, it is highly recommended that the novice boatman join a club, because the benefits are many.

Among the more obvious advantages of club membership are opportunities to make friends with people who have interests in common with you; the availability (in most cases) of club facilities and a place to keep your boat; opportunities to learn from lectures, training programs, or contact with experienced boatmen; and the availability of club and interclub programs or activities such as junior training, organized cruises, races, and social events. A less-known benefit of membership is that many of the better yacht clubs have reciprocal arrangements that permit a member of one club to visit another for a few days or longer, during which time he will receive membership privileges at the club he is visiting. This often means that he will receive free docking or will be put on a guest mooring, that he can use the showers or other facilities, and that, in general, he will be treated with great hospitality. When visiting a strange club, be sure to fly your yacht club *burgee* (flag), and, of course, ask the harbormaster if you can pick up a guest mooring, make fast to the dock, or use the facilities ashore.

Speaking of burgees, a few words should be said about the flags most frequently flown from a small cruiser. The yacht club burgee, which is generally a triangular flag, is flown from the *truck* (the topmost cap at the head of the mast) on single-masted yachts or at the foremost truck on yachts with two or more masts. The *United States ensign* (the U.S. national flag) or the *U.S. yacht ensign* (the American flag with thirteen stars circling a fouled anchor) is flown during daylight hours (in port, between 8 A.M. and sunset). Originally, the yacht ensign was intended only as a signal for federally registered (documented) yachts and certain other vessels that were exempt from entering and clearing at custom houses, but now it is customary for all yachts, even those numbered and with state registrations, to fly the yacht ensign. If visiting a foreign country, however, the U.S. ensign should be flown astern, while a smaller national flag of the country being visited is flown from the starboard spreader. Until quite recently, the ensign was flown from the leech of the aftermost sail on U.S. boats, but now the ensign is properly flown from a staff at the stern whether at

FIGURE 10-4: SELECTED SINGLE FLAG SIGNALS
(from International Code of Signals'' — HO 102)

A (WHITE & BLUE)
I have a diver down; keep
well clear at slow speed.

(Also, a red square flag with a diagonal
white stripe warns that a diver is down.)

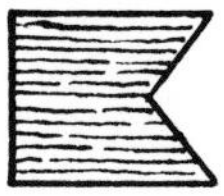

B (RED)
I am taking in or discharging
or carrying dangerous goods.

(Also the protest flag for racing yachts.)

C (BLUE & WHITE WITH
RED MIDDLE STRIPE)
Yes (affirmative).

D (BLUE & YELLOW)
Keep clear of me; I am
maneuvering with difficulty.

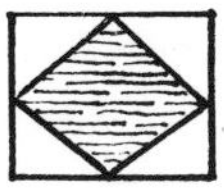

F (WHITE & RED)
I am disabled.
Communicate with me.

G (YELLOW & BLUE)
I require a pilot.

K (YELLOW & BLUE)
I wish to communicate
with you.

N (BLUE & WHITE
No (negative).

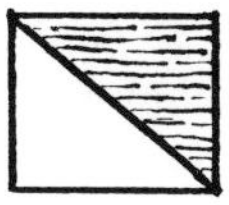

O (YELLOW & RED)
Man overboard.

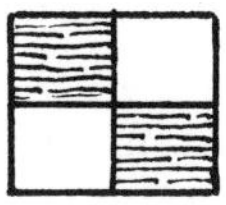

U (RED & WHITE)
You are running into
danger.

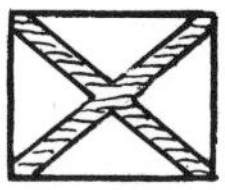

V (RED & WHITE)
I require assistance.

W (BLUE & WHITE WITH
RED CENTER)
I require medical assistance.

SPECIAL CLUB SIGNALS (should be flown under club burgee so as
not to be confused with International Code)

T

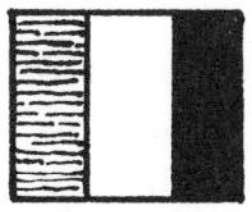

(RED, WHITE & BLUE)

Tender needed. Send club launch.
(Under HO 102: Keep clear of me,
I am engaged in pair trawling.)

M

(BLUE & WHITE)
Doctor on board.
(Under HO 102: My vessel
is stopped and making
no way through the water.)

Q

(YELLOW)
Come within hail.
(Under HO 102: My vessel
is healthy and I request
free pratique.)

anchor or under sail. The rule of thumb for proper ensign size is approximately one inch on the *fly* (the length from the edge that is secured to the edge that flaps) per foot of the boat's length overall, and the ensign's *hoist* (height of the flag from top to bottom) is two-thirds of its fly. By this rule, the ensigns seen on many yachts are slightly undersized.

The other most frequently flown flag is the *private signal* or *house flag* (the owner's personal flag). This flag may be any shape, though it usually has a swallow tail, and it can be flown from the truck in lieu of the club burgee on single-masted boats without a bow staff. On two-masted boats, it is flown from the aftermost truck.

Figure 10-4 shows a few single-letter signal flags that are a handy and simple means of sending a message to another boat or to shore. Most of those signals are from the *International Code of Signals,* HO 102, published by the U.S. Naval Oceanographic Office; however, the three boxed-in flags illustrated are not HO 102 signals but are commonly accepted yacht club signals, and they should be hoisted under the yacht club burgee so that they will not be confused with the International Code. Note that the Q flag may ask another boat to come within hail under a yacht club code, but under International Code it has to do with quarantine and signifies: My vessel is healthy and I request free *pratique*—permission to use the port (after coming from a foreign country). Especially handy is the T flag, which signals for a club launch when a boat is moored or anchored off a yacht club. It is customary to hoist the flag and then blow a horn three times when asking for tender service. If there is no question of which boat the horn blasts came from, the T flag may not be needed.

Although many yacht clubs have docks or slips for berthing boats, other clubs have offshore moorings. As said earlier, in very crowded areas it is sometimes necessary to restrict the swing of a moored boat by anchoring her from the bow and stern, but in most harbors, boats are moored from the bow only, which is a far more desirable arrangement.

A typical mooring is illustrated in Figure 10-5. The mushroom anchor shown in the illustration has tremendous holding power in a bottom sufficiently soft to allow it to become fully buried. If the harbor bottom is hard, however, multiple anchor arrangements or very heavy weights such as concrete blocks are often used.

With the shortage of swinging room in most of

FIGURE 10-5: A MOORING

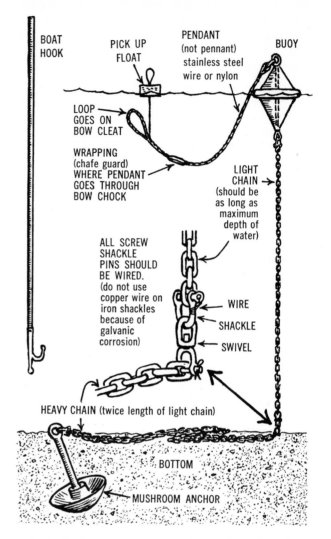

today's harbors, scope must be limited, but there should be sufficient chain to allow for the extremely high tides that usually accompany hurricanes. The light chain shown in the illustration should be inspected periodically, at least once a season. The heavy chain, which adds weight to the mooring and acts as a shock absorber in heavy weather, needs regular inspection, too, but not so often. A thorough inspection of the heavy chain often requires that the anchor be lifted, and if it is a mushroom type, the lifting should seldom be done during the boating season when the mooring is being used because of the lengthy time it usually takes for the anchor to become buried again. In moderate winds and currents, some light displacement boats will ride to the light chain only, without picking up the heavy chain, while large, heavy boats having a lot of windage may stretch out the heavy chain even in mild weather. This fact should be considered carefully when boats of contrasting displacement and size are moored in close proximity. When screw shackles are used, they should be wired to assure that their pins will not unscrew, and the wire should not be of a metal dissimilar to that of the shackle. In other words, the two metals should be galvanically compatible to avoid corrosion in salt water. Don't use copper wire on a galvanized iron or steel shackle. On shackles with pins that are secured with cotter keys, the latter should be extra heavy, and they too should be made of a compatible metal. It is important to use a heavy swivel between the light and heavy chains to prevent them from becoming twisted when the boat swings around in circles. The swivel and shackles should be lifted and carefully inspected at least once a season.

The pendant shown in Figure 10-5 should have a length of about three times the boat's freeboard, and it is generally made of stainless steel or nylon cable. The latter material has the advantage of providing some elasticity, but of course it will chafe, and so it must be well protected with a chafe guard (preferably the type that resembles a rubber sleeve) where the line passes through the bow chock. Incidentally, the chock and bitt or cleat intended for a stainless

steel cable should be designed and installed in such a way that no sharp bend is put in the cable when it is under strain. Also, chafe guards on a stainless steel pendant should be removed periodically in order that the wire can be inspected for possible damage from shielding corrosion. A cable tightly encased under a chafe guard may be deprived of the oxygen necessary to form the corrosion-retarding oxide film that protects the stainless steel. While on the subject of pendants, it should be mentioned that the word is often misspelled "pennant" even by very authoritative boating writers. A pennant is a flag, while a pendant is a short, single piece of rope or chain, usually hanging.

Anchorages

When picking an anchorage away from a marina or yacht club, study the chart very carefully to determine the depth of water, the anchor-holding characteristics of the bottom, and the protection afforded for the weather anticipated. If possible, study the local cruising guide, which will discuss the merits of most anchorages in your area. And always listen to weather reports for predictions of wind direction and storm warnings.

It is not easy to find an almost completely land-

This boat appears to have dragged aground during the night. Unless it has dragged onto jagged rocks or coral, however, damage will probably be minimal.

locked harbor, but a crescent-shaped cove with one exposed side will usually suffice if the wind direction can be foretold with reasonable accuracy. In most U.S. cruising areas during the summer months, winds often prevail from one direction (see Chapter 8), or else their shifting is fairly predictable, and sudden thunderstorms most often come from one quadrant, usually from westerly directions. In very hot weather, the prevailing weather system wind may be opposed or reinforced by a sea breeze during the late morning and afternoon—that is, the hot air rising above the land will often suck in the cooler air over the sea, causing an onshore wind, and sometimes the wind direction will be almost reversed at night after the land cools. Of course, every attempt should be made to keep the boat anchored under a windward shore, especially in heavy weather (or anticipated heavy weather), so that there will not be sufficient *fetch* (distance of open water over which the wind blows) for a strong wind to produce sizable waves; but on the other hand, the boat should not be so close to the shore that she is completely blanketed and those on board are deprived of breezes in hot weather. A position

very close to shore also might put the boat in a vulnerable position in the event of an unexpected 180-degree wind shift during a sudden squall. Another consideration is that when you are very near shore, especially a marshy one, you are often susceptible to mosquitoes or other insect pests.

In some harbors that are open to the sea on one side there may be a surge or swells rolling into the anchorage even when the wind is from offshore. In this case, and also when there is a steady stream of motorboats powering through the harbor, many monohulled boats at anchor will develop an unpleasant rolling motion. One solution to the problem is to use the roll control mentioned in Chapter 1 and illustrated in Figure 10-6. This device, which consists of a flat metal frame covered with a flexible plastic, is suspended overboard from the end of a boom. As the boat rolls, the device alternately rises and sinks in the water. When it sinks, flap valves in the plastic open, but the valves close when the device rises, and thus it resists the rolling motion. Of course, it is more effective to use two roll controls, one on each side of the boat. The spinnaker pole might be used for a suspension

A snug gunkhole that offers a peaceful anchorage. The yawl is the famous ocean-racing cruiser, the *Finisterre*.

FIGURE 10-6: ROLL CONTROLLERS (FOR BOATS AT ANCHOR)

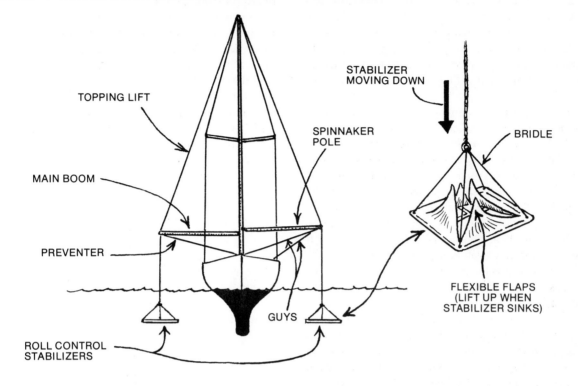

TOPPING LIFT

STABILIZER
MOVING DOWN

BRIDLE

SPINNAKER
POLE

MAIN BOOM

PREVENTER

GUYS

FLEXIBLE FLAPS
(LIFT UP WHEN
STABILIZER SINKS)

ROLL CONTROL
STABILIZERS

FIGURE 10-7: YAW CONTROL AT ANCHOR

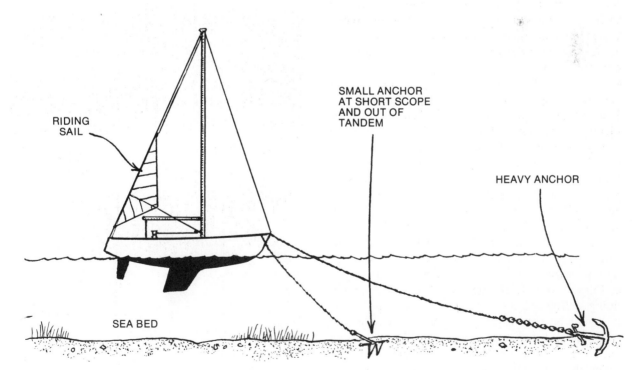

RIDING
SAIL

SMALL ANCHOR
AT SHORT SCOPE
AND OUT OF
TANDEM

HEAVY ANCHOR

SEA BED

boom on one side and the main boom on the other side, as shown in the illustration. The guys and preventer are rigged to hold the booms steady and prevent them from swinging fore and aft. Very simple homemade roll controls without valves might be made from small sheets of waterproof plywood, about two feet square, that are weighted to make them sink.

Some modern boats swing around or yaw quite a bit in fresh winds when at anchor with all sails furled. If there is a lot of windage forward from a high bow or a tall mast and the boat has a cutaway forefoot, her bow will often blow off and she will begin to "sail" until she is pulled into the wind by her anchor line. Then she will tack and sail off in the other direction. All of this back and forth motion may bring the boat dangerously close to other craft nearby, and it may even break out the anchor. There are several ways to alleviate this problem. The simplest solution might be to anchor by the stern instead of the bow, which also may be the most effective way to ventilate the boat in hot weather. Another method that can be partially effective is to rig a spring line on the *rode* (anchor line) in the manner suggested previously in the discussion of compass adjusting (see Figure 8-2), or, of course, you can anchor by the bow *and* stern. Another method of preventing excessive yawing is the so-called *hammerlock moor*, which utilizes a second anchor put out from the bow at short scope. When using the hammerlock system, drop the heavy anchor in the customary way, pay out ample scope, and then wait for the boat to yaw. At the end of the most extreme yaw, drop the second, lighter anchor, and pay out enough scope for it to dig in thoroughly. Then shorten the scope of the second anchor slightly. A hammerlock is most effective when the two anchors are well out of tandem—i.e., when there is a wide angle between the two rodes.

Still another solution to the yaw problem is to hoist a small *riding sail* aft. A riding sail may also be helpful in keeping the boat head-to-wind when there is a current that opposes the wind. The riding sail can be the mizzen sheeted flat on a yawl or ketch, but a single-master sometimes can use a jib set backward on the permanent backstay as shown in Figure 10-7. It is preferable, of course, that a riding sail be made specifically for riding purposes. It should be cut very flat and have a wire in the leech. A full-length batten or two will help keep the sail quiet. Be sure, by the way, that there is a toggle under the backstay turnbuckle to assure that the

fitting will not fatigue due to alternating lateral pressures from the sail.

The most popular anchors in use today seem to be the lightweight Danforths, Northills, and plow types, but under certain conditions the older yachtsman type (sometimes called a fisherman or kedge anchor) is still superior. All of these anchors are illustrated in Figure 10-8. Which type you choose will depend primarily on the kind of seabed in your cruising area. Opinions among experienced yachtsmen vary somewhat concerning the most suitable anchor for each kind of bottom. By and large,

A lovely schooner comes to anchor in a New England cove. She has a yachtsman type anchor with Herreshoff palms, an ideal "hook" for rocky and heavily weeded bottoms.

however, Danforths are considered superior in very soft bottoms; the yachtsman type is usually most appropriate in rock, shell, hard sand, or weed-covered bottoms; and many experienced boatmen consider the plow to be the best all-purpose anchor for a great variety of bottoms. I have used a plow exclusively for the last five years in sticky mud, sand, shell, and weedy bottoms, and have dragged only twice—once when the bottom was very soft ooze and again when I carelessly failed to make sure that the anchor was properly dug in.

A good anchor selection for the average boat that will cruise in a number of different areas having a variety of seabeds might be: a lightweight Danforth (preferably the "Hi-Tensile" type), a medium weight plow for general usage, and a heavy *Herreshoff type* yachtsman that can be used as a storm anchor. The latter type is sometimes made so that it can be disassembled for easy stowing. The Herreshoff palm is fairly broad for reasonable holding power in soft bottoms, but the fluke attaches to the arm in somewhat the same manner that a paddle blade attaches to its shaft, and this helps prevent the possibility of the anchor line fouling the fluke that is not buried in the bottom.

As for the proper anchor weight, a simple rule of thumb is that there should be a half pound of anchor weight per foot of the boat's overall length for the light anchor and one pound of anchor weight per foot of overall length for the heavy working anchor (not the storm anchor). Another rule for the weight of the light anchor is 2 percent of the square of the boat's length. For instance, a thirty-foot boat would take an eighteen-pound light anchor by this rule. At least one prominent yachtsman feels that the lightweight modern anchors, such as Danforths, used on yachts today are unnecessarily heavy. It is true that once a Danforth or plow is dug into a bottom that is not too soft, it has tremendous holding power. Because there must be sufficient anchor weight to make those anchors penetrate a hard bottom, however, I would rather err on the heavy side than on the light side in order to enjoy a worry-free night's sleep. One means of adding weight to a light anchor is with a short length of heavy chain, perhaps ten or more feet long, shackled between the anchor and its rope line. This will also help the line absorb sudden shock loads, aid in keeping the angle of pull low so that the flukes will dig in, and prevent a rope rode from chafing on a rocky bottom. A storm anchor probably should be at least a third heavier than the heavy

FIGURE 10-8: ANCHOR TYPES

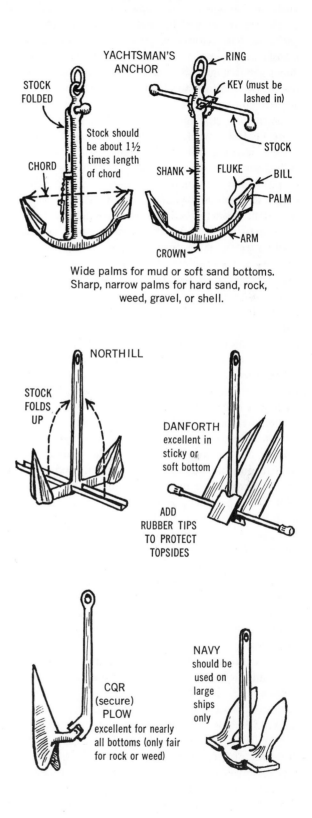

Wide palms for mud or soft sand bottoms. Sharp, narrow palms for hard sand, rock, weed, gravel, or shell.

working anchor, especially if the former is the yachtsman type.

The favorite anchor rode of many American yachtsmen is nylon rope. Nylon is strong, easy to handle, resistant to rot, and highly elastic, which reduces shock loads. Of course, many experienced sailors prefer nothing but chain, and it is true that chain affords some advantages in chafe resistance, extra weight, easy stowage, and a large catenary for a more favorable angle of pull; furthermore, it affords good shock absorption up to a point. Still, I remember riding out one storm behind a chain rode at full scope when the chain was periodically stretched taut with clanking jolts as the bow lifted to a heavy sea. Of course, this kind of jolting might have been alleviated with a heavy rubber shock absorber holding some slack in the chain. My choice of rode is a short chain between the anchor and a nylon rode. According to one school of thought, the nylon rodes found on most American boats are too large in diameter, especially for use with light anchors, because a light line will stretch sooner and thus be more capable of absorbing shock loads that might loosen the anchor's grip on the bottom. While there may be justification for this thinking, the rode should be sufficiently heavy to resist surface wear and chafing where it cannot be well protected with chafe guards, and it is safest to use fairly heavy line with extra long scope for a heavy anchor. Proper anchor line diameter for the heavy anchor will depend on the boat's displacement and on such other factors as the amount of windage, but very generally speaking, I would not have a heavy anchor's nylon rode lighter than one-half inch on a cruiser just under thirty feet long overall, three-quarters of an inch on a boat thirty to forty feet long, and one inch on a boat forty to fifty feet long.

The ideal ratio of scope to water depth is six or preferably seven to one (that is, a length of anchor line equal to six or seven times the depth of water where the boat is anchored), but in many anchorages this ideal cannot be achieved because there simply is not enough swinging room. A five to one ratio is usually acceptable, however, if the harbor affords satisfactory protection and there is good holding bottom. Small cruisers should probably carry at least 150 feet of heavy anchor line; cruisers from twenty-five to forty feet long should have at least 200 feet of line, and larger boats should have 250 feet or more. In addition to the heavy rode, be sure to carry a spare, lighter anchor line.

I find it handy to carry a long anchor rode in two or three pieces, each of which has eye splices around metal thimbles at both ends in order that the lines will be a convenient length to handle and can be easily coiled (when the rode does not run through a hawsepipe). When long scope is needed, the pieces can be shackled together. A well-made eye splice will only weaken the line by about 5 percent. Another convenient arrangement for medium-sized to large boats is to have the heavy anchor line feed through a hawsepipe in the foredeck from a reel mounted in the boat's forepeak. Most rode reels are operated by spring tension to wind up the rode automatically as it is pulled in when the anchor is being weighed.

Usually it is desirable, especially for a small boat, to anchor in fairly shallow water if the tidal range permits, because shoal water requires less scope for a given scope-to-depth ratio. In addition, of course, it is important to anchor away from thoroughfares and areas where larger craft that require a lot of swinging room are located. A further benefit is that currents generally are far weaker over shoals than in deep water or channels.

In rocky waters or in areas where there may be mooring chains on the bottom, some sailors rig a trip line from the crown of their anchor to a small buoy that floats almost directly over the anchor. If a fluke becomes lodged in a rocky crevice so that the anchor cannot be weighed by hauling in on its rode, then it usually can be dislodged by hauling on the trip line. In areas where there is a considerable range in tide and strong currents, however, trip lines can become fouled rather easily. This problem is avoided by using an anchor with a sliding ring that can be pulled from the top of the shank to its bottom, or the anchor can be *scowed*—have its line secured to the crown, then lightly lashed at the ring so that the ring lashing can be broken and allow the anchor to be lifted from its crown. These latter methods are not perfect solutions, though, because there is a slim chance that the anchor might break out accidentally. In most cases, when anchoring over a rocky bottom, I would use a yachtsman anchor that leaves one fluke exposed; then if the other fluke became jammed, I would power or sail in great circles around the anchor, wrapping the short length of chain between the anchor and rode around the exposed arm. After this, the anchor probably could be extricated by hauling straight up on the rode. When using the yachtsman anchor, of course, one should be alert to the possibility of its accidentally fouling in this manner. Such a fouling is possible when there are several 180-degree wind shifts or when the boat is alternately controlled by wind and current so that she swings 540 degrees around her anchor.

One effective means of avoiding the use of a buoyed trip line is to use a short trip line, say three fathoms, with one end secured in the usual manner to the anchor's crown but with the other end secured to the three-fathom mark on the rode. Then the hauling end of the trip line can be reached easily when the rode is pulled up.

In regions where there are strong currents and crowded anchorages, it is sometimes necessary to put down two anchors. A popular means of doing this is to use the so-called *Bahamian moor* illustrated in Figure 10-9. To lay out the anchors, drop the first one and drift back (or make sternway under power) as you normally would when using one anchor, but pay out all, or almost all, of your scope and drop a second anchor from the bow. Then haul in on the first line until you are located halfway between the anchors. Notice in the illustration that your circle of swing will be little more than the boat's overall length, and you will be protected from accidentally breaking out an anchor or fouling it during 180-degree wind shifts or when winds and currents oppose each other. The only real problem with this anchoring system is that some modern boats with deep fins can foul their keels on the rode that leads astern. A weight attached to this line as shown in Figure 10-9 will help hold the rode down when it is not under strain so that it will be clear of the keel. Or, of course, sometimes the boat can be anchored from her bow and stern.

Occasionally in a crowded anchorage you may find that after swinging to a wind shift, your boat is a little too close to a neighboring boat. Very often it may be difficult to weigh anchor and drop it in a new location that will allow better clearance of all boats no matter which way the wind shifts. In this case, the simplest solution is often to carry out a second anchor in the dinghy in a direction away from your closest neighbor. This is illustrated in Figure 10-10. The dashed lines show your boat's position after the second anchor has been dropped and its scope has been shortened slightly. Be careful, however, not to drop your anchor on top of or very close to a neighbor's anchor, and figure how your boat will lie during any possible wind shift.

A final word of advice on anchoring is to be sure the "hook" is properly dug in. Never simply drop an anchor and expect it to hold. If you are under

FIGURE 10-9: BAHAMIAN MOOR

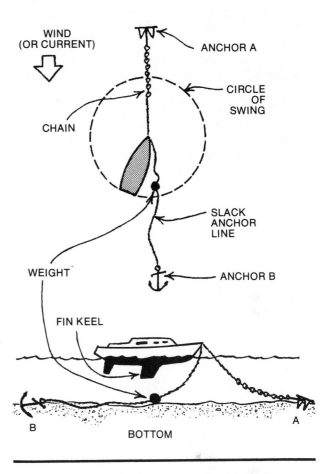

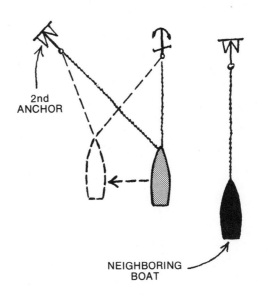

FIGURE 10-10: OBTAINING MORE CLEARANCE WITH TWO ANCHORS

power, lower the anchor and after it strikes bottom, back the engine, pay out considerable scope, snub the line around the bow cleat, and wait for the anchor to catch hold and dig in so that it brings the boat to a sudden stop. When coming to anchor under sail, of course, it is just as important to carry headway or sternway long enough to allow the flukes to become buried. Quite often it is wise to drop the anchor while headed downwind under shortened sail, or sternway may be obtained by holding the main or mizzen boom forward so that the mainsail or mizzen can drive the boat backward until the anchor digs in. After you have anchored and paid out all necessary scope, be sure to take cross bearings, and keep a watch for fifteen minutes or so to be sure you are not dragging.

The closing of this chapter concludes the book. If the reader is still with me, I sincerely hope he chooses the right boat and has many happy cruises in her. May he nose his vessel into many a perfect gunkhole, the kind that is uncrowded, unpolluted, and unspoiled by "progress."

Appendix A

Federal Equipment Requirements*

Part 175 — Equipment Requirements

Subpart A — General

§ 175.1 Applicability.

This part prescribes rules governing the use of boats on waters subject to the jurisdiction of the United States and on the high seas beyond the territorial seas for boats owned in the United States except —

(a) Foreign boats temporarily using waters subject to U.S. jurisdiction;

(b) Military or public boats of the United States, except recreational-type public vessels;

(c) A boat whose owner is a State or subdivision thereof, which is used principally for governmental purposes, and which is clearly identifiable as such;

(d) Ship's lifeboats.

§ 175.3 Definitions.

As used in this part:

(a) "Boat" means any vessel manufactured or used primarily for noncommercial use; leased, rented, or chartered to another for the latter's noncommercial use; or engaged in the carrying of six or fewer passengers.

(b) "Recreational boat" means any vessel manufactured or used primarily for noncommercial use; or leased, rented, or chartered to another for the latter's noncommercial use. It does not include a vessel engaged in the carrying of six or fewer passengers.

(c) "Vessel" includes every description of watercraft, other than a seaplane on the water, used or capable of being used as a means of transportation on the water.

* "Part 175 — Equipment Requirements" lists the latest requirements for personal flotation devices. It is taken from the *Federal Register*, vol. 37, no. 195 (October 6, 1972). The remainder of Appendix A consists of excerpts from the Coast Guard's pamphlet CG-290, entitled *Pleasure Craft*, dated February, 1972. This is the most up-to-date copy of the pamphlet available at the time of publication.

(d) "Use" means operate, navigate, or employ.

(e) "Passenger" means every person carried on board a vessel other than —

(1) The owner or his representative;

(2) The operator;

(3) Bona fide members of the crew engaged in the business of the vessel who have contributed no consideration for their carriage and who are paid for their services; or

(4) Any guest on board a vessel which is being used exclusively for pleasure purposes who has not contributed any consideration, directly or indirectly, for his carriage.

(f) "Racing shell, rowing scull, and racing kayak," means a manually propelled boat that is recognized by national or international racing associations for use in competitive racing and one in which all occupants row, scull, or paddle, with the exception of a coxswain, if one is provided, and is not designed to carry and does not carry any equipment not solely for competitive racing.

Subpart B — Personal Flotation Devices

§ 175.11 Applicability.

This subpart applies to all recreational boats that are propelled or controlled by machinery, sails, oars, paddles, poles, or another vessel except racing shells, rowing sculls, and racing kayaks.

§ 175.13 Definitions.

As used in this subpart:

(a) "Personal flotation device" means a device that is approved by the Commandant under 46 CFR Part 160.

(b) "PFD" means "personal flotation device."

§ 175.15 Personal flotation devices required.

(a) Except as provided in §175.17, no person may use a recreational boat less than 16 feet in length or a canoe or kayak unless at least one PFD of the following types or their equivalents listed in Table 175.23 is on board for each person:

(1) Type I PFD.

(2) Type II PFD.

(3) Type III PFD.

(4) Type IV PFD.

(b) No person may use a recreational boat 16 feet or more in length, except a canoe or kayak, unless at least one PFD of the following types or their equivalents listed in Table 175.23 is on board for each person:

(1) Type I PFD.

(2) Type II PFD.

(3) Type III PFD.

(c) No person may use a recreational boat 16 feet or more in length, except a canoe or kayak, unless at least one Type IV PFD or its equivalent listed in Table 175.23 is on board in addition to the PFD's required in paragraph (b) of this section.

§ 175.17 Exceptions.

(a) A person using a canoe or kayak that is enclosed by a deck and spray skirt need not comply with § 175.15 if he wears a vest-type lifesaving device that —

(1) Has no less than 150 separate permanently inflated air sacs made of not less than 12 mil polyvinylchloride film and has not less than 13 pounds of positive buoyancy in fresh water, if worn by a person who weighs more than 90 pounds; or

(2) Has no less than 120 separate permanently inflated air sacs made of not less than 12 mil polyvinylchloride film and has not less than 8½ pounds of positive buoyancy in fresh water, if worn by a person who weighs 90 pounds or less.

(b) A Type V PFD may be carried in lieu of any PFD required in § 175.15 if that Type V PFD is approved for the activity in which the recreational boat is being used.

Proposed Rule Making

§ 175.19 Stowage.

(a) No person may use a recreational boat unless each Type I, Type II, Type III, or Type V PFD required by § 175.15 or § 175.17 is readily accessible.

(b) No person may use a recreational boat unless each Type IV PFD required by § 175.15 is immediately available.

§ 175.21 Conditions; approval; marking.

No person may use a recreational boat unless each device required by § 175.15, or each device allowed by § 175.17, is —

(a) In serviceable condition;

(b) Legibly marked with the approval number as specified in 46 CFR Part 160 for items subject to approval; and

(c) Of an appropriate size for the person for whom it is intended.

§ 175.23 Personal flotation device equivalents.

Table 175.23 lists devices that are equivalent to personal flotation devices.

Numbering Requirements

The Federal Boating Act of 1958 establishes a uniform system for the identification of pleasure

---

TABLE 175.23

Devices marked		*Are equivalent to*
160.002	Life preserver	Performance Type I personal flotation device
160.003	Life preserver	Performance Type I personal flotation device
160.004	Life preserver	Performance Type I personal flotation device
160.005	Life preserver	Performance Type I personal flotation device
160.009	Ring life buoy	Performance Type IV personal flotation device
160.047	Buoyant vest	Performance Type II personal flotation device
160.048	Buoyant cushion	Performance Type IV personal flotation device
160.049	Buoyant cushion	Performance Type IV personal flotation device
160.050	Ring life buoy	Performance Type IV personal flotation device
160.052	Buoyant vest	Performance Type II personal flotation device
160.053	Work vest	Performance Type V personal flotation device
160.055	Life preserver	Performance Type I personal flotation device
160.060	Buoyant vest	Performance Type II personal flotation device
160.064	Special purpose water safety buoyant devices	A device intended to be worn may be equivalent to Type II or Type III. A device that is equivalent to Type III is marked "Type III Device—may not turn unconscious wearer." A device intended to be grasped is equivalent to Type IV.

craft. Undocumented vessels are to be numbered by the State in which the boat is principally used. If a boat is propelled by machinery of over 10 horsepower, and is used principally on navigable waters of the United States in New Hampshire, Washington, Alaska, the District of Columbia, or Guam, the Certificate of Number will be issued by the Coast Guard. When a vessel is used principally on the high seas, it is to be numbered in the State in which it is usually docked, moored, housed, or garaged.

Certificate of Number

The identification number issued to a vessel is shown on the Certificate of Number. With each Certificate issued by the Coast Guard, two color coded validation stickers will also be issued. The Certificate of Number must be on board whenever the vessel is in operation.

Display of Number

The identification number should be painted on or attached to each side of the forward half of the vessel (the bow), and no other number may be displayed thereon. Numbers are to read left to right, be in block characters, be of a color contrasting with the background, and be not less than 3 inches in height. There shall be a hyphen or space between the prefix letters and numerals and between the numerals and suffix letters. The hyphen or space shall be equal to the width of any letter except "I" or any number except "1".

The validation sticker must be placed three inches beyond, and level with, the last letter of the identification number.

CORRECT: DC 1234 AB or DC—1234—AB

INCORRECT: DC 1234 AB or *DC 1234 AB*

State Numbering Requirements

State fees are fixed by State law. A number issued by a State may be valid for not more than 3 years. The State may require the numbering of vessels of less than 10 horsepower.

Information about State numbering systems is available from State agencies, Coast Guard units, and marine dealers.

Each state with an approved numbering system must recognize for a period of at least 90 days the validity of a number issued a vessel by the Coast Guard or by another State having an approved system.

Applying for a Coast Guard Number

For the States shown above, except for Guam, applications for Number are made to Commandant (BD-1), U.S. Coast Guard, Washington, D.C. 20590. Application forms for Coast Guard numbers are available at post offices and Coast Guard facilities in those States. Applications for Certificates of Number in Guam are made to the local Coast Guard Officer in Charge, Marine Inspection Office.

Coast Guard numbering fees are: original numbering including sticker, $6; renewal of number including sticker, $6; reissue of lost or destroyed certificate of number, $1; reissue of lost or destroyed sticker 25¢. Fees must be paid by check or money order, payable to the U.S. Coast Guard, and forwarded with the application.

Documentary proof of title and ownership is not required by the Coast Guard with an application for number, but the applicant declares (under penalty for false certification) that he is the owner. A certificate may be canceled for false certification in the application.

A number awarded by the Coast Guard is valid for 3 years from the date of the owner's birthday next occurring after the certificate is issued, and must be renewed before the expiration date. Renewal applications are mailed to applicants 90 days before expiration. If not renewed within 1 year after expiration date, the number will be voided and a new number may be assigned at later application.

Upon sale or transfer, where the vessel continues in use in the same State the old number will be issued to the new owner. Numbers may not be transferred from one boat to another, except for the special dealers' and manufacturers' numbers issued for demonstrating, transporting, or testing boats.

Notification of Changes Required

When a vessel is lost, destroyed, abandoned, or transferred to another person, the certificate must be surrendered to the issuing authority within 15 days.

If the Certificate of Number has been lost or destroyed, notice to that effect must be given to the issuing authority.

Changes of address must also be reported.

If the State of principal use is changed, the owner must make application for a number in the new State and surrender the old certificate within 90 days.

Coast Guard Approved Equipment

"Coast Guard Approved Equipment" is equipment which has been approved by the Commandant after it has been determined to be in compliance with the various Coast Guard specifications and regulations relating to the materials, construction and performance of such equipment.

Personal Flotation

Prior to 1972, only motorboats were required to carry personal flotation devices. Now all boats (with a few exceptions) must carry these devices. See chart . . . .

LIFE PRESERVERS. Kapok, fibrous glass, or unicellular plastic foam is used as flotation material in life preservers. They are either of the jacket or bib design and are acceptable for use on all types of motorboats and vessels. Adult sizes for persons 90 pounds and over, and child sizes for those less than 90 pounds are available. Coast Guard approved life preservers bear markings showing flotation material used, size, and U.S. Coast Guard approval number. All Coast Guard approved life preservers manufactured after 1949 are Indian orange.

BUOYANT VESTS. Coast Guard approved buoyant vests use the same flotation materials as life preservers, but may be any color. Approved buoyant vests come in three sizes: adult, child medium, and child small. Weight ranges of the child sizes are included in the Coast Guard approval markings. It should be noted that buoyant vests provide less buoyancy than life preservers do. They are not acceptable on motorboats 40 feet in length and over or on vessels carrying passengers for hire.

BUOYANT CUSHIONS. Buoyant cushions approved by the Coast Guard contain kapok, fibrous glass, or unicellular plastic foam. They come in a variety of sizes and shapes and may be any color.

Cushions are not acceptable on motorboats 40 feet in length and over or on vessels carrying passengers for hire.

Approved buoyant cushions are marked on the side (gusset) showing the Coast Guard approval number, and other information concerning the cushion and its use. Buoyant cushions are intended for grasping and should never be worn on the back.

RING BUOY. Ring life buoys can be made of cork, balsa wood, or unicellular plastic foam and are available in 30-, 24-, and 20-inch sizes. Their covering is either canvas or specially surfaced plastic foam. All buoys are fitted with a grab line and may be colored either white or orange.

Cork and balsa wood ring buoys must bear two markings, the manufacturer's stamp and the Coast Guard inspector's stamp. Plastic foam ring buoys bear only a nameplate marking.

SPECIAL PURPOSE WATER SAFETY BUOYANT DEVICES. Approved special purpose water safety buoyant devices are manufactured in many designs depending on the intended special purpose, such as water skiing, hunting, racing, etc. Additional strength is added where needed for the intended purpose of the device.

Special purpose devices include those to be worn and those to be grasped. They are acceptable on Classes A, 1 and 2 motorboats not carrying passengers for hire. Devices to be worn are available in adult and child sizes. All special purpose devices show U.S. Coast Guard approval number E25/160.064 . . . , include instructions on use and care, and other necessary information. The devices intended for grasping also are marked with the wording: "Warning—Do not wear on Back."

Fire Extinguishers

Approved types of fire extinguishers are identified by any of the following:

(a) Make and model number on extinguishers manufactured before 1962. Check markings on nameplate with the Coast Guard.

(b) "Marine Type" marking. Check nameplate marking on Underwriters' Laboratories, Inc., listing manifest showing the words, "Marine Type USCG" followed by the Coast Guard classification such as "B-I, B-II."

(c) Coast Guard approval number. Check for marking of Coast Guard approval number on nameplate.

Stored pressure dry chemical extinguishers manufactured after June 1, 1965, that have the propellent gases and extinguishing agent in the same bottle, must have a visual pressure indicator—a pressure gauge or similar device that shows the state of internal pressure charge.

EQUIPMENT REQUIREMENTS
Minimum Required Equipment

EQUIPMENT	CLASS A (Less than 16 feet)	CLASS 1 (16 feet to less than 26 feet)	CLASS 2 (26 feet to less than 40 feet)	CLASS 3 (40 feet to not more than 65 feet)
BACK-FIRE FLAME ARRESTER	One approved device on each carburetor of all gasoline engines installed after April 25, 1940, except outboard motors.			
VENTILATION	At least two ventilator ducts fitted with cowls or their equivalent for the purpose of properly and efficiently ventilating the bilges of every engine and fuel-tank compartment of boats constructed or decked over after April 25, 1940, using gasoline or other fuel of a flashpoint less than 110° F.			
BELL	None.*	None.*	One, which when struck, produces a clear, bell-like tone of full round characteristics.	
PERSONAL FLOTATION DEVICES†	One approved life preserver, buoyant vest, ring buoy, special purpose water safety buoyant device, or buoyant cushion for each person on board or being towed on water skis, etc.			One approved life preserver or ring buoy for each person on board.
WHISTLE	None.*	One hand, mouth, or power operated, audible at least ½ mile.	One hand or power operated, audible at least 1 mile.	One power operated, audible at least 1 mile.
FIRE EXTINGUISHER —PORTABLE When NO fixed fire extinguishing system is installed in machinery space(s).	At least One B-1 type approved hand portable fire extinguisher. (Not required on outboard motorboat less than 26 feet in length and not carrying passengers for hire if the construction of such motorboats will not permit the entrapment of explosive or flammable gases or vapors.)		At least Two B-1 type approved hand portable fire extinguishers; OR at least One B-11 type approved hand portable fire extinguisher.	At least Three B-1 type approved hand portable fire extinguishers; OR at least One B-1 type *Plus* One B-11 type approved hand portable fire extinguisher.
When fixed fire extinguishing system is installed in machinery space(s).	None.	None.	At least One B-1 type approved hand portable fire extinguisher.	At least Two B-1 type approved hand portable fire extinguishers; OR at least One B-11 type approved hand portable fire extinguisher.

Fire extinguishers manufactured after 1 January 1965 will be marked, "Marine Type USCG Type _____ Size _____ Approval No. 162-028. . . ."

*NOTE — Not required by the Motorboat Act of 1940; however, the "Rules of the Road" require these vessels to sound proper signals.

†NOTE — With a few exceptions, all boats (not just motorboats) are *now* required to carry personal flotation devices.

**NOTE — Toxic vaporizing liquid-type fire extinguishers, such as those containing carbon tetrachloride or chlorobromomethane, are not accepted as required approved extinguishers on uninspected vessels (private pleasure craft).

Dry chemical extinguishers manufactured prior to June 1, 1965, without pressure indicating device are still acceptable if: (1) inspection record shows weight check within the past six months, (2) weight is within one-fourth ounce of weight stamped on container, (3) external seals or disc in neck are intact, and (4) there is no evidence of damage, use or leaking.

Fire Extinguishers Required

Each fire extinguisher is classified, by letter and number, according to the type of fire it may be expected to extinguish, and the size of the extinguisher. The letter indicates the type of fire: ("A" for fires in ordinary combustible materials; "B" for gasoline, oil, and grease fires; "C" for fires in electrical equipment.) Extinguishers approved for motorboats are hand-portable, of either B-I or B-II classification.

Fire Extinguishers

CLASSIFICATION (type-size)	FOAM (minimum gallons)	CARBON DIOXIDE (minimum pounds)	DRY CHEMICAL (minimum pounds)	FREON (minimum pounds)
B-I	1¼	4	2	2½
B-II	2½	15	10	—

NOTE: Carbon tetrachloride extinguishers and others of the toxic vaporizing-liquid type such as chlorobromomethane are not approved and are not accepted as required fire extinguishers.

Flame Arresters
(Backfire Flame Control)

Flame arresters are not required on gasoline inboard engines installed prior to April 25, 1940. Installations of backfire flame arresters made before November 19, 1952, need not meet the latest requirements of approval, and may be continued in use so long as they are in good condition. Automotive air breathers and containers with steel wool however, are not acceptable. Engines installed after November 19, 1952, must have a Coast Guard approved flame arrester fitted to the carburetor or bear a label indicating that the Coast Guard has approved the use of that engine without an arrester.

To meet the requirements, flame arresters must have flame-tight connections, clean elements, no separation of grid elements which would permit flames to bypass the grid elements and be Coast Guard approved. The flame arrester's name and model number can be checked with the Coast Guard, or the arrester will have a Coast Guard approval number on the grid housing.

Exceptions are: (1) engines accepted for use without a flame arrester and so labeled by the U.S. Coast Guard and (2) situations where attachments to air intake system or the location of the engine will disperse backfire flame to open atmosphere clear of the vessel, persons on board, nearby vessels and structures.

Status of Formerly Approved Equipment

(a) General. With few exceptions any equipment which has ever been approved by the Coast Guard or the former Bureau of Marine Inspection and Navigation will be accepted as legal equipment so long as it remains in good and serviceable condition. When no longer serviceable, or when the approval stamps are no longer legible and the equipment cannot otherwise be identified as being approved, such equipment must be replaced with currently approved equipment. Any questions regarding the status of approval of any item of equipment should be directed to a Coast Guard District office or an Officer in Charge, Marine Inspection Office, together with a complete description of the device and its markings.

(b) Exceptions. Certain fire extinguishers are not acceptable as noted under the classification table for fire extinguishers. Also, lifesaving devices which use kapok or fibrous glass not encased in a heat-sealed plastic liner are not acceptable.

Loading Your Boat

A boat's stability is affected by the moving about of people on board. For safety, there are several things that should be remembered when loading a boat. Distribute the load evenly; keep the load low; don't stand up in a small boat; don't overload.

Many boat manufacturers display a plate on their boats showing recommended weight capacity usually in *number of persons* as well as in the *number of pounds for persons, motor, fuel and gear*. These are only recommended values for fair weather and do not relieve the boatmen of the responsibility for exercising individual judgment.

In the absence of capacity plates, there is a double

check which, if properly used, will help prevent overloading of boats of normal shape.

First, a check of the number of persons.

$$\frac{L \times B}{15} = \underline{\hspace{2cm}} \text{ number of persons}$$

L = Overall Length
B = Maximum Width (both dimensions in feet and tenths of feet)

The result, or the next smallest whole number if the result is a fraction, gives the *number of persons* that can be put aboard without crowding in good weather conditions.

Second, one must *also* check the weight-carrying capacity to be certain the boat is adequate for that number of persons, taking into account their actual weight as well as the weight of engine, fuel, and equipment.

The *weight-carrying capacity* can be checked by determining the allowable weight in pounds from the expression:

$$7.5 \times L \times B \times De = \quad \text{pounds for persons, engine, fuel, and equipment}$$

L = Overall Length
B = Maximum Width
De = Minimum Effective Depth of the boat

Measure De at the lowest point that water can enter. This takes account of low transom cut-out or credits an acceptable engine well. All dimensions are in feet and tenths of feet.

The weather and water conditions should be taken into account, too. If the water is rough, the number of persons carried should be reduced. A more comprehensive and detailed method used to determine safe loading capacity is included in Appendix 6 to the Recreational Boating Guide (CG-340).

Suggestions for Safety

1. Gasoline vapors are explosive and being heavier than air will settle in the lower parts of a boat. All doors, hatches, and ports should be closed while fueling, galley fires, and pilot lights extinguished, smoking strictly prohibited, and the filling nozzle kept in contact with the fill pipe to prevent static spark. Avoid spilling. Do not use gasoline stoves, heaters, or lights on board. Whenever possible, portable tanks should be fueled out of the boat.

2. After fueling, thoroughly ventilate all compartments and check the machinery and fuel tank areas for fumes before attempting to start the motor. Remember that the electrical ignition and starting system could supply the ignition to any accumulation of explosive vapors. Take time to be safe. Keep fuel lines tight and bilges always clean. Check your fuel supply system; see that the tanks are vented outboard, that the fill pipes are located outboard of coaming and extend to near the bottom of the tank. Have an adequate filter on the fuel line.

3. Do not overload or improperly load your boat. Maintain adequate freeboard at all times; consider the sea conditions, the duration of the trip, the predicted weather, and the experience of the operator. Do not permit persons to ride on parts of the boat not designed for such use. Bow riding and seat back or gunwale riding can be especially hazardous.

4. Keep an alert lookout. Serious accidents have resulted from failure in this respect.

5. Be especially careful when operating in any area where swimmers might be. They are often difficult to see.

6. Watch your wake. It might capsize a small craft; it can damage boats or property along the shore. You are responsible. Pass through anchorages only at minimum speed.

7. Keep firefighting and lifesaving equipment in good condition and readily available at all times.

8. Obey the Rules of the Road. Neglect of this is the greatest single cause of collision.

9. Always have children wear lifesaving devices. Always check those intended for young children for fit and performance in the water on each individual child. Never hesitate to have "all hands" wear lifesaving devices whenever circumstances cause the slightest doubt of safety.

10. Know your fuel tank capacity and cruising radius. If necessary to carry additional gasoline do so only in proper containers and take special precautions to prevent the accumulation of such vapor in confined spaces.

11. If you ever capsize, remember that if the boat continues to float it is usually best to remain with it. You are more easily located by a search plane or boat.

12. Good housekeeping is even more important afloat than ashore. Cleanliness diminishes the probability of fire.

13. Know the meaning of the buoys. Never moor to one — it is a Federal offense.

14. Consider what action you would take under various emergency conditions — man overboard, fog, fire, a stove-in plank or other bad leak, motor breakdown, bad storm, collision.

15. Have an adequate anchor and sufficient line to assure good holding in a blow (at least six times depth of water).

16. Boat hooks are not required equipment but they are valuable when mooring or when needed to retrieve pets, preservers (and people) "over the side."

17. Know the various distress signals. A recognized distress signal used on small boats is to slowly and repeatedly raise and lower the arms outstretched to each side.

18. Storm signals are for your information and safety. Learn them and be guided accordingly.

19. Water ski only when you are well clear of all other boats, bathers, and obstructions and there are two persons in the boat to maintain a proper lookout.

20. Falls are the greatest cause of injury both afloat and ashore. Eliminate tripping hazards where possible, make conspicuous those which must remain, have adequate grabrails, and require proper footwear to be used on board.

21. Always have up-to-date chart (or charts) of your area on board.

22. Always instruct at least one other person on board of the rudiments of boat handling in case you are disabled—or fall overboard.

23. Keep electrical equipment and wiring in good condition. No knife switches or other arcing devices should be in fuel or engine compartments. Allow ample ventilation around batteries.

24. Before departing on a boat trip, you should advise a responsible friend or relative about where you intend to cruise. Be sure that the person has a good description of your boat. Keep him advised of any changes in your cruise plans. By doing these things, your friend or relative will be able to tell the Coast Guard where to search for you and what type of boat to look for if you fail to return. Be sure to advise the same person when you arrive so as to prevent any false alarms about your safety.

25. Do not test fire extinguishers by squirting small amounts of the agent. The extinguisher might not work when needed. Always follow approved instructions in checking fire extinguishers.

26. A special flag hoist (red flag with white diagonal) flown from boat or buoy means skindiving operations. Approach area with caution and stay clear at least 25 yards.

Appendix B: Chesapeake Bay Foundation Ecology Cruise Guide

A Layman's Tool for Studying the Chesapeake Bay
by James R. Howard, III, John T. Gookin, Nancy G. Dimsdale, David K. Martin, and John Page Williams, Jr.

I. Introduction

A success story! This cruise guide, matured over a period of several years and substantially revised, is in its fourth printing at the time of its publication in this appendix.

James R. Howard, III, Chairman of the Department of Science at the Park School and a valued adviser to CBF, contributes a thoughtful analysis of water studies applicable to an estuarine system. The glossary is also his. Our own staff biologist, Nancy Dimsdale, adds comments and figures relating particular findings and measurements to average and healthy conditions. John Page Williams, Jr., presently a biology teacher at St. Christopher's School, Richmond, and soon-to-be CBF educational director, contributes a section on the pleasures of gunkholing along tidal shores and marshes. CBF Student Coordinators John Gookin and Dave Martin round out the presentation with practical descriptions of beach studies and instructions for the use and fabrication of simple, do-it-yourself ecological testing equipment.

Together, the contributions present a set of instructions, guidelines, observations and information designed to be used as a practical tool for your better observation and understanding of the Chesapeake environment. We sincerely hope you, your family and friends, will use it.

Should anyone question his scientific ability and grow faint before such apparently taxing phrases as Secchi disks and aerobic organisms, take heart! Prior to my becoming engulfed in the affairs of CBF, I thought myself a daring and ingenious fellow if I ventured the opinion, after careful scrutiny with a binocular, that I had sighted a Great Blue Heron. Unfortunately, I'm not exaggerating. Now, having referred to this guide many times (not always with exacting results), I can assure you I take my place at a LaMotte dissolved oxygen test kit with complete confidence.

So please don't put this Report aside with the thought, "It's not for me." It is for you. It was originally put together for use on our ecology cruises.

But when we saw what fun and excitement, what a new dimension in enjoyment of the Bay the cruises opened up to skippers and their young crews, we redesigned the guide to be used by anyone on the water or shore disposed to explore on his own.

Sensory enjoyment of an intriguing environment like the Bay is easy. It takes more—something like "work"—to cultivate an understanding of the system. It takes time and attention to learn to appreciate what "tends to preserve" its integrity, stability and beauty. We hope this guide tempts you in that direction. If it does, we think it will help you contribute to the sound management of our natural resources.

Arthur W. Sherwood

II. Significance of What You Are Going to be Doing and Observing

During the time you spend studying and observing the Chesapeake Bay, you will learn many things. But you may well ask, how does this relate to me and to my community? Why should we study it? What can we find out that will be of lasting importance in our lives?

First of all, any time spent on the Chesapeake Bay will enrich your life, enlarge your understanding, and increase your appreciation of the natural areas that we are trying so hard to preserve. We hope it will inspire you to work with us in this effort.

For an in-depth understanding of the Chesapeake Bay, you need to know how the system works—what are the food webs, what are the habitat requirements, and what changes will occur or have occurred due to man's intervention. Only then can you recommend sound procedures for preserving these resources.

The material which follows is designed to assist you in this kind of learning process. By measuring and observing, for yourself, the physical, chemical and biological characteristics of a given area of the Bay, you can become more aware of the complexities of this ecosystem. This knowledge can be helpful in predicting the effects of various projects located on the Bay. It is sure to increase your awareness of environmental problems and give you some expertise in the discussion of these problems.

Whether your interests are broad environmental understanding, specific knowledge, pollution abatement, or simply the fun of investigating the area where you spend your recreational moments, we think this guide will prove an enjoyable and useful aid.

III. Water Studies

The following list of suggested activities is provided as a guide. You may or may not wish to take data on all of these factors.

DATE AND TIME. The importance of dating data collection in any scientific investigation cannot be overemphasized. By including a date and time with data collected, comparisons can be made over a period of time, i.e., hourly, daily, weekly, seasonally, etc. Inclusion of a date and time also permits one to readily go back and locate information from a specific time in the past.

DEPTH OF READING. Whether a sample of water to be tested is taken at the surface, bottom, or somewhere in between is of utmost importance. Animal and plant life varies according to depth. The temperature, volume of dissolved gases such as CO_2 and O_2, salinity, and turbidity all vary according to depth. The amount of light penetration is governed by the depth and this, in turn, affects the physical and biological characteristics of the sample under investigation. See instructions for lead line construction.

H_2O TEMPERATURE. Differences in H_2O temperature are caused by seasonal, daily, and hourly changes in atmospheric conditions (cloud cover, precipitation, air temperature, wind, etc.). In turn, animal and plant life, dissolved gases, and various chemical factors change according to temperature. Various plants and animals can tolerate wide differences in temperature, while others are killed off by a change of only a degree or two. The fact that the amount of dissolved gas varies with temperature is probably best evidenced by recalling the "pop" one hears in opening a warm bottle of soda compared with a refrigerated one. Cold water is able to hold more dissolved gases than warm water. An ordinary outdoor thermometer may be used to determine both the air and water temperatures.

SALINITY. Salts make up most of the dissolved minerals in water, particularly seawater. Ocean water contains about 3.5% or 35 ppt (parts per thousand) dissolved minerals, while inland ponds and streams contain very minute quantities. Salinity in the Bay varies with depth, and proximity to the ocean and various freshwater tributaries. Most aquatic plants and animals cannot tolerate wide differences in salt content. To take a sand shark from the lower Bay region and transport it to the Susquehanna would surely kill it. The concentration of salts (salinity) in different areas in the Bay varies, and the native plant and animal life varies accordingly. Salinity is easily determined with a LaMotte salinity test kit.*

Temperature and salinity follow three basic patterns in the Chesapeake Bay. In the period from March to August, warmer, fresher water flowing into the head of the Bay overlies colder, saltier water entering from the ocean; the months of September to December exhibit colder, fresher water overlying warmer, saltier water; and the two winter months of January and February both demonstrate cold, fresh water overlying cold, salty water.

In the following Table, temperature and salinity measured at a depth of 20 feet in mid-channel are recorded for three areas of the Chesapeake Bay at two month intervals. Additional data for other locations, depths and times is available upon request. Figures were taken from the Chesapeake Bay Institute's report, "Temperature and Salinity Distributions in Vertical Sections along the Longitudinal Axis of the Chesapeake Bay," September 1971.

DISSOLVED OXYGEN (D.O.). Oxygen-breathing organisms are referred to as aerobic, while non-oxygen-breathing organisms are called anaerobic, e.g., tetanus bacteria which can only survive in deep, airless puncture wounds. The majority of organisms common to us breathe oxygen by various means, i.e., gills, lungs, absorption through the skin, etc. Even the green plants, which produce oxygen (O_2) through the process called photosynthesis, breathe in O_2 at night when a light source is no longer available. The amount of D.O. in a water sample varies according to temperature, presence and amount of animal and plant life, turbulence, depth of reading, etc. By collecting data on D.O. one can determine how well a community is balanced between green plants (oxygen producers) and animals (oxygen consumers).

---

* The LaMotte Chemical Co. (Chestertown, Maryland 21620) produces the three test kits described in this guide.

TEMPERATURE (F°) AT 20 FT., MID-CHANNEL

	January	March	May	July	September	November
Baltimore	35°	43°	57°	75°	74°	47°
Cedar Point (off Patuxent River)	36°	41°	58°	75°	74°	50°
Norfolk	38°	48°	59°	73°	72°	52°

SALINITY (ppt) AT 20 FT., MID-CHANNEL

	January	March	May	July	September	November
Baltimore	15	14	10	8	15	11
Cedar Point	17	18	12	13	17	18
Norfolk	29	23	22	25	27	24

D.O. is most easily measured using a LaMotte dissolved oxygen test kit.

Acceptable dissolved O_2 levels have been set at not less than 4 ppm (parts per million) in waters for general use and not less than 5.0 ppm in areas used for the propagation of fish and other aquatic life, except in areas where lower levels occur naturally.

pH. pH is a measure of how acidic or how alkaline a water sample is, and is dependent on the concentration of hydrogen (H^+) ions; it is measured on a scale ranging from 1 to 14 with 7 representing neutrality. Hydrogen ions (H^+) and hydroxide ions (OH^-) are present in equilibrium in all water ($H^+ + OH^- = H_2O$). pH readings below 7 indicate a high concentration of (H^+) and an acid condition; the closer the pH is to 1, the more acid the sample. A pH above 7 means the solution has a higher concentration of (OH^-) than (H^+) and the solution is basic. As the pH approaches 14 the sample becomes severely basic. Most plants and animals exist within a certain pH range; an environment with a higher or lower pH is likely to cause death. Animals give off carbon dioxide during respiration. This reacts with water to form an acid. Therefore, a water sample with an acidic pH value may indicate an overabundance of animals or a lack of green plants. Industrial effluents may also cause acid or basic conditions in various bodies of water. pH is easily measured with pH test paper, available at tropical fish supply stores or in a LaMotte pH test kit. Normal pH values in the Chesapeake Bay range from 6.0 to 8.5.

It might be well to mention at this point that these tests do not just yield abstract figures. Salinity measurements of 15 ppt indicate the ideal environment for oysters. Fish kills can result from low (less than 4 ppm) dissolved oxygen levels. pH indicates the levels of plant and animal activity and imbalances of the two. An understanding of the effect of salinity, D.O., and pH levels on the ecological community can increase your appreciation of the complexity of Bay environmental problems.

TURBIDITY. The amount of suspended particulate matter (particles) in a body of water is directly related to the turbidity or cloudiness of the sample. Suspended particles may result from nearby soil erosion, and from industrial, sanitary, and storm drainage systems emptying into the water system under study. Turbidity can also be caused by high concentrations of phytoplankton (microscopic plant life) which may result from the fertilizing effect of sewage effluents and agricultural runoff.

Suspended particles cause the sunlight hitting the water to be scattered or absorbed rather than penetrating to lower depths. Hence, depending on the amount of turbidity, many physical and biological factors can be affected. Turbidity is most readily measured with a Secchi disk.

TYPES OF FISH NOTED. Fish can usually be observed from the shore or boat. Large quantities of various species can be caught using a seine (inexpensively purchased in local hobby or bait-tackle stores). Rather than identifying specific fish as to their species (although this is encouraged if time permits) identify their size, numbers, and depth at which they are found. Also, try to learn something about what they are feeding on, whether they feed at the surface, on the bottom, or both. If you wish to preserve your catch make certain you take but one of each species and return the remainder of your catch to the water immediately. Make sketches of those fish you wish to return to the water and want to identify at a later time. Pay particular attention to shape, fins, tail, and markings.

TYPES OF PLANT LIFE NOTED. Plants can be roughly divided into three groups—submerged, emergent, and floating. Submerged and emergent plants are generally rooted in the bottom with the submerged plants being entirely covered by water and the emergent plants having underwater roots and a stem exposed to the air. Floating plants may or may not be rooted, but their mass is mostly on the surface. Plants can be identified using one or more of the excellent identification books on the market covering aquatic life (see Part VIII, Resource Material). If such specific identification is undesirable, plants can be grouped according to their size, relative numbers, location, and whether they are floating, emergent or submerged. Collected specimens can be pressed between newspaper and weighted down to drive out the moisture, or placed in a typical plant press. The finished product should be labeled and mounted on white paper and covered with clear plastic contact paper, available in most hardware stores.

PLANKTON. Plankton are microscopic plants (phytoplankton) and microscopic animals (zooplankton) normally swimming or suspended in open water. These microscopic organisms represent the fundamental food for larger animals; what they lack in size they readily make up for by their tremendous numbers. There are many fine identification books which permit rapid classification. Interesting comparisons can be made on where plankton are located in greatest abundance and at which time of the day, year, etc. Simple identification may be made according to whether the plankton is phytoplankton or zooplankton. Plankton nets represent quite an expense if purchased through a scientific supply house. A simple, inexpensive, and readily constructed net may be made by consulting Part VI, Instructions for Water Test Equipment.

IV. Beach Studies

ZONES OF STUDY. It is important to realize that there are many regions of a beach. The effect of the adjacent water on one region may closely correspond or widely differ from the effects on another. Try to keep in mind the relationships between these regions; how they are interdependent and how they work together in their ecosystem.

Spray Zone. This zone is constantly being sprayed by water (and consequently salt) from wave action. Though this zone is practically nonexistent in smaller tributaries, it extends much farther than it may seem where waves occur. It may extend into bordering grasslands, dune areas or beginnings of a forest.

Intertidal Zone. Perhaps the most interesting region affected by the water, this area is doused by tides twice a day. The length of time that each area within this zone is covered varies according to its elevation. When studying this zone note adaptations for breathing and eating. How does the submergent-emergent cycle affect the life of the plants and animals? Note whether tide is in or out. How can you determine this?

Submerged Zone. Though this zone might be considered better classified under water studies, it may also be studied here because this region has several characteristics similar to those on the beach. It is inhabited by tall plants whose roots are constantly underwater, but whose stems and leaves occasionally extend into the air. It is frequented by swans, herons, etc., adapted with long legs and necks.

Perhaps at the location which you are studying, there is no beach, but cliffs which drop swiftly at the water's edge. When trying to gain an overall viewpoint of the water, think of the effects of such a formation. Consider the fact that there are no grasses growing here, no shelter for small fish and no wave action to help provide dissolved oxygen. Whichever kind of border is formed at the water's edge, note what materials (silt, sand, clay, earth, rock) make it up. How and to what extent does this material provide nutrients for life?

EQUIPMENT. There are many tools which can be used when conducting your beach studies. Though observation by means of your various senses is undoubtedly of the highest importance, the use of these tools can be quite helpful. Binoculars can be quite helpful to identify birds. Use a sieve to extract organisms from the wet mud or sand. A seine net can be used to investigate the shallows. Trotlines and crab nets can be used to find the presence of crabs in the water farther out. Devise your own equipment to investigate the waters. Refer to Part VI for more information.

ANIMALS AND PLANTS. Note and identify as many as possible. Don't forget the birds. How does each one interrelate with its environment? Where does each fit in a food chain? Look for adaptations such as mouths, feet, roots, etc., which enable each plant and animal to live more easily in its niche. How do the plants and animals that you observe depend upon each other, the water, land, air, beach? What would be the effect on each should the water become covered with ¼ inch of *oil*?

MAN. Is the water you are studying being used commercially? Has it been changed by man by dredging, clamming, crabbing, etc.? Has it been changed by developing its shores, destroying natural marshes? Is there foreign matter (litter) in the water? Have you seen anything discharged into the water? Are there any indications (dead fish, birds, or plants) of pollution? How is man affecting this natural area, this part of our Bay? How are you affecting the Bay?

V. Marshes

More and more we are finding that marshes are both interesting and important. They are natural sediment traps—this means that they tend to be much more stable than beaches. But, even more important, they trap nutrient-rich sediments suspended in slowly flowing water. Thus, marsh soil is fertile. It is not, however, an easy place for plants to live. They must withstand high concentrations of salt; also they must withstand having their roots alternately flooded and dried out as the tide rises and falls. In a rigorous situation like this, it is common to find that a few species do very well. They are present in large numbers, while other species are rare. This is true of the Chesapeake's salt marshes. They are dominated by grasses of the genus *Spartina*, especially *Spartina alterniflora*, which is tall and coarse and grows where it is flooded twice a day by the tides; and *Spartina patens*, salt hay grass, which is shorter and finer and grows higher on the marsh where it is flooded less often.

The *Spartina* grasses are the dominant plants on the marshes. Thus they are the base of the marsh food web—they provide the food for the marsh community. But very few of the marsh animals eat marsh grass directly. Instead, the system is based on detritus, a mixture of partially decayed marsh grass and decay bacteria. Marsh grasses have tough, indigestible outer coverings, but bacteria can break them down after the grass dies. This decaying grass adds to the fertility of the marsh soil for future generations of *Spartina*. But it also adds to the fertility of the water. These bits and scraps of digested grass provide food for a variety of animals that live in the waterways of the marsh. Some, like clams, oysters, periwinkle, and microscopic animals, eat the detritus directly. Others, like crabs, juvenile fish, and some adult fish, eat the animals which feed on the detritus.

Beyond directly providing habitat and food, marshes contribute some of their accumulated dead organic material to surrounding deeper waters. This material furnishes food there for filter feeders like oysters and nutrients for microscopic plants (phytoplankton) upon which food webs there are primarily based. Thus the contribution of marshes to a large body of water is substantial.

Incidentally, it is worth noting here that the very success of the *Spartina* grasses implies instability in the marsh food web. A web based on only one or two species of plant can collapse if anything destroys the marsh as a habitat for those species. Pollution or draining of a marsh can ruin its stands of *Spartina*.

There are some larger animals that live and feed either part- or full-time on the marshes. The most common mammals are the raccoon, which feeds primarily on clams and fiddler crabs, and the muskrat, which feeds on roots and makes lodges of the stems of the marsh grasses. Others, rarer and more retiring, include mink, otter, and, if the marsh is large or close to woods, white-tailed deer. Among the birds, the fish-eating herons are most common. These include the great blue heron, the smaller green heron, and the American egret. Other fish-eating birds include kingfishers, ospreys, and a few bald eagles, as well as small shorebirds like sandpipers.

The most useful tools for looking at a marsh are, again, the senses. Walk a marsh, or move through it slowly and quietly in a boat. Look and listen. As you move, look into the water and at the edge of the bank. Look around the base of the grasses and anywhere else where there is shade for small animals in the summer. On open patches of sand or mud, look for tracks of mammals and birds. Take a pair of binoculars and a book like *A Field Guide to the Birds* and try to identify the birds you see. But remember to watch them and their activities too. Identifying is not the same thing as observing. Low tide is a good time to look at a marsh. Much is visible then that is not visible later. Sunrise and sunset are also good times to be around. Mammals especially do not spend much time actively on the marshes during the day. Try also to visit a marsh at different seasons of the year.

Other techniques besides walking and looking are also useful. In shallow water mudflats, look for small round holes. These are siphon holes for clams. If you like, try to dig with one hand down into the hole to catch the clam. But dig fast—clams can burrow very well. And be prepared to get yourself wet. Buy a minnow seine from a sporting goods store and pull it in shallow marsh lagoons. Crabs, juvenile fish, killifish—it is always amazing what turns up in a seine. Run some chemical water tests too. Because of decaying materials and summer sun warming shallow water, dissolved oxygen levels get low sometimes, but the flushing action of the tides tends to minimize this.

Finally, look at the transition areas where the marsh land gets higher and therefore flooded less often by the tides. Conditions in these areas are less rigorous for plants, so there is more diversity. These areas are interesting as they change from marsh land to upland and woods.

FORAGING. Marshes that are fertile ground for so many food finfish and shellfish are also good for the person who enjoys foraging wild foods. Clams, mussels, oysters, crabs, and periwinkles are abundant, as are some edible marsh border plants like orach, sea rocket, and sheep sorrel. Foraging is a profound way for man to relate to his environment.

While you are in the mood to forage, remember crabs and larger fish. Some directions for crabbing are included later in this guide, in case you are not already experienced as an amateur crabber. Fishing is a large topic. If you have no experience at it, your best bet is to check with a local sporting goods store. Probably the easiest way to get started is to rig a hand line with a sinker at the bottom and two hooks, 6 and 12 inches above the sinker. Bait the hooks with bits of bloodworm or peeler crab and fish over areas where the bottom is hard sand, preferably 10-25 ft. deep. Fish with the sinker on the bottom and the line tight above it. Set the hook with a snap of the wrist when a fish bites. Trout and spot, and less frequently, croakers, rockfish, and bluefish can be caught in this way. All are fine for eating. Another technique that will sometimes take blues and rock in the summer and early fall is to trail a handline from a sailboat. This is called trolling and should be done with a bucktail or metal spoon as a lure. It is most productive in areas where the fish are feeding on the surface, usually on schools of marsh-bred shiners (silversides). Such areas are marked by gulls feeding on scraps left behind by the fish. By the way, if you catch a blue, beware his sharp teeth—a caught blue is not above snapping at his captor.

Again, remember that the above instructions are minimal. Seek advice from tackle dealers, marina operators, and fishermen. Many will be glad to help get you started.

Two other notes about marshes and their environs. Look at birds and at the trees in the uplands beyond the marsh. Many species of birds call the Bay home or highway at different seasons of the year. One particularly enjoyable time to watch them is summer; ospreys, herons, and their kin are mentioned above. In fresher water marshes, the male red-wing blackbird is conspicuous. Another time is late fall, winter, and early spring. Then the Bay harbors several species of attractive or amusing ducks, including mallards, teal, canvasbacks, redheads, mergansers, buffleheads, ruddy ducks, and old squaws. Even more spectacular are the Canada geese and the whistling swans.

VI. Instructions for Water Test Equipment

SECCHI DISK. Lower in the water until it can no longer be seen. If there is glare then try looking at it from different angles. Record the level at which it disappears. Lower it another 1-2 feet and begin raising it slowly. Record the level at which it reappears. Add the two readings and divide the sum by 2 to get the average turbidity for that spot. (See illustration.) Readings of 4′ to 8′ are most common.

SAMPLE BOTTLE NO.1. (For samples near surface only.) Place bottle just above surface of water. Quickly lower it to a 1-2 foot depth and hold it there until air bubbles stop surfacing. This will give a sample with most of the water from the depth of the *top* of the bottle when submerged.

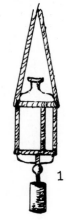

INSTRUCTIONS FOR FABRICATING ECOLOGICAL STUDY EQUIPMENT

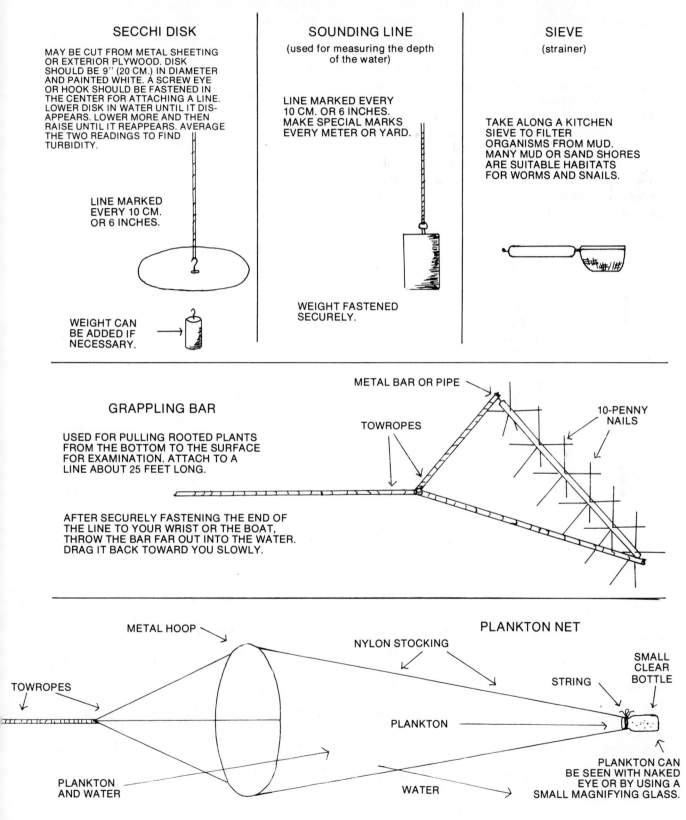

SECCHI DISK

MAY BE CUT FROM METAL SHEETING OR EXTERIOR PLYWOOD. DISK SHOULD BE 9" (20 CM.) IN DIAMETER AND PAINTED WHITE. A SCREW EYE OR HOOK SHOULD BE FASTENED IN THE CENTER FOR ATTACHING A LINE. LOWER DISK IN WATER UNTIL IT DISAPPEARS. LOWER MORE AND THEN RAISE UNTIL IT REAPPEARS. AVERAGE THE TWO READINGS TO FIND TURBIDITY.

LINE MARKED EVERY 10 CM. OR 6 INCHES.

WEIGHT CAN BE ADDED IF NECESSARY.

SOUNDING LINE
(used for measuring the depth of the water)

LINE MARKED EVERY 10 CM. OR 6 INCHES. MAKE SPECIAL MARKS EVERY METER OR YARD.

WEIGHT FASTENED SECURELY.

SIEVE
(strainer)

TAKE ALONG A KITCHEN SIEVE TO FILTER ORGANISMS FROM MUD. MANY MUD OR SAND SHORES ARE SUITABLE HABITATS FOR WORMS AND SNAILS.

GRAPPLING BAR

USED FOR PULLING ROOTED PLANTS FROM THE BOTTOM TO THE SURFACE FOR EXAMINATION. ATTACH TO A LINE ABOUT 25 FEET LONG.

AFTER SECURELY FASTENING THE END OF THE LINE TO YOUR WRIST OR THE BOAT, THROW THE BAR FAR OUT INTO THE WATER. DRAG IT BACK TOWARD YOU SLOWLY.

METAL BAR OR PIPE

TOWROPES

10-PENNY NAILS

PLANKTON NET

METAL HOOP

NYLON STOCKING

STRING

SMALL CLEAR BOTTLE

TOWROPES

PLANKTON

PLANKTON AND WATER

WATER

PLANKTON CAN BE SEEN WITH NAKED EYE OR BY USING A SMALL MAGNIFYING GLASS.

SAMPLE BOTTLE NO. 2. (For samples from a specific depth.) This is the same as No. 1 except that it has a cork in the hole with a string attached. The cork should be placed in the hole with only a little bit of pressure. Under water you may not be able to release the cork if it's in too securely because of the inward pressure of the water. Lower the bottle to the desired depth and give the string (to cork) a sudden jerk. This will release the cork if it isn't in too hard and the lines are clear. Often the cork string and line to the bottle will get tangled. It may help to use a heavier weight and have the two lines further apart at the surface. To obtain an accurate temperature reading leave the bottle, filled with water, at the desired depth for 10-15 minutes.

PLANKTON NET. Make sure that all lines are fastened very securely. Tow slowly through water so as not to put too much pressure on the net. The faster you go the more plankton you collect but if you go too fast you could possibly lose the rig. By dragging the net slowly or by attaching weights, deep-water plankton collections may be made. (See illustration.)

TEST KITS. We highly recommend that a layer of newspapers be placed under the kits during use to protect the surface under it. Some of the chemicals in use will leave permanent stains on a surface— even fiberglass.

General Test Kit Instructions: Loading a Syringe (see illustrations).

1. Pull out the plunger most of the way to fill the syringe with air.

2. Insert syringe into the fitting on the cap of the bottle.

3. Press plunger in all the way to push the air into the bottle.

4. Invert bottle. Then pull plunger about halfway out and push back about 3 times rapidly. This should get any air bubbles out of the syringe. If it doesn't, then try tapping the syringe to make them rise. Then try pulling it in and out again.

5. Pull syringe plunger out to last mark.

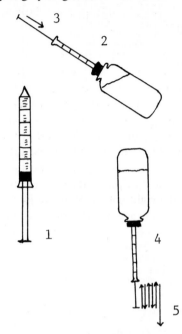

Titrating. Carefully add the titrant drop by drop to the solution. Between each drop mix the solution thoroughly. To compare the color be sure and use a consistently colored white background. When the solution suddenly changes you have reached the "endpoint."

Dissolved Oxygen Test Kit. Follow instructions *very* carefully. It is better to read the directions and then go back reading them step by step as you do them. Be sure that your glassware (sample bottle, syringe, burette, etc.) is very clean. If possible scrub and rinse thoroughly with distilled water. To get a better reading rinse out the sample bottle with part of the sample first, then fill it until it overflows. When adding the acid you may need to add a little extra to get the precipitate (solid parts formed in sample) to dissolve. Be sure in adding more than one buretteful of titrant (sodium thiosulfate) that you only push the burette to "20" and don't go to the end. Also be sure and keep track of how many times you refill the burette, and don't forget to add both amounts (before and after iodine is added) of sodium thiosulfate to figure your ppm (parts per million).

Salinity Test Kit. Be *extremely* careful with this kit. One of the chemicals is silver nitrate, which stains very badly and cannot be removed from decks. Remember in this kit to use the red lettered syringe for adding the sample and the black lettered one for adding the titrant. Also remember to use distilled water in the titration tube and add .5cc of the sample.

PH Test Kit. Fill one tube to the line with the sample. Remember: the closer to the line you are, the more accurate your reading. If you look carefully at the surface of the water you will see a curve called a miniscus. Be sure and use the *bottom* of this curve and *not the top.* Carefully add 10 drops of pH indicator. After mixing, place test tube in one hole in the top of the comparator. Find the closest color. You may have to put it into the other hole to get it between the right colors. You can give your readings with more accuracy by guessing how much difference there is between the colors. This way you can get readings like 7.6 and 8.3.

SEINE. A minnow seine can be bought in a good hardware or sporting goods store for $2, but you'll have to get some poles (mop handles are perfect). Drag the seine (weights down/floats up) along the bottom in a shallow area up onto a beach. You must have two people working it. Keep the bottoms of the poles about one foot ahead of the tops so that the poles lean backwards. Make sure that the weights drag along the bottom but also try to keep the floats near the surface. In other words— ideally the water should be a little shallower than the width of the net.

CRABBING.

1. *Crablines.* Take some cotton string in lengths about 1½ to twice the depth of the water and tie one end to a piece of crab bait and the other end to a boat or dock. Toss the baited end away from you out into the water and let it rest on the bottom for 5-10 minutes. Pull it in *very* slowly and steadily. *No* sudden jerks. Pull the crab (if you've got one) as close to the surface as you can and scoop it quickly.

2. *Trotline.* Two people in an ordinary dinghy can manage a trotline without difficulty. One rows along the line slowly and quietly. The other does the dipping. Dip with decision, and deftly. Blue crabs hanging onto chicken necks are fortunately careless of their lives, but they can be disturbed by clumsy dipping. The line should be drawn over the bow, or an oar, without jerks or any other sudden moves. In the prime times—early morning and late afternoon—the line can be frequently worked. Remember to set the floats and anchors to take advantage of the tide, and be sure to allow the bait to rest on the bottom. Crabs caught in this fashion come out fighting mad. They can be dumped into the bottom of the dinghy, but not when bare toes are exposed.

3. *Crab Bait.* Fish heads, chicken necks (actually any chicken parts) or pieces of salted eel work fine.

4. *Ring Nets; Crab Pots.* A notably peculiar characteristic of the Bay region is the way in which local custom and tradition have developed different techniques for harvesting seafood. Crab pots predominate in the lower Bay; trotlines in the upper Bay. Stranger yet, by and large, the ring net is not used at all.

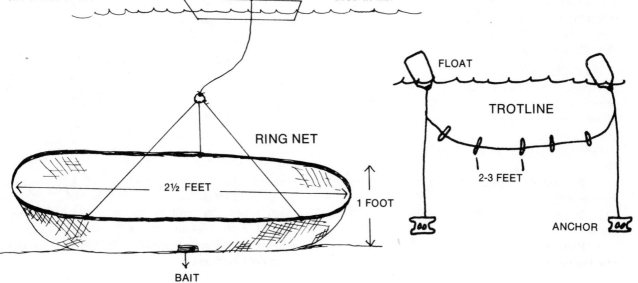

RING NET — 2½ FEET — 1 FOOT — BAIT — FLOAT — TROTLINE — 2-3 FEET — ANCHOR

For yachtsmen, the ring net is ideal, because it's easy to stow. It consists of a ring of wood or metal from 2′ to 3′ in diameter, to which is attached a shallow net, 1′ to 2′ in depth. To use, simply attach crab bait to the center of net and lower to the bottom. A three-line halter is attached to the ring. In lively waters, raise the net after it has rested on the bottom 15 minutes, more or less. It's not unusual to catch as many as 4 or 5 crabs at a time. The renowned forager Euell Gibbons advises us that a ring net often produces an entire meal for a couple of hearty eaters from a single haul.

Crab pots are wire cages, usually used with a float to mark the spot where they have been dropped. Too large to take on most pleasure boats, they are best worked by those who have easy access to the water with small boats.

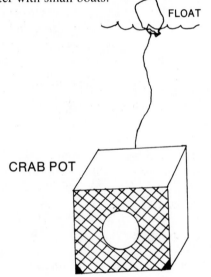

FLOAT

CRAB POT

VII. Afterword

The experiments you conduct are related to the following conditions, each of which has a significant bearing on the health of Bay waters.

1. Eutrophication (excessive enrichment causing dissolved oxygen depletion). *Turbidity, dissolved oxygen, pH.*

2. Industrial pollution (thermal, chemical, oil from plant and storm drainage). *Temperature, water samples.*

3. Agricultural runoff (pesticides and herbicides and inorganic fertilizers). *Dissolved oxygen.*

4. Fish kills (oxygen depletion, acidity, weather). *pH.*

5. Algae blooms. *Secchi disk, pH, dissolved oxygen.*

6. Microscopic animal and plant productivity. *Plankton net.*

7. Bird and fish life. *Binoculars, seine nets, trotlines, etc.*

8. Plant life. *Grappling hooks, spade.*

9. Turbidity (cloudiness). *Secchi disk and plankton nets.*

10. Shore development, Bay population. *Observation and all tools.*

Good luck!

VIII. Resource Material: Useful Handbooks for Identification of Bay and Shore Life

Fresh Water Biology, Ward and Whipple, John Wiley & Sons, Inc.

Golden Nature Guide Series, Golden Press, New York:
Birds of North America, Chandler S. Robbins.
Fishes, A Guide to Fresh and Salt-water Species, Zim and Shoemaker.
Flowers, Zim and Martin.
Insects, Zim and Cottam.
Pond Life, Reid and Zim.
Seashores, A Guide to Animals and Plants Along the Beaches, Zim and Ingle.
Trees, Zim and Martin.

A Guide to the Study of Fresh-Water Biology, Needham and Needham, Holden Day Inc.

Gymnosperms, Charles J. Chamberlain, Dover Publications Inc., N.Y.

Manual of the Trees of North America (Volumes 1 and 2), Charles S. Sargent, Dover Publications Inc., N.Y.

Our Northern Shrubs, Harriett Keeler, Dover Publications Inc., N.Y.

Phytoplankton of the Chesapeake Bay, Ruth Griffith, Ches. Biological Lab., Solomons, Md.

The Peterson Field Guide Series, Houghton Mifflin Company, Boston:
A Field Guide to the Animal Tracks, Olaus J. Murie.
A Field Guide to the Birds, Roger Tory Peterson.
A Field Guide to the Ferns, Boughton Cobb.
A Field Guide to the Insects, Borror and White.
A Field Guide to the Mammals, Bart and Grossenheider.
A Field Guide to the Reptiles and Amphibians, Roger Conant.

A Field Guide to the Rocks and Minerals, Frederick H. Pough.

A Field Guide to the Shells (Atlantic and Gulf Coasts), Percy A. Morris.

A Field Guide to the Shrubs, George A. Petrides.

A Field Guide to the Wildflowers, Peterson and McKenny.

Picture-Keyed Nature Series, William C. Brown Company:

How to Know the Freshwater Algae, G. W. Prescott.

How to Know the Freshwater Fishes, Samuel Eddy.

Putnam's Nature Field Books, G. P. Putnam and Sons, New York:

Field Book of American Wildflowers, F. Schuyler Mathews.

The New Field Book of Fresh Water Life, Elsie B. Klots.

Field Book of Insects, Frank E. Lutz.

Field Book of Marine Fishes of the Atlantic Coast, Charles M. Breder, Jr.

Field Book of Nature Activities and Hobbies, William Hillcourt.

Field Book of Ponds and Streams, Ann Haven Morgan.

Field Book of Reptiles and Amphibians, Cochran and Goin.

Field Book of Trees and Shrubs, F. Schuyler Mathews.

The Reptiles of North America, Raymond L. Ditmars, Doubleday & Co., N.Y.

Water Pollution and Environmental Studies, The Tilton School Water Pollution Program, Environmental Protection Agency.

Suggested Reading Materials:

The Bay, Gilbert Klingel, Dodd-Mead & Co., N.Y.

The Closing Circle, Barry Commoner, Knopf.

The New York Aquarium Book of the Water World, William Bridges, American Heritage Press.

Sail and Power, Richard Henderson with Bartlett S. Dunbar, Naval Institute Press.

Stalking the Blue-Eyed Scallop, Euell Gibbons, David McKay Co.

Wild Season, Allan W. Eckert, Little, Brown & Co., Boston.

Bibliography:

Blair, C. H., & W. D. Ansel. 1970. *Chesapeake Bay Notes & Sketches.* Tidewater Publishers.

Gibbons, Euell Theophilus. 1964. *Stalking the Blue-Eyed Scallop.* David McKay Co.

Klingle, G. C. *The Bay.*

Peterson, R. T. 1947. *A Field Guide to the Birds.* Houghton Mifflin Co.

Shurtleff, B. P., & G. C. Klingel. 1971. *Seeing Chesapeake Wilds.* International Marine Publishing Co.

Teal, J. & M. 1969. *Life and Death of the Salt Marsh.* National Audubon Society. Ballantine Books.

Wass, M. L., & T. D. Wright. 1969. *Coastal Wetlands of Virginia: Interim Report of the Governor and General Assembly.* Special Report No. 10 of the Virginia Institute of Marine Science.

IX. Glossary of Terms

AEROBIC. Able to live or grow only where oxygen is present.

ALGAE BLOOM. An overproduction of algae usually caused by fertilization of the water.

ANAEROBIC. Able to live and grow where there is no air or free oxygen.

AQUATIC. Growing or living in or upon water.

BASIC. Alkaline in reaction.

BENTHIC. Relating to, or occurring at, the bottom of a body of water.

BURETTE. A graduated (marked) tube used for measuring small quantities of liquid or gas.

CO_2 (CARBON DIOXIDE). A colorless, odorless gas, somewhat heavier than air. It is exhaled from the lungs of animals and absorbed by plants.

CM. (CENTIMETER). A unit of measurement in the metric system meaning one one-hundredth of a meter.

CC. (CUBIC CENTIMETER). A unit of volume measurement in the metric system equal to one one-thousandth of a liter.

DISSOLVED MINERALS. Minerals which have liquefied or merged into a solution.

DISTILLED WATER. Purified water. Water which has had all dissolved minerals removed from it.

D.O. (DISSOLVED OXYGEN). Oxygen which has merged into water and is most readily available to water-breathing organisms.

DIURNAL. Having a daily cycle.

ECOSYSTEM. The relationship between the physical environment and the community of living organisms for a specific location.

EFFLUENT. Flowing out or forth such as the outflow of a sewer or sewage tank.

E.G. (Latin) *exempli gratia*, for the sake of example; for example.

EMERGENT. An outgrowth from beneath.

ENDPOINT. That point in a chemical reaction where a given amount of one substance completely reacts with an unknown amount of another substance; usually made visible by the use of liquid indicators which change colors when the endpoint is reached.

ENGULF. To swallow up; overwhelm.

EQUILIBRIUM. A state of balance or equality.

EROSION. Wearing away gradually; disintegration.

ESTUARY. An inlet or arm of the sea where the tide and salt water meet the freshwater currents from the draining land.

EUTROPHICATION. Overenrichment of nutrients in a water body causing an algae bloom. As the algae die from overcrowding and a lack of sunlight, the water becomes stagnant from a lack of oxygen.

FOOD CHAIN. The step-by-step progression of one organism depending on the next for food. Example: grass → cow → human.

FORAGER. A person who searches for his own food or provisions in the wild.

HERBICIDE. A chemical used to kill plants.

H_2O. Chemical symbol for water.

I.E. (Latin) *id est*, that is.

INTERDEPENDENT. One organism depending on another and vice versa; both organisms depending on one another.

INTERTIDAL ZONE. The zone of a beach which is alternately covered and uncovered by water as the tide rises and falls.

ION. An electrically charged atom or group of atoms, the electrical charge of which results when a neutral atom or group of atoms loses or gains one or more electrons (negative charges surrounding the nucleus).

LITER. Basic unit of volume in the metric system; slightly more than one quart.

LONGITUDINAL. Running lengthwise.

MG/L. Milligrams per liter—measurement of weight per volume.

MINISCUS. Horizontal upper surface or boundary of any liquid in a container. One should always read the bottom of this horizontal bubble.

NICHE. A way of life (in ecology); an organism's way of life or "occupation." The sum of all the relationships between any species of organism and its environment.

NON-POINT SOURCE. Originating from many locations with no clearly defined source, such as land runoff.

O_2. Oxygen gas.

PHOTOSYNTHESIS. The process by which green plants use light to form carbohydrates from water and carbon dioxide.

PLANKTON. Microscopic animal and plant life found floating or drifting in the ocean or fresh water, used as food by fish.

POINT-SOURCE. Originating from one identifiable and highly localized source, such as an industrial effluent pipe.

POLLUTION. Contamination or alteration which impairs the legitimate beneficial use of such land or water and may endanger wildlife or man.

PPM. Parts per million.

PROPAGATION. To reproduce itself; raise or breed.

PROXIMITY. Nearness in space, time, etc.

RESPIRATION. Process of breathing; inhaling and exhaling air.

SALINITY. The quality or degree of being saline; salty; saltiness.

SEINE. A large fishing net with floats along the top edge and weights along the bottom.

SIEVE. A utensil having many small meshed openings of a size allowing passage only to liquids or to finer particles of loose matter; sifter; strainer.

SOUNDING LINE. A line or cable weighted at one end and used for measuring the depth of water.

SUBMERGED. Underwater.

TETANUS. Lockjaw; an acute infectious disease caused by the toxins given off by non-air-breathing bacteria.

TITRATION. The process of finding out how much of a certain substance is contained in a solution by measuring how much of another substance it is necessary to add to the solution in order to produce a given reaction.

TITRANT. The substance of known strength which is being added to the unknown solution.

TROTLINE. A strong line suspended from distant floats, with short, baited lines hung from it at intervals; trawl line.

TURBULENCE. Agitated; disturbance; disorderly.

> Greater than.

< Less than.

INDEX

ABYC
  see American Boat and Yacht Council
Accessibility
  and inspection, 50
  and safety, 25
Accommodation plans
  for large cruisers, 32, 33
  for medium-sized cruisers, 30
  for small cruisers, 28-30
Accumulative rolling, 1, 2
  and multihulls, 12
Activities, miscellaneous cruise, 98-106
Aeronautical beacons and RDF, 121
Aesthetic balance, 4
Aft sections, U-shaped, 4, 5
Air vent valve on bilge pump, 24, 25
Alternator, engine-driven, 60
Aluminum construction, 21
  and cautions concerning antifouling paint, 22
American Boat and Yacht Council, 23, 65, 67, 96
American Practical Navigator
  see Bowditch, Nathaniel
Anchor
  chain inspection, 148
  and digging in, 155, 156
  dislodging, trip line for, 154, 155
  Herreshoff type yachtsman, 153
  line, proper diameter, 154
  line, amount of, and boat size, 154
  rode, choice of, 154
  scowed, 154
  selection for average boat, 153
  types, 152, 153
  weight, rule for proper, 153
Anchorage, choice of, 149
Anchoring under a windward shore, 150
Anchors, 152
  obtaining more clearance with two, 155
Anemometer, 56
Antenna, stern-mounted loaded whip, and safety, 68
Apparent wind indicator, 60
Aspect ratio, 9

Autopilots, 139
Auxiliary cruising sailers, 32
Awning, 76, 77
Azimuth scale, 113

Back-siphoning prevention, 67
Bahamian moor, 155
Ballast
  bonding to keel interior, 21
  external, bolts, and inspection accessibility, 21
  external, and Lloyd's recommendations, 21
  external, and lowest center of gravity for given weight, 21
  movement or detachment prevention, 21
  one piece of lead as, 21
Barometer warnings of extratropical lows, 92
Batteries, 60
  location, 60, 62
  and security, 60
  size, 60
  and three-way master switch, 60
  ventilation, 60
Beacon, sending
  location of, 121
  and signal identification, 121
Beam and draft, 6
Beam/LWL, 5, 6
Bearing, 109
Bearings
  magnetic, using the sextant, 115
  taking, 114, 115
Bell as fog signal at anchor, 121
Berth details, 37
Berth, double V, forward, 38
Berthing capability *vs.* living comfort, 36
Bilge pump, 24, 25, 67
Bilges
  fairly flat, 3
  hard, 1, 2
  and pounding, 3
  rounded, 2, 3
  slack, 1, 2, 3
Bimini top, 76, 138
Bird identification books recommended, 104
Birds of area and local "field list," 104
Blister and air pocket discovery, 49
Blister problem and corrective measure, 51
Boating Industry Association, 65
Boat swapping service, 94
Bowditch, Nathaniel, 109, 117, 118, 123
Bow
  pulpit, 26

sharp, plumb, and plowing into head sea, 4
and stern section, extreme dissimilarity of,
    and heeling, 4
Breakaway point, 54
Breast lines, use of, in docking, 144
Britton, Wright, 133, 135
Broadcast stations, standard, and RDF, 121
Brush, 54
Builder, choice of, 22
Bunk
    athwartships, and heeling, 39
    boards, 36, 37
    dimensions, 36
    width variation, 36, 37
Buoyage system details, 123
    bands, 123, 124
    intracoastal waterways, and conventional U.S.
        system conflicts, 125
    lights, 123, 124
    shapes, 123, 124
    solid colors, 123, 124
    sounds, 123, 124
    vertical stripes, 123, 124
Buoys, basic U.S. types, 123, 124

Cabin
    double, plan, 28, 29
    tops, adjustable, 28
    and use as camper, 30
Camber, constant, and hydrodynamic efficiency, 3
Camper-cruisers, 30
Cans (buoys) 123, 124
Cape Cod Canal, 89
Carter, Richard, 9
Catamaran
    see Multihulls
Ceiling, 21
Centerboard boats and beam size, 6
Centerboards
    retracting, 6
    tandem, 7, 9
Center of effort
    forward of designed total center of effort, 136
    under full sail, 128
Channel preferred, buoy indications of, 123, 124
Chart books, 86
Chartering
    bareboats, 95
    crewed boats, 95
    restrictions, 95
Charts, 109-111
Chart table and navigator's niche, 32

Chesapeake Bay Foundation Ecology Cruise
    Guide, 104, 165-177
Chopper gun, 18
Circle of position, 116, 117
Citizen's band (CB) radiophone, 68
    lack of contact with Coast Guard, 68
Cleat jamming and natural fiber sheets, 74
Cleats, quick release jam vs. anvil types, 74
Cloth, 18
Cloud identification illustrations, 93
Cloud warnings
    of extratropical lows, 92
    of isolated, air mass thunderstorms, 92
Coamings, high, and raked outboard, for spray
    protection, 42
Coastal passages, special cautions, 90
Coastal Warning Facilities charts, 121
Coast Guard
    and dinghy regulations, 82
    and engine and fuel systems regulations, 65, 67
    lack of direct contact with, through CB
        radiophone, 68
    List of Lights and Other Marine Aids, 109
    Local Notice to Mariners, 109
    PFD regulations, 72
    standards and requirements for the Rules of
        the Road, 27
    statistics on boating fatalities, 82
Coast Pilot books, 86, 87
    directly related to National Ocean Survey
        charts, 87
Cockpit cover
    see Bimini top
Cockpit drainage, 23
Cockpit volume, 23, 24
    NAYRU limits, 23
Cockpit comfort, 42
Cockpit scuppers, 23, 24, 42
    minimal total area recommended by ABYC, 23
    minimal total area required by NAYRU, 23
Cockpit well, dimensions, 42
Cofferdam, 70
Collision mat, 73
Comfort equipment, 76-81
Communications
    long distance, 68
    short-range, 67, 68
Companionway
    dodger, 42, 76, 77
    at forward end of after cabin, advantages of, 34
    sill safety, 23
Companionways, double, 37

Compass, 111-114, 120
  example of correcting, 113-114
  flat-top, fitted with sighting vane, 114
  hand bearing, 109
  location, 111
  roses, 109, 110, 113
  variation error avoidance, 113
Condensation minimization in fuel tanks, 64
Construction features, 18-22
Cook's snap-on strap, 43
Corners
  in fiberglass, 20
  rounded for safety, 47
Course protractor-plotter, 109
Crabbing, 102
Crown, excessive, 26
Cruise planning, 86-98
"Cruising Cal 36," 32
Cruising *vs.* competitive features, 1-3
Cruising guides, 86
  current issue, 86
  procurement, 86
Cuddy, 28, 29
Current observed against buoy and "wrong
    way" lean, 89
Current, strength of, and weather, 89
Currents, U.S. locations of strong, 89, 90
Cutter rig, 127

Dagger board, 83, 84
Danforth anchor, 152, 153
Dead reckoning (DR), 109, 118, 120
  derivation of term, 118
  and making allowance for leeway and current,
    120
Deck
  color, 48
  gear, optional, 74-76
Deflection when crossing a current, 120
Depth recorders and navigation, 68
Depth sounders, electronic, 68-70, 109
Deviation
  card, 111-113, 120
  and compass adjusting, 111-113, 120
  errors, finding, 111
  periodic check, 113
Dew point and fog forewarning, 94
Diesel engine
  exhaust fumes, 63
  fuel consumption rule of thumb, 63
  starting difficulties, 63, 64
  stopping difficulties, 64

Diesel oil wood penetration, 63
Dinette, 7, 28, 29
  convertible to double bunk, 30, 31, 38, 39
  L-shaped, 31, 32
Dinghy
  capacity plate, 81
  choice of, 81
  Coast Guard regulations, 82
  materials, 83
  oarlock positions, 83
  sailing, 83, 84
  towing attachment, 82
Directional instability, 1
Directional stability, 3
  and skeg, 3
Displacement
  heavy, 3
  light, 1
Displacement hull, 16
Displacement/keel ballast, rule of thumb, 9
Distance determining
  bow-beam bearings method of, 118, 119
  by doubling the angle on the bow, 118, 119
  with a log, 118
  with a sextant, 116, 117
  with a speedometer, 118
  with a speed-time-distance calculator, 118
Distance finding stations and calculations from
    signals, 121
Distant cruising areas, 94-98
Dividers, 109
Dock lines used when lying alongside a peer,
    144, 145
Dodger
  see Companionway dodger
Doghouse, 16
Dorade vents, 76, 78
Double cabin with stateroom forward, 30, 31
Draft
  and beam, 6
  controllable, in a keel-centerboarder, 7
  rule of thumb relation of, to LWL, 7
  shoal, and reserve stability, 10
  variable, 6-9
Drifter, 130, 131
Drift tendency, importance of knowledge of, 57
DSB-AM (double sideband-amplitude modulation)
    radiotelephones, 67

Ecology Cruise Guide, Chesapeake Bay
    Foundation, 104, 165-177
Ecology studies, 104

Electrical system of a 30 ft. LWL cruising
    sailboat, 61
Electrolysis, 68
Encasement, solid hard woods and conventional
    planking as materials for, 18
Engine accessibility, 64
Engine cooling
    keel cooler *vs.* heat exchanger, 64
    sea water *vs.* closed fresh-water system, 64
Engine power, auxiliary, 16
Engine service without fuel spilling, 67
Engines
    auxiliary, 62
    diesel *vs.* gasoline, 63
    outboard *vs.* inboard, 63
Engine unreliability and water in the fuel, 64
Ensign size, rule for proper, 148
Entrance and exit from after cabin, alternate
    means of, 34
Equipment, federal requirements, 157-164
Excessive noise as strain indications, 56
Exhaust system, desirable features, 64, 65
Exit, alternate through forward hatch, 23
Eyeball navigation, 122
    tips, 123

Fatalities, boating, Coast Guard statistics, 82
Fathometers
    see Depth sounders, electronic
Fatigue cracking prevention, 20
FCC (Federal Communications Commission), 67
    regulations and license requirements, 68
Federal equipment requirements, 157-164
Fender protection when lying alongside a pier,
    144, 145
Ferrocement
    see Steel-reinforced concrete construction
Fiberglass boat deck-to-hull junction, 18
    use of pop rivets with bonding, 18
    use of self-tapping screws without bonding,
    18, 19
Fiberglass
    construction, 18-21
    and undetectable internal cracks, 21
Fiddles, 14, 41
Fill pipes, 65
Fire extinguisher in galley, 45
Fix, 116, 117
    from one object, 117
    running, 117, 121
    from three lines of position, 115
Fitting attachment, 19, 20

Fitting out cost estimation rule of thumb, 72
Flag codes, conflict in, 148
Flashing lamp depth indicator, 68, 69
    location, 70
Flotation, 23
Flow separation, indication of early, and drag,
    54
Fog
    advection, 92
    formation of, 94
    radiation, 94
    as regional, seasonal problem, 92, 93
    tactics, 94
Fog piloting, 120, 121
Foresail, 128
Foreign cruising and diesel power advantages, 63
Foreign waters buoyage system, 125
Forward sections, V-shaped, 4, 5
Foul weather gear, 107
Four berth single cabin, 28, 29
Freeboard/beam, 5, 6
    and reserve stability at moderate heel, 6
Fuel
    fumes vented overboard, 66, 67
    shut-off valve accessibility, 45
    system features, 65, 66
    tank capacity, 41

Galley, 28, 29
    athwartships after, 30, 31, 43
    counters, 47
    details, illustrated, 44
    fire prevention precautions, 45
    fore and aft layout opposite dinette, 30, 31, 43
    hand grips and grab rails, 47
    L-shaped, 31, 32, 43
    stowage, 47
Galvanic corrosion, 21, 25, 130, 149
    and inspection, 50
Garboard, 20
Gasoline engine fuel consumption rule of thumb,
    63
Gear stowage, 83, 85
Gel coat, 18
    examination, 48
Genoa, cruising, 131
    vs. racing, 128
Gimbals, 14
    see also Stove, gimbaled
Gin pole, 97, 98
Grab rails, 26
Great cabin, 36

Great Lakes and lighting exceptions, 27
Grounding
  on hard bottom and keel damage, 21
  intentional, 3
  simple hints for extricating boat, 125, 126
Ground plates and electrolytic corrosion, 68
Group rendezvous, 98, 100

Hammerlock moor, 152
Hammond, Paul, 133
Hard spots on hull
  and new boat inspection, 50
  and two possible remedies, 19, 20
Hard spots on sails, 130
Hatch fasteners, 24
Hauling on marine railway, 3
Head door jamming due to downward thrust of
  mast, 56, 57
Head pendant on jib, 130
Heads, 28
  location, 40
  ventilation, 40
Headsail, 128
Headsails, specialized *vs.* one roller furling
  sail, 133
Heaters, 81
Heel, low angle of, 2
Heeling
  and athwartships bunk, 39
  and athwartships seats in dinette, 39
  minimized on multihull, 13
  resistance to initial, 11
  and roll out, 6, 7
  and rudder forces, 5
Helm
  balance check, 53
  excessive quickness on, 3
  management check, 54
  position of, 42
  sluggish, 4, 5
Helmsman's seat and visibility, 26
Helms, two identical, 34
Hobbyhorsing, 4
  minimized, 127
Horn
  blast significance, 121
  sounding intervals, 121
Horseshoe buoy, 72, 73
Hose clamps, 23, 24, 67
Hot-weather rig, 138
House flag, 148
Hull-deck, acceptable attachment methods, 19, 20

and new boat inspection, 50
Hull reinforcement, fiberglass, 19
Hull rigidity lacking, indications of, 51
Hull shell
  core and outer skin, 18
  gradual thickening of, rule for, based on
    Lloyd's scantlings, 20
Hulls, displacement or nonplaning on motor
  sailers, 16
Hung-up blade and stern tube or shaft log
  damage, 57
Hurricane cautions, 90, 91

Icebox
  drainage, 43, 44
  insulation, 43
  location, 43
  size, 43
Inland waterways and uniform state aids to
  navigation, 125
Inspection list, summary, 57-59
Inspection of new boat, 48-51
International Code of Signals, HO 102, 148

Jam cleats, automatically releasing, 12
Jib, 128
  boomed, and trimming advantages, 132, 133
  boomless, 129
  with luff wire and twist stopper, 133, 135
  reaching, 131
  self-attending, 132, 133
  sheet winches, power of, 56
  storm, 128
  working, 53, 131
Jibs, high-cut, 26
Johnson, Irving, 39

Keel-centerboarder, 6, 7
  compromises, 6, 7
  shoal-draft, 7
Keel depth/rig size on motor sailers, 16
Keel fouling on rode with two anchors, 155
Keel misalignment, indications of, 53
Keels
  all-metal fin, bolted to hull, 20
  ballasted, 6
  deep and beam size, 6
  deep-draft, heavily ballasted, 7
  drop, and altering draft, 7
  hollow, integral with external ballast, 20, 21
  hollow, integral with hull and with internal
    ballast, 20, 21

long, 3
nonfouling, 3
retractable, 1
retractable, ballasted, 7
scimitar-shaped, 3
shoal-draft, ballasted, 6
short, and directional instability, 1
short, and minimal wetted surface, 3
swing, 7
twin, 9
twin, and trailering, 1
Ketch rig, 127, 128

Labor-saving gear, 132-136
old-fashioned, 137, 138
Laminate
building up by hand layup, 18
composition, 18
Latches and dogs and safety, 23
Lateral planes, extreme and moderate for deep
single-keel boats, 1, 4
Launching sites, suitable, 98
Lead line, 109, 123
Leeway reduction
without deep draft, 9
and rudder, 4, 5
Legal requirements, 27
Lifeboat
dinghy's limitations as, 83
inflatable rubber, 83
Life jacket accessibility, 41
Life lines and stanchions, 26
Lightning protection, minimal, 25-27
Lights required under international rules, 26, 27
Limber holes, 21
Line of position (LOP), 116
Listing, 48
Lloyd's Register of Shipping rules for construction,
20, 21
Load waterline length (LWL), 4
Lobster pot buoys, 120
Locator beacons, 68
Logs, 70
reliability, 71
Long Island Sound, 89
Loop antenna, 121
LP-gas, rules for safe use of, 46
Lubber line, 111, 114
"Luders 33," 3
Luff wire, 133-135
Lying ahull, 57

Mainsail, 131
full, 128
reefed, 128
sailing with, alone, 128
Maneuvering while lashed side-by-side, 101, 102
Man-overboard pole, 72, 73
Marina, 143
strange, entering, 144
typical dockage charges, 144
Marine life identification guide, 104
"Mariners Library," 106, 107
Marine Surveyors, National Association of, 23
Marine surveyor's services for boat buyer, 21,
22, 50
Mast, raising and lowering on small cruiser,
97, 98
Mat, 18
Mattresses, 80
Medical supplies, 108
Medium frequency (2-3 MHz) radiotelephones, 68
Mercator projections, 110, 111
Metal compatability and avoidance of galvanic
corrosion, 21, 25, 130, 149
Midship hatchways and structural support, 20
Midship section, 3
Mizzen, 128, 131
Mizzen staysail, 130, 131
Moderation in design, 1
Monohull, 9
positive stability through great angles of
heel, 11, 12
Mooring boats of contrasting displacement and
size in close proximity, 149
Mooring
cleats, position of, 74
offshore, 143
typical, illustrated, 148
Moray eels, 103
Mosquito screening, 79
Motor sailers, 16, 32
Multihulls, 11-14
beaching capability, 14
with centerboards for windward performance, 14
deck and accommodation space of, 14
extreme beam of, and railway hauling, 14
extreme beam of, and wave straddling, 12
and gunkhole cruising, 14
and heeling, 12
masthead flotation for, 132
and offshore vs. coastal cruising, 12
stability curves for, 12

Museums, marine, 98
Mushroom anchor, 148
Mystic Seaport Museum, 98

National Ocean Survey, 86, 87
Navigation book suggestions, 109
Navigation-related publications, 109, 123
NAYRU
   see North American Yacht Racing Union
"Newporter," 32
Noise, engine, 63
Nonslip surfaces, 26
North American Yacht Racing Union, 23
Northill anchor, 152, 153
Nuns (buoys), 123, 124

Offshore safety equipment, 73
"Ohlson 38," 3
Ovens, 46
Overhangs
   length of, rule of thumb for, 4
   long, and hobbyhorsing, 4
   moderate, and reserve buoyancy, 4
   and pitching, 4, 5

Pacific Northwest current, 89, 90
Paint peeling or chipping and inspection, 50
Parallel rules, 109
Pelorus, 109
   shadow, 113
   used to take relative bearings, 114
Pendant, 148, 149
PFD (personal flotation device), 72
Piloting, 109
Planking
   narrow, edge-nailed and glued, 21
   wide, and glued seam construction, 21
Plank-on-frame wood construction, 21
Plastic filler treatment for sail stretch
   minimizing, 128
Plastic hose for water, 67
Plow type anchor, 152, 153
Plywood construction limitations, 21
Pointing ability and leeway approximation,
   54-56
Polyconic projection, 111
Pooping, 6
"Pop-tops," 35
   see also cabin tops, adjustable
Portuguese man-of-war (Physalia), 103, 104
Position discovery in poor visibility

by chain of soundings, 121
by RDF, 121
Positive stability range, 9
Pounding, 1, 2
Power requirements rule of thumb for auxiliary
   sailboat, 63
Power-sailing, 16
Privacy in accommodation plan, 32
Propeller
   folding or feathering, 50
   hand rotation to minimize drag under sail, 65
   installation, 3
   pitch, 65
   torque and unmanned helm, 51, 52
Proportion of boats relative to size, 1

QME self-steerer, 140
   and crossing steering lines, 140
   limitations, 140
   operating, 140, 141
   and weight of counterbalance, 140
Quarter berths, 28, 29
   and location at point of minimal pitching
    motion, 38
   and ventilation ports, 38
Quarter wave and boat's resistance to forward
   movement, 54, 55
Quoit, 72

Radar reflector, 72, 73
Radio direction finder, 109
   portable, used as a pelorus, 114
Radiotelephones, single sideband, 67
Rafting, 98
   cautions concerning, 100-102
   leaving, 101, 102
Rainy weather activities, 106
Raised-deck cabins and safety drawbacks, 28
Range, 111, 116
"Ratio of Boat Speed to Current Speed" table, 120
RDF navigation, 121
   factors affecting accuracy of, 121, 122
Rectifier for conversion to shore current, 60
Red Rooster, 9
Reduced sail performance testing, 53, 54
Refrigeration
   ammonia boiling, 71
   electric, 71
   with eutectic holding plates, 71
Refrigerators, kerosene- or gas-operated, and
   safety, 45

Regattas, 98, 100
Regulatory markers, uniform state, 124, 125
Requirements, federal equipment, 157-164
"Rhodes Reliant," 34
Righting
   arm, 11
   capabilities of multihull *vs.* monohull, 12
   moments at various angles of heel, 11
Rig safety features, 130, 132
Rigs, cruising, popular, 127, 128
Rode reels, 154
Roll control, 16
Roll controllers for boats at anchor, 150-152
Roll-dampening sail function on motor sailer, 16
Roller furling, 132, 135
   on mainsails, 134
   vs. rod luff with no headstay, 133
   on sails attached to booms, 134
   on twin headsails, 133, 135
"Roller Jeni Wings," 134
Rolling motion
   easy, 2
   quick, in beam seas, 1, 2
Roll out and loss of steering control, 6
Rudder
   balanced, 3
   balanced spade, 3
   control from propeller wash, 16
   drag indications, 53
   forces, 4, 5
   inspection, 50
   keel-attached with raked axis and leeway
     reduction, 4, 5
   keel-separated and skeg, 3
   loss of bite and angle of heel, 53
   stalling, 3
   and vertical turning axis, 3

Sacrificial zincs, check of, 50
Safety belts, 72
   for bunks, 36
Safety equipment, nonpermanent, 72, 73
Safety features, 23-28
Safety Standards for Small Craft, 65, 96
Sailing Directions for foreign cruises, 87
Sail/mechanical power percentages, 16
Sail reduction, 132-136
Sails
   cruising, 131
   selection of, 128-130
   special purpose, 130
   stowage of, 41

Saloon
   aft, 30, 31, 32
   companionway, 32
Sandwich construction, 18
San Francisco Bay, 89
Schooner rig, 127
Scope to water depth ratio, 154
Scudding, 16
Sculling, 56
Scuppers
   see Cockpit scuppers
Seacocks, plug-type, on through-hull pipelines,
   23, 24, 67
Seasons for regional cruising, 90
Seating width, 36
Sea urchins, 103
Self-steering, 102
   devices and tillers, 75
   methods, 139
   systems, 139
   with tandem centerboards, 9
Seven-eighths rule, 118
Sextant, 109, 115
   and determining distance from object of
     known height, 116, 117
   for taking bearings, 114, 115
Shaft log, 57
Shark protection rules, 103
Sheer
   conventional, 5, 6
   powder horn, 5, 6
   reverse, 5, 6
Shooting, 57
Short-handed sailing, 138, 139
Shower operation, 40
Signals
   selected single flag, 147
   special club, 147
Single fin and effective lift at low drag, 9
Sink in galley, 43
Six berth arrangements, 30, 31
Skeg, 3
   reinforcement, 21
   and stalling, 3
Sleeping on heeled boat, 36
Slide magazines, 134, 137
Sliding gunter rig, 83, 84
Sling psychrometer and fog probabilities, 94
Slip, maneuvering an auxiliary into, with a
   crosswind, 144-146
Sloop rig, 127, 128
Snorkeling, 102, 103

Society of Automotive Engineers, 96
Speed made good (Vmg), 55, 56
Speedometers, 70
   reliability, 71
Spinnakers, 131
   without excessively wide shoulders, 130
   handling, 138
   parachute, 130, 138
Spitfire sail, 130, 131
Stability
   curves, comparison of, 10, 11
   high initial, 1
   high initial and strain on rigging, 12
   indication of initial, during inspection, 48
   low initial, 1
   negative, 12
   ultimate, lack of, 11
Stalling, rudder, 3
Stanchions, 26
Standing headroom, 28
Star watching, 104
   recommended nontechnical books, 106
   rough guide, 105
Staysail, 128
Steamers, law against hampering in narrow
      channel, 54
Steel-reinforced concrete construction, 22
Steering
   ease and rudder placement, 3, 4
   lines, 138
   wheel *vs.* tiller, 75
Stern
   pulpit, 26
   squat at high speeds, 54
   tube, 57
Stiffness, 6
Sting rays, 103
Stocking up, 107, 108
Stock model, requesting changes from, 48, 50
Storm mainsail, 130, 131, 134
Storm sails, 130
Storms, extratropical, typical tracks of, 91, 92
Storm trysail, 130-132, 134, 136
Stove, gimbaled, 14, 44, 46
Stoves
   cooking with vaporized alcohol, 45
   electric, 46
   flare-ups, 45
   LP-gas, and safety, 46
   priming, 45
   and securing pots, 46
   Sterno, regulation of, 46

Sterno "swing," 44, 46
Stowage, 41
   space check, 49
Stress distribution on laminate shell, 20
Stuffing box, 25
   inspection and servicing, 65
Sump, keel, 19, 20
Surge, 12
Swan neck, 64, 65, 67
Swimming ladder, 80

Tacking
   and jibing tests, 56
   and tandem centerboards, 9
Taff rail log, 70
Tanks
   fuel, lacking sufficient baffles, 56
   location and stability, 40
   materials, 67
   and piping illustrated, 66
   removable, 42, 67
TCE (total center of effort)
   on cruising boat, 53
   on ketch, 53
   on sloop, 53
   on yawl, 53
Tender service
   alternative to, 143
   flag signal for, 148
Throttles, recessed, 26
Tidal current charts and graphic presentation of
      direction and velocity of flow, 89
Tidal Current Tables, 87
   and times of slack water and times and velocities
      of maximum currents, 89
Tidal ranges
   mean, defined, 87
   spring, defined, 87
Tide
   change interval, 87
   and current information, up-to-date, 87
   and dock line adjustment, 145
   estimation of height of semidiurnal, at any
      given hour, rule for, 88, 89
   estimation from previous tides, 87
   extreme, and twin keels, 1, 10
   illustration, 88
   table accuracy and weather conditions, 87
   Tables, 87
Tides
   diurnal, 89
   mixed, 89

neap, 87
semidiurnal, 89
Tiller
quivers and size of propeller aperture, 51
S-curved, 42
Toilets
flow-through chemical, and Coast Guard EPA
certification, 40
flow-through, and state restrictions on the use
of, 40
and holding tanks, 40
macerator-chlorinator, 40
marine, care of, 67
marine and EPA performance standards, 40
Topsides, distorted reflections on, as indications
of irregularities, 48
Track switch, 134, 137
Trailerable cruiser
construction and safety standards, 96
launching, 98
and state legal regulations, 96
Transducer location, 69, 70
Transom berths, sliding, 36, 37
Transom seat-pilot berth arrangement, 30
Travel lift, 3
Trial sail, 51-57
Tri-cabin arrangements, 32-35
Trimaran
see Multihulls
Trolling, 102
Trunk cabin vs. raised deck, 28, 35
Turning turtle, 12
Twelfths rule, 89
Twin-keeler, 1, 9, 10
with all-metal fins, 20
stock, drawbacks of, 9
Twin wing, self-steering sails, 141, 142

United States ensign, 146
U.S. buoys and channel markers, 123
variation in, 123, 125
U.S. Inland Rules, 27
U.S. Naval Oceanographic Office, 87, 148
Notice to Mariners, 109
U.S. yacht ensign, 146
Unitized construction, 25

Ventilation, 21
hot weather, 152
plans, 78, 79
Ventilators, removable, 23
VHF-FM (very high frequency-frequency
modulation) radiotelephones, 67

Waller, Otway, 133
Wash basin location, 40
Water
box, 70
depth, judging by boat's shadow, 122
depth, planes of reference on east and west
coasts, 110
hot, 81
light, 72, 73
tank capacity, 41
tanks, 67
trap box, detachable, 76, 78
Weather
bureau forecasts, continuous, 94
pattern of cruising area, advance knowledge
of, 90
regional, 90-92
U.S. generalized, 91
Weather cloths, 73
Webster Reflectograph, 116
Weems Position Finder, 116
Wetted surface
defined, 1
excessive, 4, 5
high, 2
low, 1-3
minimal and short keels, 3
Width, combination sleeping and seating, and
sliding transom berths, 36
Winches, geared two-speed, 74
Wind vanes for moving helm mechanically, 139
with horizontal axis, 140
with vertical turning axis, 139
Wind sensor, 60
Windlass, 74
Window safety, 23, 36
Winds, surface, simplified pattern of U.S.
summer, 91, 92
Windsail, 77, 79
Wing deck, 14
Wood construction precautions, 21
Woodwork, cabin, psychological aspects, 49, 50
Workmanship in construction, indications of
quality of, 50
Woven roving, 18

Yacht clubs, 143, 146
burgee (flag), 146
reciprocal arrangements, 146
Yachtsman anchor, 152, 153
Yankee, 39
Yaw control at anchor, 151, 152
Yawl rig, 127, 128